THIS BOOK IS DEDICATED TO
MY GIFTED CHILDREN
MEGAN AND MADISON

I LOVE YOU DEARLY

First Edition 'Beyond Doorways' The Mysteries Revealed
First printed in Australia, April 2005

Keeper of the Crystals Pty Ltd
PO Box 536
St Ives NSW 2075
email: beyonddoorways@transferencehealing.com
fax+ 61 (2) 9402 5850

Design, Graphics and Publication Management by

LIVLIF® Publications and Management
www.livlif.com

Editing: Karen Stuart

Cataloguing: Cartwright, Alexis
  Beyond Doorways: the mysteries revealed
Includes Index.
  ISBN 0-9750628-1-6

ACKNOWLEDGEMENTS

Firstly I would like to thank Irene Payne from the bottom of my heart for supporting me on a personal and spiritual level with the daily activations that occur through the channelling and anchoring of this energy onto the planet. I feel that she gives me the strength to endure all that is necessary to continue to evolve and grow.

I would also like to give my love to my children, Megan and Madison; for their continual love and support.

Thank you to Karen Stuart for her commitment and expertise as the principle editor of all material involved in this book. Her dedication in supporting the information getting 'out there' was remarkable.

I would also like to thank Lucy Lyne for her expertise on the energetic nature of Chiron and the astrological influences that it makes. Her chapter is not only informative but very supportive for all who read this book.

This book would not be able to represent the frequency of Transference and the channelling that I have brought through, without the kind support of all those involved in the graphic art design work. Therefore I would like to thank:

Helen Longhurst for her creative drawings on Lady Nada and the elemental and galactic Pleiadian beings. Her insight into the inner nature of these Divine beings was remarkable and the quality of her artistic work, profound.

I would like to thank Anita Pavlovic for creating the vision and managing the design of the cover of this book, it refects the energy contained within this book with great accuracy.

Thank you again to Anita for the graphic design work of the two 'Animal Magic' cards provided in this book, the Dragon and Raven, her commitment to these cards is remarkable. I would also like to acknowledge her team, Stuart from Net-Tek services for the technical support that he gave and also Irene Payne for her input on symbols, crystals and colour.

I would like to thank John Rundle for photographing the clear quartz pyramid with pyrite, seen at the beginning of chapter 3 and also on the front cover of the Lightbody Kit Book.

The book sustains many other designs and templates and I would now like to personally thank Rebecca Taubert, not only for her originality of the design and layout of the book, but for the way that she was able to transfer the images that I had in my head out into the world in such a way, that they instil such magical and healing qualities.

This book would not have been birthed in the way that it has been without the expertise and support of Kyrona and her team at LIVLIF Publications and Management. Her commitment to this energy and educating the world about it, is profound.

I would like to finally thank all my Sponsors, Graduates and Clients for the encouragement and belief that you have in myself, Transference and its teaching.

Finally I must thank you the reader, for having the courage to enter into the realms of possibilities, by reading the material in this book.

Thank you,

Alexis

" The most
beautiful thing
we can experience is
the Mysterious "

Albert Einstein

PREFACE

hroughout my life, I have been internally driven to understand who we are, where we are going and the meaning and purpose of our Soul's existence, the 'Alpha Omega'.

MULTIDIMENSIONAL REALITY

Every human being has experienced many different dimensional realities, at different points in time, within different parallel universes while being sustained within different bodies consisting of the elemental compounds of different frequency levels of matter and light, we are multidimensional beings.

Even though we have a specific DNA coding system sustaining us within an individual physical body within the 'human' species as a whole, every Soul within humanity has hidden aspects of individuality that are 'unique.' Through working with such deep levels of a client's energy system and DNA, I have obtained a unique understanding of the *hidden* evolutionary patterning that exists within the human body and consciousness.

Through this multidimensional, evolutionary process we have been able to express the *nature* of our consciousness at specific times of incarnation. All the individual memories of our evolutionary process and progress are encoded geometrically within the complex helix system of the DNA, which sustains the many aspects making up our consciousness.

(By tuning into the **DNA** or attuning to the **Akashic Records** we can receive all the information necessary, to understand the true nature of anything or anybody).

The Akashic Records are etheric codes full of specific information that is mathematically indexed, formatted, programmed and sustained within different etheric frequency levels within ether and space. **Attuning** is the process of connecting to higher consciousness and while doing so altering and enhancing our sensory perception, as we open our *clairaudient* channel. We can then filter into consciousness specific information stored within these codes which lie within the ethers of the universe- and therefore obtain universal information. At this level of consciousness we are hearing and telepathically communicating the 'language of light'.

The very high frequencies of sound, which resonate from this coding system, *cannot* be heard through the normal sensory channels. So the sound is 'filtered' down through the higher chakra system and specific dimensions of the brain, pineal, pituitary glands and the upper central nervous system, allowing relevant information from specific codes to be downloaded into human consciousness

Dolphins and whales utilise the same process of *attuning,* but on a different level when they filter through sound frequencies and inputs of sensory information from the third dimensional solar-based system of the world. This enables them to communicate with each other across hundreds of miles and navigate by attuning to the grid line system within the etheric levels of the Earth, Ocean and Space - which cannot be seen by most of humanity. This crystal and light grid line system is the coding system of the Universe that I call the **Global Grid Matrix** *(explained further in chapter 2)*.

DOORWAY WORK

Through higher consciousness, we can therefore retrieve, remember and access anything we choose to know. I call this **'Doorway work'.** I began to master this process by tuning into the coding system of a client's **DNA** when performing a healing and on a parallel level, tuning into the Global Grid Matrix (**coding system of the universe**). Through this process I have not only been able to access relevant and intuitive information for the client but have also explored many dimensions, gone through many Doorways and conquered the restrictions of time and space. This has enabled me to understand more of the **mysteries** of the human body, Nature and the universe.

When I tune-in to facilitate a Transference Healing, I am able to understand what clients have experienced at different times of incarnation, whether it is a time and existence within the third dimension on Earth or existences within other times and dimensions within the parallel universes. Whatever is relevant at the time. When channelling the relevant healing energies and information for clients, I have experienced many 'inter-dimensional reality shifts' to help them understand, release and heal past, painful experience. They can then heal current symptoms and circumstances that might be occurring in their lives, at that particular time of the healing.

PAST, PRESENT AND FUTURE

It is important to heal the past so we can co-create a better state of being for the future, *at the present point in time*. If we are unable to go into the deeper dimensions of the etheric body and DNA to heal core weakness, past weaknesses ultimately surface through different, stressful circumstances in life. The necessary symptoms or karmic situations are then created so the internal restrictions can be 'cleared', in order to heal and grow.

A TRANSFERENCE SHIFT

Through developing the Transference Healing technique, of which Doorway work is an aspect, I have been able to master clearing subliminal weaknesses on many energetic levels of the body and consciousness. It creates such a deep energetic healing response that clients consequently begin to release and heal **genetic** blocks and painful memories stored within their etheric body and DNA.

Transference Healing has enabled me to support others to heal and transform. They can then **exist** within higher levels of consciousness without going through so many learning curves and struggles in their daily lives. The healings and realisations transfer them from one state of being into another and therefore change painful and difficult symptoms and circumstances within their body, reality and life. At the same time they can preventatively clear possible weaknesses, symptoms and issues that might come into manifestation within the near future.

The depth of the healing determines its duration. It can preventively care from three months to three years into the future. It can also create more and more profound levels of healing and enlightenment 'in the moment', depending on how much they choose to surrender and *allow* change and transformation into their own body, consciousness and reality. A conclusive transference shift can happen rapidly, no matter the sickness, issue or personal growth process.

INTERDIMENSIONAL HEALING

Through the Doorway work of a Transference Healing session, clients embody more inner peace and wellness and gain insight about themselves. In return I gain a greater understanding of the hidden mysteries, origins and functions of the etheric/physical body, DNA and consciousness. I have come to understand more conclusively *the many dimensions, within the human body and consciousness, as well as in space, time and the universes.* Transference Healing clears this inter-dimensional wounding, unresolved karmic issues and energy blocks from within the DNA, the different levels and layers of consciousness, the etheric body, and physical anatomy so we can evolve and become more whole, complete and 'one with all that is'.

PERSONAL HEALING SESSIONS

Channelling personal readings and healings for clients enables them to understand more of the complexity of their own divine and inner nature- to see the reason behind circumstances in their lives and the outcome to these circumstances. It also allows them to see the source of their physical ailments, and through the healing, clear the internal weakness so they can physically heal and create a complete shift in consciousness.

When they experience the energetic impact of a 'transference shift' through the healing session, they begin to see the wonder of their life force and existence and feel how it impacts the Universe. As they heal through a channelled Transference Healing they naturally become more 'enlightened' in body and consciousness.

INFORMATION GAINED THROUGH TRANSFERENCE HEALING

I have experienced many revelations while healing others through Transference Healing. The insights I have gained over the years have given me a deeper understanding of the complexity of our DNA and etheric body and consequently a greater understanding of the origins of our existence. As we all become conscious of our Higher Self through healing within, Doorways will eventually open to connect us to the co-existing worlds and dimensions that are part of the totality of our DNA.

These realities or dimensions are constantly being revealed to me and allow me to explore the wonders of the Universes. Healing others has also enabled me to see dimensions of our past and future selves and to travel through Doorways into worlds that no longer exist or even worlds that are still to come into existence through our ascension process.

I have also been given an in-depth understanding of the changes that will occur within and around humanity over the next millennium as our *physical bodies* evolve into a new anatomy and lightbody system and our *consciousness* into higher levels of reality.

THE TIME OF TRANSITION 1999-2012

The global transference shift, occurring at this time, was foreseen by the ancients and referred to as the 'Shift of the Ages' or 'Time of no Time'. It is the transition period of *the fourth dimension* and creates an illusion of being stuck in a time warp as Earth goes through a rapid shift in time and space. Earth and humanity will enter *the fifth dimension in 2013,* after making radical changes within the frequency, and corresponding alchemical makeup, of our planet, body and consciousness. The world that we know will continue to go through radical changes so we can live in this new dimension already beginning to manifest within our reality. *We are entering into a whole new way of being.*

'BEYOND DOORWAYS': SURVIVAL THROUGH THE EARTH AND COSMIC CHANGES

I was intuitively guided to write 'Doorways' to share a general understanding of certain procedures necessary for mastering health and the ascension process during this critical time of transition. The fundamental procedures available in this book are to be used every week and are necessary for maintaining general health and wellness through the ever constant Earth changes occurring during this shift into the next dimension.

The basic procedures and spiritual tools shared through this book will support each person using them to re-balance, align and shift the frequency of their body to sustain a general level of wellness. By working the procedures herein they will begin to alleviate the general lightbody symptoms that everyone seems to be suffering with, to different levels and degrees.

It is important however that readers are aware the procedures offered in this book only hold a small aspect of the healing powers that the Transference modality can provide. So if you wish to master your wellness throughout our current 'transition' to the fifth dimension while continuing to awaken and grow as effectively as possible, I would recommend that in addition to running these procedures on yourself weekly, you either receive regular Transference Healings from a certified practitioner or empower yourself by becoming a self-healer through learning the Transference Healing Fundamental teachings *(refer to page 485 for more information)*. Either approach will allow you to access the complete spectrum of Transference Healing energies needed at this time. Follow your inner guidance as to determine which approach is the correct path for you.

This revision of 'Doorways' gives more insight into some of my channelled teachings that I feel are relevant at this time and also a deeper understanding of the nature of Transference Healing so people can feel and understand the energy.

I hope this material inspires more people to experience Transference Healing to empower themselves to break through their own limitations and see beyond the restrictions of old belief systems. How much we master and manifest within this lifetime, at this vital time of transition, is a matter of individual choice.

Thank you for allowing me to share part of this journey with you.

Love and Light

Alexis

ABOUT SYMBOLS AND THE COMMENCEMENT AND COMPLETION RITUALS RECOMMENDED FOR EACH CHAPTER OF BOOK.

Symbols are very effective tools for healing, spiritual growth and transformation. They can be seen as "etheric enzymes" as they catalyse specific reactions in the etheric and subtle bodies and consciousness. This is because our etheric body is energetically created through the technology 'geometric formations' of light. Light itself sustains a mathematical coding system 'symbols' that sustained the laws that form the building blocks of our universe.

Each symbol also emanates specific sound waves that can only be heard on a clairaudient level. Some people therefore hear symbols emanating different vibrational tones. Because symbols do create subtle sound waved they are *instruments* of light and when formatted together, they resonate an aspect of the universal 'language of light'.

This explains how each symbol has its own specific vibration and technology and therefore sustains a unique and powerful creative force. By connecting with a symbol you are able to access and align with a specific facet of the life force energy and also filter through into your consciousness, universal knowledge. Symbols therefore create not only a self-healing process, but also awakening and self-empowerment processes.

This explains why it is helpful to meditate on the formation and meaning of symbols. In this book I have written an individual formation of symbols for each chapter, each formation reflecting the nature of the chapter. I recommend that before reading each chapter you follow its' *Commencement Ritual* by running your fingers along the line of symbols given from left to right. When you finish reading each chapter you should undertake the *Completion Ritual* running your fingers along the line of symbols from right to left. This will enable you to encode the essence and healing powers of each chapter and thereby support your healing, enlightenment and ascension process at this time.

CONTENTS

Chapter 1   Transference Healing 23

Chapter 2   The Global Grid Matrix: The Key to Ascension .. 51

Chapter 3   The History and Use of Crystals 101

Chapter 4   Revelations of the Christ 147

Chapter 5   The New Dimension 199

Chapter 6   Self-Help Techniques and Tools for Healing
             and Maintaining the Body and Facilitating
             Self-Transformation 223

Chapter 7   Channelled Teachings of the Christ 271

Chapter 8   The Prayer of the New Millennium 303

Chapter 9   Chiron: The Planet and Mythology 315

Chapter 10   Raven Power, the Black Madonna
             and Black Ray of the Goddess 341

Chapter 11   Dragon Power 357

Chapter 12   Children of the Light 373

Chapter 13   The Earth and its Doorways into Co-Existing
             Angelic, Elemental and Galactic Dimensions 391

Chapter 14   The Earth's Grid Point Connections to the
             Parallel Dimensions of the Angelic, Elemental
             and Galactic Worlds 445

Chapter 15   Lightbody Essences 487

HAS A PARTICULAR GRAPHIC IN THIS BOOK GRABBED YOUR ATTENTION?

Would you like to use a particular graphic for your new brochure or website?

Would you find it useful to place a chakra poster on your wall or to offer posters to clients and/or students?

Would you benefit from the energy of an Animal Magic Card Poster, A Master Christ Template or Lady Nada Template being integrated into your home or office?

Many of the original Beyond Doorways artworks are available for you to purchase either as a poster or as digital artwork supplied under license.

Note: For your convenience the table of diagrams on the opposite page, identifies the graphics that are available for purchase. Simply look for the $ symbol after the diagram name.

Visit the www.TRANSFERENCEHEALING.com
for more information and to place orders.

TABLE OF DIAGRAMS

2.1 - The Global Grid Matrix § 57

2.2 - Sacred Site of Stone Henge 58

2.3 - The Etheric Body § 61

2.4 - The Transference Crystal Cross Christ Template § 62

2.5 - The Flower of Life Symbol § 72

2.6 - Thoth § 76

2.7 - Earth Chakras as Mapped on the Human Body § 85

2.8 - The Chalice and the Holy Grail Grid Point:
      'Key to Immortality' 89

2.9 - Lady Nada § 92

3.1 - Crystal Skull 111

3.2 - Aboriginal Drawing Depicting the Translucent Lightbody.. 124

4.1 - The Astrological Template of the Grand Cross 155

4.2 - The Astrological Template of the Grand Square 156

4.3 - The Rider Waite Tarot - Wheel of Fortune Card 157

4.4 - The Dimensions of the Anatomy Affected by the
      Astrological Influence of the Planet/Venus - at the
      Time of the Grand Cross § 159

4.5 - The Dimensions of the Anatomy Affected by the
      Astrological Influence of the Star/Sun - at the Time
      of the Grand Cross § 162

4.6 - The Dimensions of the Anatomy Affected by the
      Astrological Influence of the Planet/Pluto - at the
      Time of the Grand Cross § 164

4.7 - The Dimensions of the Anatomy Affected by the Astrological Influence of the Planet/Uranus - at the Time of the Grand Cross § 166

4.8 - The New Age: 26,000 Tun Cycle 177

4.9 - The Astrological Template of the Star of David Activation, 8 November 2003 183

4.10 - The Astrological Template of the Venus/Transit Sun Activation, 8 June 2004 185

5.1 - The Negative and Positive Polarity Shifts of the North and South Pole.§ 200

5.2 - The Gravity Line of the Planet § 201

5.3 - The Gravity Line and Three Main Lines of Force in the Body § 204

6.1 - The Electromagnetic Lines of Force and Corresponding Elements § 225

6.2 - The Gravity Line, Three Lines of Force and the Categories Harmony Alignment Points Technique §..... 231

6.3 - The Seven Master Glands Within the Endocrine System § 235

6.4 - The Glands and Third Eye Chakra: Creating a Universal State of Enlightenment § 240

6.5 - The Lords Prayer Template: Colour/Gland and Planetary/Sound Healing Meditation § 246

6.6 - The Chakras and Corresponding Anatomy § 251

7.1 - Third Dimensional Physical Body Symbol § 282

7.2 - Sixth Dimensional Lightbody Symbol § 283

7.3 - Fifth Dimensional New Anatomy Body Symbol § 284

7.4 - Seventh Dimensional Celestial Body Symbol § 286

8.1 - The Centaur Chiron § 313

10.1 - The Raven Card from the Transference:
'Animal Magic Deck' § 340

11.1 - Dragon Card from the Transference Healing
'Animal Magic Deck' § 356

11.2 - Dragon Power Symbol § 361

12.1 - Inner Child Soul Portrait 380

13.1 - Becker-Hagens Earth Star 395

13.2 - The First Chamber of the Heart Chakra § 411

13.3 - The Second Chamber of the Heart Chakra § 412

13.4 - The Third Chamber of the Heart Chakra § 414

13.5 - The Eleven Chakras § 415

13.6 - The Master Christ Template Set § 429

14.1 - The Lyran Grid Point, Gateway and Constellation 449

14.2 - The Arcturian Grid Point, Gateway and Constellation 451

14.3 - The Pleiadian Grid Point, Gateway and Constellation. 454

14.4 - An Elemental Version of a Pleiadian Being § 459

14.5 - A Galactic Version of a Pleiadian Being § 461

14.6 - The Sirian Grid Point, Gateway and Constellation 464

14.7 - The Orion Grid Point, Gateway and Constellation 465

15.1 - The Complete Transference Healing Lightbody Kit.... 492

IMPORTANT: *Commencement Ritual*

*Before reading chapter 1, run your finger from **left to right** across the sacred language below.*

Your action, intent and the sacred vibration of this powerful language, will ensure that you are fully open to receiving and integrating the information within.

These symbols are the 13 elements of power symbols used in Transference Healing. In order from left to right, these symbols are Primal Matter/ Earth, Philosophic Sulphur/ Gold, Philosophic Mercury/ Silver, Salt, Philosophic Egg or Seed, Thermal Cycle, Death/Rebirth, Rainbow/ Rebirth, Purification, Divine Love, Oneness, Perfection and Alchemy.

When reading these symbols they create an internal alchemical healing and ascension process.

TRANSFERENCE HEALING

FROM THE AUTHOR

In 1992 I was divinely guided by the spiritual hierarchy to channel and establish the Transference Healing Modality onto the planet, by 1995 I had completed this task. I am entrusted with the Transference Healing frequencies, principals and teachings.

I am actively supporting the spiritual hierarchy to help heal and erase dis-ease from the global body and consciousness at this time of transition from the third to the fifth dimension. I am also assisting to anchor and channel through the necessary resources to create the *New Anatomy*, supporting humanity's Divine ascension process at this vital time of transition.

I am now keenly focused on facilitating global understanding of the Transference Healing Modality and creating global access to it. I have been guided, encouraged and supported in manifesting this book so that global understanding, acceptance and use of its' healing energies can be achieved as quickly as possible, allowing Transference to support humanity through the Earth changes.

Transference Healing moves people from one place to another (thus the name). It is transformational and empowering, encouraging everyone to become a self-healer. It incorporates all healing modalities within it and for this reason is of a very high vibration and very effective.

Everyone can benefit from a healing and everyone can learn how to be a Transference Healer if they are so inclined. *It is a healing of hope, light and love, enhancing a spiritual awakening and conscious connection through the Christ back to the God/Goddess.* It has and will continue to achieve profound results. The aim of this chapter is to create a foundation for the rest of this book, to explain how and why Transference has re-emerged onto the planet at this time, as well as, how and why Transference Healing works.

Thank you,

Alexis

CHAPTER OVERVIEW

In this chapter you will learn that:

- We are now in this *time of transition*, which is due for completion in 2012. Radical and magical alchemical changes are occurring within the *etheric* foundations of all matter, at the sub-atomic level of the human body and planet. We are all now experiencing a *divinely orchestrated process of co-creation*, which will enable us to shift from a three dimensional homo-sapien (holographic body and reality) into the '*Adam Kadmon*,' fifth dimensional (holographic body and reality). We are therefore taking a quantum leap forward in our evolutionary process.

- Our etheric body, DNA, chemical & hormonal make-up is quickly changing, resulting in *lightbody symptoms* such as; new illnesses, viruses, diseases, emotional and mental disorders, dissatisfaction, unexplained or increased severity of symptoms and in many cases ineffectiveness of traditional methods of treatment.

- Alexis was guided to channel through the Transference Healing modality to provide an opportunity for humanity to begin to work on themselves at this time of transition. The procedures and spiritual tools made available through this book will support each person using them to re-balance, align and shift the frequency of their body to sustain a general level of wellness.

- To achieve and maintain wellness individuals need to regularly clear, realign and balance all their energetic bodies, to heal deep emotional woundings, genetic weaknesses and shift to higher levels of consciousness.

- Transference Healing is unique because:
  - It works on an energetic level to heal and repair the DNA and etheric/physical body, as well as working with the electromagnetic field and lightbody system that interplays within the body so that it can ascend at this vital time of transition.

- It unifies all Eastern, Western, Indigenous, Mystery School and ancient Pagan healing principles and powers into *one holistic, universal and conclusive in-depth form of healing*. This was made possible through the support, wisdom and consciousness of *Chiron* and its planetary influence.
- It integrates more of the *Feminine* Principle, Goddess power and principles onto the Earth.
- During a healing Earth and cosmic inter-dimensional healing energies are channelled and filtered into and through the whole etheric/lightbody system to repair and heal the physical anatomy and shift consciousness into a new and more evolved state of being.
- Of its profound ability to create rapid, dramatic, widespread and magical changes in peoples health, life and consciousness. Hence the name 'Transference' which means just that 'change from one state of being into another'.
- It has manifested onto the planet at this time, to support the planet as a whole and humanity on an individual level, to co-create the necessary healing and transference responses within our body, consciousness and reality to survive the transition.
- It is an ancient healing system that has been reborn as the new healing system of the future.

◆ The tools utilised in Transference which include:
- Colour and sound waves.
- Crystal and vibrational essences.
- The elements (ether, earth, water, air, fire).
- Alchemy and planetary symbols.
- Masters and rays.
- The Master Christ Template Set.

◆

TRANSFERENCE HEALING®

LIGHTBODY ESSENCE KIT

Amazonite	Apatite	Amber	Amethyst	Aventurine	Calcite	Carnelian	Charoite	Chrysocolla	Chrysoprase	Citrine
Clear Quartz	Danburite	Diaptase	Fulgurite	Garnet	Jasper	Kyanite	Lapis Lazuli	Malachite	Moldavite	Moonstone
Rhodonite	Rose Quartz	Selenite	Smoky Quartz	Sunstone	Turquoise	Angel	Arthritis	Asthma	Cosmic Shield of Protection	Crystal Cross
Dragon Power	Emergency	Empowering Wisdom	Fertility	Goddess	Inner Child	Karmic Pain Release	Rainbow	Raven Power	Rebirthing	Regression
Star of David	Unconditional Love	Alchemy	Death/Rebirth	Divine Love	Oneness	Perfection	Philosophic Egg/Seed	Philosophic Sulphur Gold	Philosophic Mercury Silver	Primal Matter
Purification	Rainbow Rebirth	Salt	Thermal Cycle	Jupiter	Mars	Mercury	Moon	Saturn	Uranus	Venus
Air	Earth	Fire	Water	Blue Ray	Green Ray	Orange Ray	Red Ray	Violet Ray	White Ray	Yellow Ray

TRANSFERENCE HEALING®

LIGHTBODY KIT®

The vibrational medicine of the new millennium

CHANNELLED BY
ALEXIS CARTWRIGHT

Transference Healing is a new vibrational healing modality, of very pure and high frequency, that is multi-dimensional, comprehensive and advanced! It is an energy system that unites science with spirit, because it utilises the technology and resources of energy, light and matter.

PREMONITIONS AND PROPHECIES

Since the time of Atlantis specific prophets of supreme scientific and spiritual intellect, have been attempting to discuss and educate us on the many dimensions of the etheric/physical body. Some have understood how to utilise the natural technology and universal resources available to us from within the universe, to support a natural self-healing and ascension process.

The ancients had an advance level understanding of the rotation of the planets and astrological events that occur within our solar system. Sacred texts were written prophesising certain times when radical Earth movements and cosmic events were to come about, because of Celestial forces occurring within our universe. Cosmic events create magnetic grid shifts and electromagnetic changes within the Earth, enabling the Earth, human body and consciousness to go through rotational steps and evolve into higher levels of consciousness and reality.

They understood the Celestial science behind the Universe and also the alchemical or magical properties sustained within the Earth and Nature itself. They were in particular, preparing our civilisation for a *specific* Earth and cosmic occurrence, which came to be known as the 'Grand Cross Alignment' of 1999. This astrological event and the alchemical changes that it began to make within our universe, is explained in detail in chapter 4. It marked the beginning of this *time* of *transition* when we would complete a stage of evaluation and also begin to create a new and higher level of existence.

We are now in this *time of transition*, which is due for completion in 2012. Radical and magical alchemical changes are occurring within the *etheric* foundations of all matter, at the sub-atomic level of the human body and planet. We are all now experiencing a divinely orchestrated process of co-creation, which will enable us to shift from a three dimensional homo-sapien (holographic body and reality) into the *'Adam Kadmon'*, fifth dimensional (holographic body and reality). We are therefore taking a quantum leap forward in our evolutional process.

This book provides channelled information relating to these changes and their global side effects. I have also shared specific fundamental healing techniques and channelled through a smaller Lightbody Kit to provide an opportunity for humanity to begin to work on themselves at this time. This is because the Earth and cosmic changes are occurring more rapidly than ever before and will continue to increase in intensity over the upcoming years, enforcing us to make the necessary changes within our body and consciousness to ascend into the fifth dimension. The healing procedures are specifically covered in chapters 4, 6, 8, 10, 11, 13 and 15.

The procedures and spiritual tools that I have made more available through this book will support each person using them to re-balance, align and shift the frequency of their body to sustain a general level of wellness. By working the procedures herein they will begin to alleviate the general lightbody symptoms that everyone seems to be suffering with, to different levels and degrees.

It is important however that readers are aware the procedures offered in this book only hold a small aspect of the healing powers that the Transference modality can provide. So if you wish to master your wellness throughout our current 'transition' to the fifth dimension while continuing to awaken and grow as effectively as possible, I would recommend that in addition to running these procedures on yourself weekly, you either receive regular Transference Healings from a certified practitioner or empower yourself by becoming a self-healer through learning the Transference Healing Fundamental teachings *(refer to page 485 for more information)*. Either approach will allow you to access the complete spectrum of Transference Healing energies needed at this time. Follow your inner guidance as to determine which approach is the correct path for you.

WHY VIBRATIONAL HEALING IS NOW NECESSARY

The Earth and the human body is evolving, in turn viruses, illnesses and symptoms are changing and as a result our methods of healing need to change in order to remain effective.

Our transition from third to fifth dimension is resulting in *scientifically observable* energetic changes such as the movement of the magnetic lines and poles of the Earth, dramatic increases in the electromagnetic frequencies of both the Earth and human beings, increased cosmic activity including unprecedented solar flare counts - associated magnetic tidal waves, bizarre weather changes, severe weather patterns and natural disasters.

As you will learn, human beings are not just physical in nature; we are complex multi-dimensional energetic beings with a complex, geometric, etheric template or blueprint underlying and sustaining us, which regulates the automatic function of the body's self-healing system.

For this reason the energetic changes of the Earth, are co-creating alchemical changes within matter and light, which in turn is changing the fundamental make-up of our body, planet and reality as a whole. Our etheric body, DNA, chemical & hormonal make-up is quickly changing, resulting in lightbody symptoms such as; new illnesses, viruses, diseases, emotional and mental disorders, dissatisfaction, unexplained or increased severity of symptoms and in many cases ineffectiveness of traditional methods of treatment.

> **To achieve and maintain wellness individuals need to regularly clear, realign and balance all their energetic bodies, to heal deep emotional woundings, genetic weaknesses and shift to higher levels of consciousness.**

COMMON LIGHTBODY SYMPTOMS BEING EXPERIENCED AS A RESULT OF EARTH AND HUMAN CHANGES

- Respiratory discomfort, tightness in the lungs, asthma, flu like symptoms, hay fever, colds, runny noses and sneezing for up to 24 hours.

- Inflammation and or aching of bones and joints.

- Headaches or even migraines not alleviated by painkillers.
- Occasional diarrhoea.
- Dizziness, ringing in the ears, co-ordination imbalances.
- Heart palpitations.
- Lack of circulation, loss of muscular power and brief periods of weakness.
- Tingling in the arms, hands, legs and feet.
- Hormonal imbalance.
- Strange skin irritations.
- Feelings of dé·jà vu, intense fear of separation and loss.
- Immune & lymphatic system changes.
- Short periods of intense tiredness.
- Mood swings and bouts of short term depression.
- Strange symptomatic pain, especially through the back and vertebrae area.
- Dreams and strange sleeping patterns, night sweats.
- Hypersensitivity.
- Vagueness in the head and an empty feeling in the stomach.

THE MAGICAL PROPERTIES OF TRANSFERENCE HEALING

Transference was channelled through at this time to *shift* our perception on the alchemical particles and properties of the etheric/ physical body and how to clear internal imbalances and distortion within, so that corresponding systematic pain, distortion or disease can also be released instantaneously from the physical body and consciousness.

Transference helps us to understand the internal technology involved within the DNA and etheric body and how to energetically work with it to filter through the necessary ethereal and vibrational elements of the ever changing Earth and Cosmos, so that the body and consciousness can shift into higher frequencies and therefore into a more evolved mechanism that sustains a more substantial lightbody system.

Transference not only gives you the know-how to tap into and understand the etheric and physiological changes that are occurring within the physical and parallel lightbody system, but is also a tool to help you understand and utilise the changes within Nature, to support a divinely orchestration but radical shift forward in your evolution process.

> **Transference Healing is therefore supporting us in creating the necessary healing responses within the etheric/physical body, while re-coding our DNA, so that we can re-connect to an integral part of our genetic heritage and retrieve information and vital elements to support our ascension process into a higher dimension and a more inter-dimensional reality.**

There are many dimensions involved in a Transference Healing process, which I have summarised here in this chapter, but one will come to understand the complexity and the energies, teachings and healing process that Transference creates within the body and on Earth, through reading the following chapters.

WHY TRANSFERENCE HEALING IS UNIQUE

There are several reasons that Transference Healing is unique in comparison to other healing modalities these include:

TRANSFERENCE AND THE ETHERIC/LIGHTBODY SYSTEM OF THE ANATOMY

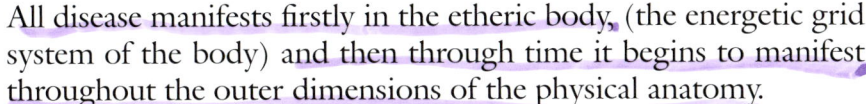

All disease manifests firstly in the etheric body, (the energetic grid system of the body) and then through time it begins to manifest throughout the outer dimensions of the physical anatomy.

It is very difficult to explain the etheric levels of the body. This is because it is a very complex energy system that co-exists within higher or more refined dimensions of the body and sustains the energetic resources that co-creates and maintains all dimensions of our physical anatomy.

It has not yet been identified with and understood totally by the technology of science and biology, because it cannot be seen by the naked eye. Actually it is very difficult to comprehend with the rational or consciousness mind. This is because you have to reach deep within and beyond the more physical levels of the anatomy, to be able tap into this 'etheric body,' which can only be felt, touched, and understood through higher consciousness and through psychic perception.

However if one stays open and sets their intent to understand and work with this level of the body they can then 'tap' into it and therefore create a more effective and conclusive self-healing response within all dimensions of etheric/physical body and consciousness.

I have developed and channelled Transference Healing onto the planet by coming to personally understand and work more *directly* with the complex levels and layers sustained within etheric body, which constitutes the many dimensions of the physical anatomy and new lightbody system.

To see a conceptual representation of the etheric body view diagram 2.3 on page 61.

The Etheric Body: The etheric body is commonly referred to as a complex energy web or system that sustains and weaves 'pranic' energies (very fine particles and ethereal properties) throughout the anatomy, so that a natural healing response can be initiated from within the body, to heal painful symptoms and diseases that are manifesting throughout the physical anatomy.

The energetic levels of the body that are more commonly worked with, when tapping into the 'etheric body', are the chakras, meridians, acupuncture and reflexology points and so on. The specific levels of the etheric body worked upon and the areas of the body in which a physical healing is obtained are usually determined by what 'Eastern medicine' technique is being applied, such as Acupuncture, Shiatsu, Chi Gong, Reiki and so on.

What makes Transference Healing so unique on a fundamental level before all else is that I intuitively channelled through all Eastern philosophic healing procedures in such a way that they became *one* holistic form of healing. My ability to do so was supported by being able to tap into and channel through the wisdom and consciousness of *Chiron* and its planetary influence, which is explained in more detail throughout the book, specifically in chapter 8.

Incorporating all energetic procedures and also focusing on channelling new information from Chiron, is what I felt was necessary to make a more conclusive *etheric* healing response within the many *energetic* dimensions of the anatomy, so that the physical body could repair and heal itself more effectively. I realised that this would not only co-create a more *holistic* healing response throughout the whole physical anatomy of the body, but also heal emotional and mental distortion or weakness held within the consciousness of the person that one was working with.

The lightbody: In channelling Transference I was also working with another energetic system that seemed to interplay within the body on different and higher frequencies levels to the energy system of the *etheric* body. I came to see and understand that this system was a vital element that needed to be addressed in order to clear the increasing number of symptoms resulting from Earth changes (lightbody symptoms).

To help clear the *transitional* symptoms my clients were experiencing, while also enabling them to shift into a higher state of consciousness, change the chemical compounds within their bodies and allow them to *ascend with the Earth* into a higher state of being, I realised that I had to work more within the complexity of the *lightbody* system.

To do this I had to reach into and understand the deeper dimension of the etheric body. This enabled me to access the higher levels of the *electromagnetic field* which actually creates the technology and resources of the lightbody system, which interplays within the etheric and physical anatomy. To understand this system it is necessary to understand the healing properties, principles and technology of light.

Transference Healing is unique in that is works on an energetic level to *heal* and *repair* the DNA and etheric/physical body, as well as working with the electromagnetic field and lightbody system that interplays within the body so that it can ascend at this vital time of transition.

THE UNION OF EASTERN, WESTERN, INDIGENOUS, MYSTERY SCHOOL AND ANCIENT PAGAN HEALING PRINCIPLES AND POWERS

Transference is unique and profound because not only are all vibrational, energetic or etheric 'Eastern' procedures are combined within it to create a more holistic *etheric* healing response within the body, but also all 'Western procedures' or healing modalities that are distributives from these more Eastern healing proprieties, philosophies and procedures, are also included.

Therefore each of the many procedures within Transference Healing were channelled through in such a way that they collate and integrate the necessary technology and energies that are sustained within Eastern and Western techniques, into *one holistic and universal form of healing*. These procedures and their therapeutic impacts work within all dimensions of the etheric/physical body and consciousness in a divinely orchestrated and synchronistic way. They include the healing properties of such techniques as: Chiropractic Care, Colour/Sound Therapy, Psychic Surgery, Chironic Healing, Acupuncture, Reflexology, Chi Gong and vibrational medicines: such as Homeopathic Care, crystal essences and alchemy symbols, to name a few. Divination charts are also available that give insight and diagnoses on the physical and spiritual attributes that need to be identified with and that are also being worked with, throughout the duration of a healing session. Transference also provides an opportunity to obtain a medical intuitive, as well as a spiritual and psychic reading and counselling.

Transference Healing also integrates more of the *Feminine Principle*, Goddess power and principles onto the Earth. The procedure when performed, manifests aspects of some of the ancient and forgotten transformative powers of the indigenous cultures, spiritual powers of the Anointed Ones or High Priests and Priestesses of the Mystery Schools and magical powers of the Magicians of ancient, pagan times.

> **Within Transference all *natural* healing principles and properties are united and channelled through to create a universal and conclusive in-depth healing response that is vital for our ascension process at this time.**

THE EARTH AND COSMIC ENERGIES UNITING HEAVEN AND EARTH WITHIN, CREATING ASCENSION.

By working energetically with both the *etheric* and *lightbody* system within the anatomy a more *conclusive* and in-depth physical healing response can be made. Earth and cosmic energies are channelled through simultaneously to weave, repair or co-create the necessary changes within enabling the etheric/physical body and consciousness to not only heal itself more effectively, but to shift into a higher state of being.

The **Earth** changes are providing the necessary ingredients such as plant, mineral or crystal vibrational properties/extracts, through to elements from within and on the planet, to heal the anatomy. This is done while performing the Transference procedures. Earth related energies are filtered and dispersed into the **physical anatomy** via the complex energy channels of the etheric web within the body.

The **Cosmos** is also currently going through many changes that are providing electromagnetic frequencies that continue to repair the *etheric* body clearing and revitalising the pranic centres, chakras, meridians and etheric levels of the DNA, so that the necessary frequencies of elements can continue to filter in creating a consistent rejuvenation process, throughout all dimensions of the etheric/physical body and co-creating the new **lightbody system.**

> During a Transference Healing, Earth and cosmic inter-dimensional healing energies are channelled and filtered into and through the whole etheric/lightbody system to repair and heal the physical anatomy and shift consciousness into a new and more *evolved* state of being.
>
> Hence the name 'Transference' which means just that, 'change from one state of being into another'.

AN ANCIENT HEALING SYSTEM REBORN AS THE NEW HEALING SYSTEM OF THE FUTURE

The Universe is now creating a healing and 'transference' shift within the body, planet and consciousness. These Earth and cosmic energies required to achieve this shift successfully are being relayed, filtered through and anchored into the body and consciousness of humanity through the procedures that I have channelled, anchored and now teach within this new modality, 'Transference Healing'.

I believe that this form of healing was on the planet during the latter time of Lemuria, supporting them at a vital time in their evolutionary process. I also believe that it was on the planet when the civilisation of Atlantis was being birthed and also during the time of Atlantis, when they sustained more of their lightbody system than we do now.

After the sinking of Atlantis, this healing process was handed down and practiced by surviving 'initiates' that migrated into Egypt and taught within the sanctuary and seclusion of its Mystery Schools. The process was also taught to Jesus during his last incarnation of Earth, and even though I do not claim to know all aspects of this ancient technique and the extent of its healing abilities, I have been intuitively guided to comprehend some of its teachings and healing attributes, so that it can be re-established once again, back onto the planet.

This is another reason Transference Healing is unique. It is a divinely guided process that has come through from a higher source for the planet and humanity, at this *specific* time, so that a global transference process can be supported. The Earth is now going through vital changes just like the changes that occurred at the end of Lemuria and Atlantis and both our planet and humanity is now entering into a whole new state of existence.

This is a time when we are going through a global death and rebirth like these critical times in the past. We are going through a divinely orchestrated *transference* of energy, light and matter, so that a whole new state of being can be reborn within our reality, without having to experience a death process, we just have to let go and let the changes in.

Transference has come through at this time, to support the planet as a whole and humanity on an individual level, to co-create the necessary healing and transference responses within our body, consciousness and reality to survive the transition. It has also reappeared to help re-establish an ancient philosophical teaching and form of healing that is needed if we are to evolve into the future.

HOW TRANSFERENCE HEALING CREATES AND MAINTAINS HEALTH AND WELLNESS

Receiving regular Transference Healing sessions allows us to achieve and sustain a consistent level of health and wellness through the Earth and human changes. Bodies maintain longevity, while deep emotional woundings begin to heal themselves from within, as we make consistent shifts into higher levels of consciousness. We become free from the need for medical or even alternative care, because we are consistently clearing the etheric and genetic weaknesses from within our body, preventing imbalances and their symptoms.

Through the energy of Transference and the support of a Healing Facilitator, we continue to awaken and grow, obtaining the necessary internal resources to release fear and confusion, to break through illusions and restrictions, to heal and ascend. We begin to take the right steps towards improving all aspects of our lives including relationships, talents, career and income. *Transference empowers us to become a self-healer and to start to master on a daily basis, ultimately achieving our highest vision of ourselves.*

HOW TRANSFERENCE HEALING WORKS

Transference Healing does not diagnose a condition by analysing the symptom of the dis-ease, instead it looks deeply into the etheric components of the body and reads it with psychic perception.

Transference incorporates many procedures, templates and essences that filter through the new codes, energies and elements into the etheric body.

Transference Healing also works with the *electromagnetic frequency & magnetic fields* of the body.

> **It is this magnetic aspect of Transference that results in the powerful alchemical impacts experienced by our clients and provides for the truly magical qualities of this healing process!**

All dis-ease manifests from a weakness in the etheric and/or magnetic fields, which over time manifests into the physical body. By working with both the etheric body & the magnetic frequency and fields of the body, we reach deep into different levels of vibrational density unrestricted by time or space. This allows a natural hormonal & biochemical balance to occur within the body. This balance when combined with counselling, guidance, insight, and assistance from Source, universal energies, guides and physicians on higher planes creates an opportunity to achieve a much more powerful healing.

The "source" of the trauma and pain can be obtained and removed through intent from the etheric or magnetic aspects of the body, without physical intervention and the physical body then responds quickly and with ease. This also allows and enables one to work on a preventative care level. Self-healing (through enlightened intent) occurs through the energetic and alchemical makeup of the body without having to use manual or physical intervention.

Transference Healing defies the *karmic gravity force of preordained death and genetic dis-ease* that creates death itself. It integrates more of the *Feminine Principle,* Goddess power and principles onto the

Earth, while unifying all healing modalities to effect a holistic and universal healing process.

Healing tools utilised in Transference include:

+ Colour and sound waves.

+ Crystal and vibrational essences (the medicine of the new millennium).

+ The elements (ether, earth, water, air, fire).

+ Alchemy and planetary symbols.

+ Masters and rays.

+ Templates.

THE MASTER CHRIST TEMPLATE SET

While creating the Transference Healing modality I was strongly guided to channel a set of healing templates through and onto Earth, to be used as a vital support tool for the Transference healing and ascension process. There are five main templates that make up The Master Christ Template Set. These templates filter through all the inter-dimensional energies that create the properties and procedures of Transference Healing.

Some of the healing and ascension powers created by The Master Christ Template Set are:

1. They support an in-depth healing process of the DNA so that it can begin to re-weave through a more pure 22-strand DNA system. Through the healing and re-coding of this new and more perfected DNA system the internal technology is then

provided to begin healing past life or genetic weaknesses. As the genetic weaknesses are decoded and the DNA gradually perfected, a more in-depth clearing also occurs within the more subtle levels or dimensions of the etheric/physical anatomy.

2. The technology of these templates support the changes that need to occur within the etheric body so that the third dimensional human body can ascend into the new fifth dimensional Adam Kadmon body, during this vital time of transition from 1999-2012.

3. These templates also filter through inter-dimensional frequencies of light to support the anchoring and creation process of the new lightbody system. The templates were channelled through from the seventh dimensions and sustain the crystal technology necessary to co-create the divinely orchestrated changes within the body so that the body and consciousness can ascend at this time.

4. Although these templates are used as healing procedures within the Advance Level Procedures of Transference Healing, they are also powerful tools to have around your home or office. If placed in the 'cross formation' on the wall they will automatically begin to filter into the body, the Transference Healing energies beginning a more subtle but affective healing and ascension process for all who come in contact with them.

5. When placed in a 'cross formation' on a wall they also begin to clear any distorted energies from the home, while gridding the crystallised properties beneath the Earth thereby creating a more pure, clear, protected and higher frequency environment to live in.

THE TRANSFERENCE HEALING RESPONSE

Clients usually go into a three-week gestation period after a Transference Healing. During this time they experience a radical internal vibrational and alchemical healing process, which can be so profound as to be almost magical in its healing nature and power.

Symbolically, it is like being taken into the womb of the Earth where you are internally supported and nourish to grow. Clients can feel a little 'altered' through this three-week period, they may feel mild symptomatic pain release, go through identity crises and experience changes in long standing issues in their lives. They can also feel at this time, a higher source of intervention so that they begin to feel spiritually safe enough to slowly let go of the negative patterning, defence strategies and their need to control the circumstances in their lives.

During this gestation period they may also experience a healing crisis as they go through their own personal change or 'transference shift'. Their etheric bodies go through a process of purification, realignment and repair; their DNA is being de-programmed and re-coded and their sub-conscious fears are being released. Some feel strange and mild 'release symptoms' ranging from mucus release, nausea, headaches through to a need for more rest.

After the gestation period, clients begin to feel refreshed, reborn and ready to take part in a life at a new level. Passion and potential growth slowly surfaces as they embody and live more of their new selves. They feel rejuvenated, more positive, are able to sustain more passion and recognise more of their own personal sense of direction.

At this time of rapid Earth and human evolution, humanity will open to and embrace the empowering and transformational energies of Transference Healing.

IMPORTANT: Completion Ritual

*Before you stop reading this chapter, run your finger from **right to left** across the sacred language below. This procedure will assist you to finalise the energies from this chapter.*

Your action, intent and the sacred vibration of this powerful language, will greatly assist you to fully integrate the information you have just read.

THE CRYSTAL CROSS CHRIST TEMPLATE

This template awakens the Christ Consciousness within, to transfer the Earth and Humanity into a higher frequency level and the next dimension through:

- Resonating the new magnetic and electromagnetic crystal matrix into and around the Earth.

- Interweaving the Celestial Christ Divine Light Gridding System into the heart of all matter.

- Templating and interweaving a Crystal Cross of crystalline light frequency into everything within our existence.

- Interweaving the crystal properties of nature to support everything within our dimension to shift to a higher frequency.

- Templating the creation of the lightbody and creating a more ethereal form of physical body and consciousness.

Note this template is sold either individually or as part of the Master Christ Template Set of five (see page 197). It can be placed in any room within your home or workplace.

This A4 size emerald green template has been overlaid with fine gold and silver leaf, to reflect its' magnetic and electromagnetic energies and has a detailed explanation on its reverse-side.

Place your order at www.TRANSFERENCEHEALING.com

IMPORTANT: *Commencement Ritual*

*Before reading chapter 2, run your finger from **left to right**
across the sacred language below.*

*Your action, intent and the sacred vibration of this powerful
language, will ensure that you are fully open to receiving and
integrating the information within.*

0.618039887 / $1.61803\ 39887$ / $y = mx + b$ / $xy^3 + x^2 + (y\text{-}x)^2 = 6$ /
$E = mc^2$ / $y = mx + b$ / $xy^3 + x^2 + (y\text{-}x)^2 = 6$ / $E = mc^2$ / 0.618039887 /
$1.61803\ 39887$ / $y = mx + b$ / $xy^3 + x^2 + (y\text{-}x)^2 = 6$ / $E = mc^2$ /
0.618039887 / $1.61803\ 39887$ / $y = mx + b$ / $xy^3 + x^2 + (y\text{-}x)^2 = 6$ /
$E = mc^2$ / $y = mx + b$ / $xy^3 + x^2 + (y\text{-}x)^2 = 6$ / $E = mc^2$ /$6789\text{-}3954849 +$
40593949 / $594303 + y = mx + b$ / 30349548 / 54933556 / $y = mx + b$
/ $xy^3 + x^2 + (y\text{-}x)^2 = 6$ / $E = mc^2$ / $7354940 + 94837$ / 48372645069

This code consists of a random selection of numbers: numbers are symbols
that measure the geometric formation in which matter is formed in space.
The Global Grid Matrix is formed through the crystallisation of sound:
numbers. This geometric etheric template or crystal 'global gird matrix'
in turn formulated the creation process of the planet Earth and all matter
itself that came to exist within our universe.

Included in the above code is the Fibonacci numbers as well as Einstein
equations or numerological formulas of a straight line or linear and
nonlinear equations and also the equation of mass = the speed of light. By
running your fingers across the formation of numbers, you are 'tuning into'
the very fine and numerological sound structures that format the Global
Grid Matrix and all physical matter within our universe.

THE GLOBAL GRID MATRIX: THE KEY TO ASCENSION

CHAPTER OVERVIEW

The topics covered in this chapter are very broad and diverse, despite this they all relate back at some level to the Global Grid Matrix and ascension. In this chapter you will discover:

- How key sacred sites are located where the powerful grid line connection points of the Global Grid Matrix are energetically sustained by the crystal frequencies of light within and around the globe. How and why healing miracles and spiritual phenomena occur at these sites.

- How these grid line connection points disperse energies and create frequency changes in the Earth, similar to how the chakras on the human body operate.

- That the Atlantians understood this Matrix and used it for their power source, communications and technology. They also used it to create healing chambers for self-rejuvenation and longevity.

- How this Matrix not only sustains the life force, alchemical make-up and ecological balance of the planet, but also the etheric and electromagnetic bodies anchored within the human anatomy.

- How the Transference Healing Crystal Cross Matrix weaves through the necessary dimensions of the Global Grid Matrix needed for the healing process.

- In this time of *transition to the fifth dimension* (1999-2012), the *lightbody system* is actually anchoring into the physical anatomy before we die enabling us to ascend into the next level of consciousness without having to experience the death process.

- As the lightbody begins to anchor in, all of humanity will begin to master the self-healing process and begin living within a higher level of consciousness – we currently only use about 25 percent of our healing powers.

- The Matrix is etherically inter-woven and encoded within

the DNA of the central nervous system. We currently only use a small portion of this technology, which is enabling us to make the necessary alchemical changes so that the lightbody or new anatomy can begin to anchor in at this time.

- The Matrix was damaged in the fall of Atlantis and is now revitalising, healing and anchoring more into the DNA as a result of the Earth and cosmic changes, allowing us to regain access to it and heal.

- A new *12-strand DNA system* is weaving in during the transition to 2012, allowing us to alchemically change to heal and rejuvenate the anatomy and body beyond what was previously possible.

- Further the new DNA is allowing us to heal viral and past life or genetic distortions creating more effective healing, and slowly eliminating environmental and genetic disease off the planet to sustain life, longevity and wellness.

- There are another ten etheric strands of DNA relating to the lightbody system that exist beyond but parallel to the physical 12-strand system and relate to the ten steps of the 11/11 Gateway (the pathway to ascension and initiation to complete 'enlightenment' on Earth). As we master each of the fundamental 12-strands of DNA these will slowly filter in to create the more evolved 22-strand DNA system.

- There is a minority of humanity that is anchoring the extended 10-strand system they are preparing to evolve to the seventh dimension in this time of transition. A few who master the 11/11 Gateway initiations and anchor the ten etheric strands will become the founding masters of the New Age and play fundamental role in supporting humanity to create a new way of living. Everyone who exists after 2012 will begin this process. Everyone on Earth will have perfected and completed the ascension process by the year 3012.

- *Jesus* embodied the wisdom, technology and powers of the Matrix. His initial learning's were via John the Baptist's Mystery School (which taught Egyptian and esoteric secrets). He did not teach Jewish law but the sacred Egyptian teachings, he created his own Mystery School teachings and initiated the 12 apostles into his inner circle. He visited Egypt to learn more about mastering the Divine powers of alchemy and lightbody resurrection and worked to personally and spiritually master these practices so he could embody the totality of his electromagnetic/lightbody and therefore anchor in his Christbody and Consciousness while on Earth (resurrection via the Crucifixion).

- *Mary Magdalene* was a high priestess of the Black Madonna Line – a Sirian lineage of teachings from the Mystery School of Isis. She stood beside Jesus supporting his 'awakening and enlightenment process' and his mission on Earth.

- Learn about *Thoth* and how he stands behind all concepts and teachings of the planetary grid ever given to Ascended Masters on Earth. How all Mystery Schools and Golden Ages emerged from his teachings. In our time Thoth has handed his lineage of power and wisdom to Archangel Michael who is assisted by Melchizedek in this dimension.

- Learn about *Lady Nada* and how specific teachings and powers have now been handed to her, to be channelled through her to the Earth and humanity. These frequencies will heal grid lines that exist in the Earth and help us to heal the Crystal Kingdom, which will then support the frequency shifts of water over the Earth, in turn assisting the human body to heal more effectively.

- Learn about the healing 'centaur' Chiron and how it accesses the human etheric anatomy via the Chiron Point (located between the solar plexus and heart chakras, bridging them). How it has come through physically at this time to activate human and planetary healing by helping us weave the higher universal frequencies of the Global Grid Matrix into our energetic and physical existence allowing us to transfer into the new anatomy.

- Mastering Chiron consciousness and perfecting the energetic transition from the solar plexus to the heart chakra is allowing us to be released from the restrictions of time, space, duality, karma, death and reincarnation.

- The Global Grid Matrix is being healed and perfected through the awakening of the electromagnetic fields of the crystal formation of the Earth resulting from constant solar flare activity and stellar / planetary alignments.

- Enlightenment is a process that must be created within the body, not just the mind or consciousness. This is the essence of alchemy and the key to immortality.

- Learn how the *Pleiadians* were the first lightbeings to inhabit the Earth. They co-existed with the Crystal Kingdom. Their DNA mutated and their etheric bodies evolved via the technology of the crystals. They are the template and origin of the human DNA and life on Earth. At the same time the Earth establishing herself in a parallel dimension ultimately creating a reality called Lemuria.

- The human body has an 11 chakra system , as well as, multiple heart chambers, Chalice and Holy Grail points.

- The Earth has a chakra system arranged in an energetic sequence at seven key 'dome centres' around the globe that weave in the universal energies from the Global Grid Matrix.

◆

GLOBAL GRID MATRIX

This chapter explains some of the complexity of the energetic Global Grid Matrix as it impacts the healing and ascension process of our Earth, Cosmos and correspondingly our body and consciousness, at this vital time of transition into the fifth dimension.

DIAGRAM 2.1
The Global Grid Matrix

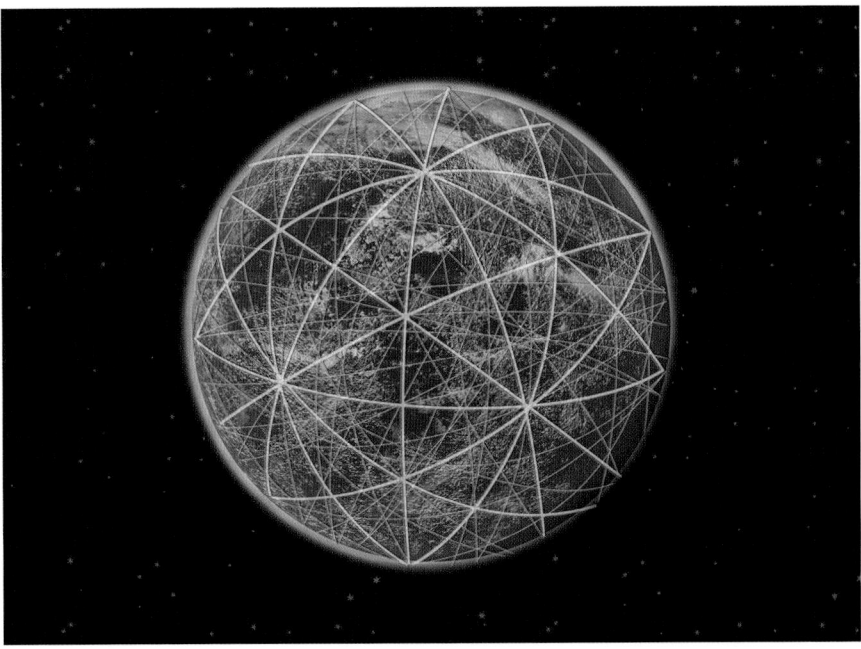

This global gridding system existed before the Earth and Cosmos was formed and was a vital tool in the creation process of our world and dimension.

PART 1

The Earth and its energies are comprised of and organised by an intelligent geometric pattern or 'web' of energy called the *Global Grid Matrix*. Imagine the Earth as a globe wired by an energetic lattice or grid of lines of light intersecting at specific points within and around the planet. These grid lines or ley lines and their connection points provided the knowledge and inspiration for the ancients to locate the sacred sites on Earth and create the geometric dimensions of their megalithic stone temples.

DIAGRAM 2.2
Sacred Site of Stone Henge

SACRED SITES

Sacred sites of stone temples, pyramids and circles, are positioned all around the planet. They were once used as places of worship

- creating an enlightenment and empowerment process for those who meditated there. Some of today's best know and often-frequented churches are built over the remains of these abandoned sites.

Healing miracles and spiritual phenomena have occurred throughout time, at these locations because they are actually located where powerful grid line *connection points* of the *Global Grid Matrix* are energetically sustained by the crystal frequencies of light, within and around the globe. Examples include profound healing within the physical body itself; sightings of the manifested lightbodies of Ascended Masters and profound revelations obtained through a 'psychic' awakening process. In some locations where water emerged from the ground, 'healing wells' were then established for the people.

These connection points disperse energies and create frequency charges into the Earth and surrounding area just as the chakras of the human etheric/physical body. Therefore, the natural 'electromagnetic energies' resonating out from these *connection points* within the crystal formation of the Earth, are absorbed by and then shift the energy system of the body. This creates a shift of frequency within the body enabling some to experience an 'enlightenment and healing' response within.

As the ancients understood the technology of the *Global Grid Matrix* these locations became sacred sites, for healings and spiritual practices. They energetically enhanced the process being performed by the practising Shaman, Initiate or Healer.

ATLANTIS

The Atlantians understood the geometries of the *Global Grid Matrix* to the extent of accessing its sacred information to create beautifully proportioned architectural buildings containing healing chambers for self rejuvenation and longevity. The whole power source and technology of Atlantis was created through their ability to access this unique energetic gridding system. It also allowed inter-dimensional telecommunication and spaceship travel. Sadly, the misuse of both the power of crystals and the ley lines of light created the final fall of Atlantis.

THE ETHERIC BODY

The complex etheric gridding system and existing ley lines not only sustain the life force, alchemical make-up and ecological balance of the planet, but also sustain the dimensions of the etheric and electromagnetic body anchored within the physical human anatomy.

1. The *etheric* body is an energetic maze of adjoining acupuncture points, meridian channels and chakra vortices which sustain the physical body in the third dimension.

2. The *Global Grid Matrix* sustains and rejuvenates the complex *etheric* body which in turn rejuvenates, sustains and creates our physical anatomy.

3. The *Global Grid Matrix* weaves in the etheric body and continues to co-create an *energetic* and also *alchemical* healing process throughout the many levels and layers of the physical anatomy. *The Matrix* therefore interplays through and between the etheric/physical body to sustain our health, life force, form and consciousness in this dimension.

The Global Grid Matrix combines the elemental compounds from and of the Earth to create the physical body and anatomy. It also continually weaves through vibrationally to slowly heal and evolve all matter into higher frequency and consciousness.

DIAGRAM 2.3
The Etheric Body

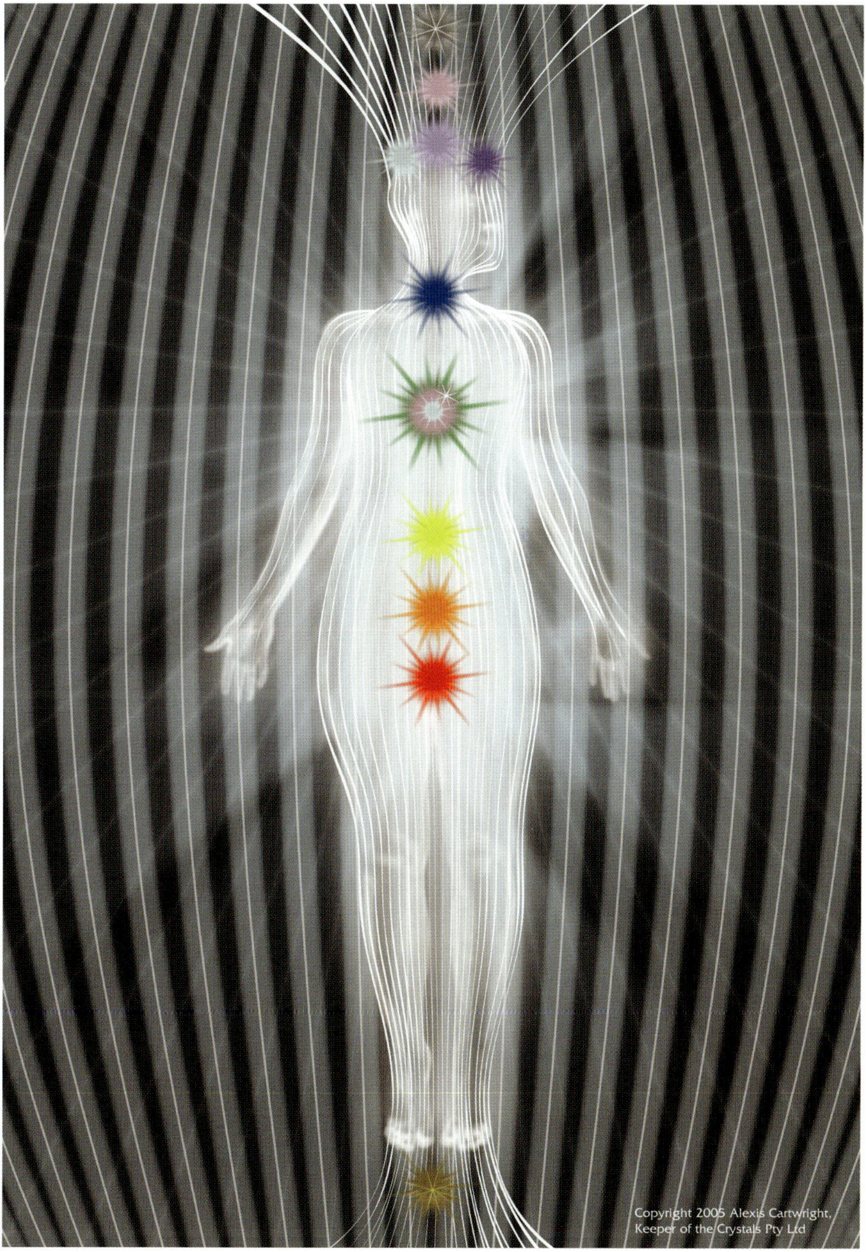

THE ELECTROMAGNETIC BODY AND THE CRYSTAL CROSS CHRIST TEMPLATE

The electromagnetic body or lightbody interconnects through the physical body via the essence and technology of the etheric body sustained by the *Global Grid Matrix*. It consists of higher or finer frequencies and specific geometries of the *Global Grid Matrix* which remain hidden and more removed from the consciousness of most of humanity.

D IAGRAM 2.4
The Transference Crystal Cross Christ Template

Copyright 2005 Alexis Cartwright, Keeper of the Crystals Pty Ltd

The Crystal Cross Christ Template filters through the frequencies of the Global Grid Matrix and combines the necessary Earth and cosmic energies, to heal and restore the etheric anatomy and physical body. It also filters through the necessary resources to resurrect the lightbody. This template also channels the crystal technology and healing frequencies of the Transference Healing procedures.

I have channelled and energetically imprinted the *Global Grid Matrix* into *the Crystal Cross Christ Template* of Transference Healing. This template is a physical healing tool which weaves through all the necessary dimensions of the *Global Grid Matrix* needed for the healing process of the *etheric/physical anatomy* of the body. It also filters or weaves through the necessary technology and higher frequencies of energies of the *Global Grid Matrix* to create and restore the electromagnetic field of the body so the *lightbody* can anchor through more during a healing session. *Refer to page 49 for more information on this product.*

THE EARTH AND HUMANITY'S ASCENSION

The *Global Grid Matrix* firstly weaves into the Earth and then into the human body, shifting consciousness and creating all the necessary energetic and alchemical changes necessary, for the body and consciousness to ascend. On a parallel level it also creates the necessary energetic and elemental changes in the Earth, so the Earth can also ascend into a higher level of existence. It therefore creates the necessary changes within all of *matter itself,* so the Earth and humanity can complete the transition into the fifth dimension by 2013. This matrix is supporting us to ascend with and through the Earth and cosmic changes so we can anchor through more of the Higher Self and therefore co-exist within a higher level of existence and consciousness.

THE GLOBAL GRID SELF-HEALING PROCESS

This matrix is not only weaving in the necessary Earth and cosmic energies and elements so we can heal and ascend but is also constantly nourishing and re-aligning *itself* through and from the Earth and cosmic changes occurring within our dimension. The re-weaving and revitalisation process of this 'web of life' is also energetically supported by the crystal formation within the Earth and also by specific star systems, constellations and planetary formations within our solar system.

THE LIGHTBODY

The electromagnetic body or lightbody transfers-in during the death process, to enable us to ascend into the next level of consciousness or dimension. This is known by the ancients as the 'After Life' and referred to by Christianity as 'Heaven'. However, at this *time of transition* from 1999-2012, the lightbody system is *now* anchoring into the physical anatomy before we die. The Earth is leaving the third dimensions and will be entering the fifth dimension in 2013.

As the lightbody system begins to anchor through, all of humanity on a global level will begin to master their own self-healing process and be able to begin living within a higher level of consciousness. As we begin to master all of this, we will slowly begin to lengthen our life span and be able to interconnect with other levels of consciousness and realities within other dimensions. We will no longer be so isolated and separated from the parallel universes and their realities and worlds. Over the next 1,000 years as we anchor and exist more and more in the fifth dimension, we will slowly break down the boundaries of time and space.

THE DNA

Certain geometric proportions of the *Global Grid Matrix* are also etherically inter-woven and encoded within the DNA of the central nervous system.

At this time we only use a small proportion of the internal intelligence of the *Global Grid Matrix* which sustains the technology of the geometry of the DNA. It heals and revitalises the body and consciousness by channelling the etheric body in such a way that all natural ethereal resources are energetically relayed throughout all dimensions of the anatomy to maintain life force, vitality and wellness in the physical body and consciousness. This internal technology of the DNA also enables the body and consciousness to make the necessary *alchemical changes* so the *lightbody* or *new anatomy* can begin to anchor or transfer in at this time.

Certain dimensions of the *Global Grid Matrix* are therefore etherically templated within the DNA to give us the innate and internal know-how to re-energise and heal the body and consciousness at any given moment - *within a moment*. The key to unlocking and working with these dimensions when performing healing procedures is to work on an etheric level.

Since the fall of Atlantis, we have only been able to access a certain amount and level of our innate healing power from within the DNA because certain proportions of the *Global Grid Matrix* were damaged through our descent into lower frequency. However, the *Global Grid Matrix* is now revitalising itself because of the radical Earth and cosmic changes occurring at this time. It is therefore re-weaving and healing itself on a global and universal level as well as within our DNA. As this gridding system begins to heal, anchor and filter through more into the DNA, body and consciousness, at this time of transition, we can regain access to it and heal ourselves.

12 AND 22-STRAND DNA SYSTEMS

12-STRAND DNA – PHYSICAL

The healing process of the *Global Grid Matrix* is weaving in the *new* 12-strand DNA system during the transition from 1999-2012. As it does, the DNA will have more internal technology and codes to obtain more universal resources to continue to *alchemically* change and heal the anatomy and body - beyond what was previously possible. These changes to the DNA system are part of what is necessary for the body to ascend with the Earth into the *fifth dimension*.

The many dimensions of the new *12-strand DNA* system will also begin to heal all *viral* and *past life* or *genetic* distortions from the DNA and body, so the **physical anatomy** can begin to heal and rejuvenate itself more effectively. In this way, all environmental and genetic diseases are being wiped off the planet and the body will be able to sustain more life force, longevity and wellness without suffering so many painful symptoms. **The 12-strand DNA system therefore prepares the body to ascend into the fifth dimension.**

22-STRAND DNA - SUSTAINING HIDDEN ETHERIC STRANDS

The *Global Grid Matrix* is really weaving through a *22-strand* DNA system as there are another ten *etheric* strands of DNA relating to the lightbody system that exist beyond but parallel to the *physical* 12-strand system. These strands are hidden within higher dimensions of the etheric formation of the DNA and this level of the DNA will take much longer to anchor through.

As we master each strand of the fundamental 12-strand DNA, by slowly activating and integrating its healing power and technology into the physical body, each one of these ten *parallel* strands begins to be activated on the etheric level. They will slowly filter in through time, thereby weaving through more and more of the **cosmic or lightbody system.**

THE 11/11 GATEWAY

These extra ten strands of DNA relate to the ten steps of the 11/11 Gateway which is a pathway of ascension and initiation to complete a state of 'enlightenment' on Earth. At each stage we are encouraged to *embody* the necessary Earth and cosmic energies, so we can shift into higher states of consciousness. While doing so we are anchoring in more ether and light into our body and therefore embodying more of our Cosmic Self. Humanity is therefore completing a state of **physical** evolution and on a parallel level creating a new more evolved state of cosmic consciousness.

THE SEVENTH DIMENSION AND THE CHRISTBODY

A minority of humanity have slowly begun to anchor through the higher and more extended 10-strand DNA system, at this vital time of transition from 1999-2012. They have chosen to consciously surrender and integrate the changes within themselves and their reality with more ease to accelerate their growth process. They are perfecting their *enlightenment* process by anchoring in the lightbody with more ease and therefore shifting into higher levels of consciousness with more consistency than others around them. They are therefore in a more rapid state of ascension and are preparing to evolve into a more *seventh dimensional reality* by 2012, while the rest of humanity is physically anchoring into the *fifth dimension*. Less than one percent of humanity will *master* this process during this transition time of 1999-2012.

Those *mastering* the 11/11 Gateway initiations which are activated by the DNA, are thereby growing at a more rapid rate than the rest of humanity. As we go through an 11/11 Gateway initiation and eventually *master* each initiation, we *crystallise* higher dimensional aspects of our lightbody thereby *beginning* to anchor in more of the *Christbody* and Consciousness while physically incarnated on Earth. Our Christbody is the embodiment of the **higher frequencies** of our **cosmic** lightbody and reflects aspects of our Higher or Cosmic Self. It is more divine and galactic in nature.

The few who master these levels of initiation, at this time of transition from 1999-2012, will become the founding masters of the New Age and play a fundamental part in supporting humanity to establish a new way of living for the next one thousand years. They are therefore helping establish the seventh and final Golden Age on Earth.

However, everybody who exists or will come to exist on the planet after 2012, will begin the process of the 11/11 Gateway initiations as they slowly learn to master through each incarnation on Earth. Global consciousness will also shift more rapidly over the next 1,000 years because of the anchoring and perfection process of the lightbody. As we live in higher consciousness on Earth and go through states of initiation, we will slowly ascend into the Christbody and Consciousness. *Everybody on Earth will have perfected and completed this ascension process by the year 3012.*

ASCENDED MASTERS

Ascended Masters have completed this ascension process into the seventh dimension on a personal level, while in a state of physical incarnation on Earth. They were ascending and anchoring the completion process of their light/cosmic body therefore embodying their Christbody to access higher levels of consciousness, realities and worlds while humanity and the world around them still existed within the lower frequency and restrictions of a third dimensional body and reality. These Ascended Masters were the key *channellers* on the planet and brought about the technical knowledge, wisdom and philosophies necessary for humanity as a whole to eventually shift into higher consciousness and also ascend.

OVERVIEW

Time is speeding up because the Earth is going through a transitional shift, leaving the third dimension and anchoring into the fifth dimension which will officially begin in 2013. (This process is explained further in chapter 4). From 2013 the Earth and humanity will live within higher levels of frequency and consciousness for the next 1,000 years. Humanity will then take only 1,000 years to *complete* the totality of this ascension process by anchoring into the seventh dimension in 3013. All our previous experiences and physical, personal and spiritual growth, before and on Earth have been necessary to build the foundations to take this vital step in our evolutionary process. *As we anchor through more and more of the 22-strand DNA system, we are becoming a **living**, **ascending master** while in a state physical incarnation. This level of ascension and growth would normally have taken 10,000 years in normal linear time in the third dimension.*

At this time we only access and use about 25 percent of the healing and manifestation powers of *Global Grid Matrix*. When we access, embody and use all the sacred powers and knowledge of the whole, we will be able to completely embody and consciously live in a reality of manifestation and reclaim an innate ability to 'heal thyself' to create ongoing wellness and longevity while sustaining a physical form.

JESUS THE CHRIST

JESUS AND THE EGYPTIAN MYSTERY SCHOOLS

The Soul of Jesus who became the 'Christ' embodied the wisdom, technology and powers of the *Global Grid Matrix*. He initially learnt about its existence and innate powers, when baptised as an initiate of the inner circle of John the Baptist's Mystery School. Egyptian teachings and esoteric secrets were the foundation of John the Baptist's mission and teachings, which later influenced the mission and teachings of Jesus.

Jesus did not preach the Jewish law even though he was born through the genetic blood line of King David. The Jewish 'Talmud' reveals he preached the sacred Egyptian teachings he was initiated into by John the Baptist. He set out to introduce these empowering, true and extremely sacred and Divine teachings firstly into the Jewish community and then into the world at large.

He eventually created his own Mystery School teachings and initiated the 12 apostles into *his* inner circle. He personally taught them the hidden mysteries of ancient Egyptian/Atlantian 'esoteric knowledge' and they in turn supported his mass healing and enlightenment process on the planet.

JESUS AND MARY MAGDALENE

Mary Magdalene was a high priestess of the Black Madonna Line – a Sirian lineage of teachings from the sacred Mystery School teachings of Isis. Magdalene was the 13th apostle and partnered Jesus in a 'sacred marriage.' She stood beside Jesus supporting him in his 'awakening and enlightenment' process and his mission on Earth.

The Egyptian influence of the gospel stories is undeniable. Jesus was fulfilling the prophesied role of a Jewish Messiah and he and Mary Magdalene were embodying the teachings and magical healing and manifestation powers of Isis and Osiris.

JESUS IN EGYPT

Channelled

Jesus visited Egypt to learn more about *mastering* the Divine powers of alchemy and lightbody resurrection. He meditated in the lightbody chambers within the Egyptian pyramids and received 'channelled information' about materialising the lightbody and the realms it can take us into. As we know the Egyptians had a fascination with the 'after life'.

The pyramids themselves are temples that sustain the geometric power and internal-technology of the Cosmos. The 'lightbody chambers' built into the pyramid create etheric Doorways geometrically aligning connection points between the Earth grid and *cosmic grid* or star constellations that are stellar gateways into other dimensions.

By lying in these 'lightbody chambers' Jesus aligned his body within a two-way channel of energy between the Earth and Cosmos - and vice verse. He then etherically integrated the energies necessary to enable the Earth and cosmic frequencies to filter and anchor through, uniting Heaven and Earth within. He was resurrecting his Higher or Cosmic Self while incarnated in a physical body on Earth

By encoding and embodying certain aspects of the *Global Grid Matrix*, Jesus accessed parallel dimensions in consciousness and essence. When he referred to the 'Kingdoms of Heaven' he was referring to these parallel realms or dimensions the lightbody can resurrect us into. *(These kingdoms are the parallel realms or dimensions that are further explained in chapter 14)*.

Jesus worked to personally and spiritually master these practices so he could embody the totality of his electromagnetic/lightbody and therefore anchor in his Christbody and Consciousness.

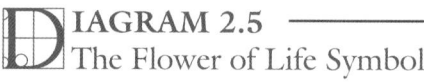

DIAGRAM 2.5
The Flower of Life Symbol

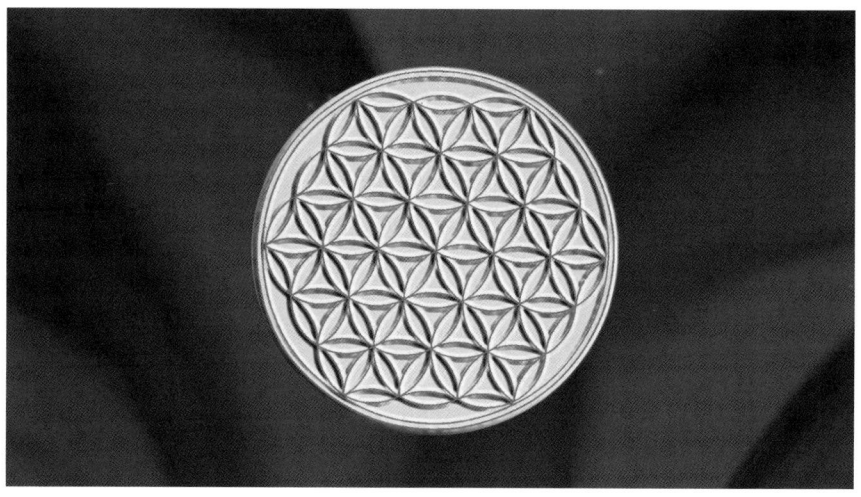

The embodiment process of the lightbody is symbolised by the geometry of the 'Flower of Life'. *Copyright 2005 Alexis Cartwright, Keeper of the Crystals Pty Ltd.*

The *Flower of Life* geometric master symbol or template sustains the technology to encode and filter through the necessary dimensions of the *electromagnetic* field to assist the lightbody to anchor in and manifest through. This geometry is also encoded into the Crystal Cross Christ Template of Transference Healing.

The universal healing and ascension process created by the Celestial Christ and the templating process of the *Global Grid Matrix* and Crystal Cross Christ Template are supporting the ascension process of our own body and the planet, at this time.

CHRIST -THE CRUCIFIXION AND RESURRECTION

Channelled

The Resurrection is a process of overcoming the limitation of gravity in the physical body, by anchoring and resonating the whole electromagnetic field of the lightbody in such a way that an alchemical *transference* process occurs on a cellular level. As each cell embodies more electromagnetic light or ether, physical mass can mineralise itself and the totality of the lightbody - the seventh dimensional *Christbody* - can anchor in. Jesus not only accessed seventh dimensional reality in consciousness, but **embodied** the totality of his *cosmic seventh dimensional lightbody system, the Christbody,* while incarnated in a third dimensional hologram and reality on Earth.

Throughout history, many initiates prepared for the process of resurrection. However, very few mastered it. Today we identify them as the Ascended Masters. Jesus not only mastered and completed this process of enlightenment and resurrection but chose to re-educate the world to come, just like Thoth had done. At the time of his Crucifixion, Jesus utilised every lesson he had learnt and mastered throughout his current and past lifetimes to achieve the resurrection of the lightbody.

The symbolism of the Crucifixion was set up so Jesus could portray to the world how to overcome the limitation of duality and gravity. While on the cross, which symbolised the sacrifice of the physical body, Jesus entered an altered and deep trance-meditative state. From this state of consciousness, he was able to continually transmute dense energy by maintaining and resonating an enlightened and compassionate level of consciousness.

As he embodied a deep and heart-felt state of enlightenment on a cellular level, a shift in mass consciousness occurred.

At this level of consciousness Jesus was able to create the necessary changes in the chakra system, kundalini and etheric body for his electromagnetic field to begin to amplify and resonate with more intensity. Corresponding to the energetic changes in the etheric body and consciousness, the necessary alchemical changes were also taking place in the physical body. Jesus *transferred* the chemical compounds of his physical body into a more ethereal form of matter, elevating himself into higher frequencies that reflected from his body like the 'halo' effect shown in Christian paintings - an example of a reflective aspect of the lightbody. This enabled him to template in his cosmic lightbody or Christbody whilst in the painful state of crucifixion. He therefore went through a complete *transference shift* allowing him to sustain his life-force while his body suffered the intensity of a near-death process.

THE TRUE TEACHINGS OF CHRIST

Summary

Jesus mastered the magical form of healing and transformation he had learnt when being initiated into the practices of the sacred and Divine 'cult teachings' of the Moon God Thoth, sustained within the Mystery Schools of Egypt. These teachings were remnants from Atlantis. The initial priests who had learned and then institutionalised these scientific and technological teachings as 'sacred' knowledge shrouded them in ceremonial mysteries and rituals to protect them from outsiders. They were then passed from initiate to initiate in an exclusive and secret tradition. This knowledge held the principles of both science and magic, and gave its possessors unprecedented mastery over the physical world. *Today they would be regarded as masters of sorcery.*

Jesus had therefore learnt to master the laws of gravity, alchemy and the properties of Nature and while doing so, showed the world the divinity and essence of the 'light'. He channelled and reflected energy and light for healing and taught about its consciousness through parables.

He also revealed the technology of what he had come to understand and master to those who were more spiritually committed, like the apostles. They then followed and supported the Christ's re-education process of the world, by healing and writing his teachings. The teachings were later collated into the scriptures of the Christian Bible. Because these teachings were also encoded within parables, the true nature and wisdom of the Christ has lain hidden from most of humanity. Only those who can access higher consciousness, Christ Consciousness, are able to decipher, read or hear the true teachings of the Christ. However these teachings are now being 'revealed' to specific people who are awakening and embodying The Light to become key channels of 'Christ Light' in support of humanity, at this time.

Isis, Saint Germaine, Buddha, Lady Nada and others, also mastered the lightbody/Christbody to become Ascended Masters. However, Jesus chose *to reveal to the world* the ancient and sacred teachings and ascension process of alchemy and the *Global Grid Matrix* so everyone could embody their divinity and release themselves from ongoing suffering and pain. He chose to master this enlightenment process and became an Ascended Master on Earth like others before him. **What is so unique about Jesus the Christ** is he chose to reveal 'the way' through which everything in existence could begin to weave through the magical alchemical healing powers of the *Global Grid Matrix* for humanity's salvation and ascension process prophesied to occur at the turn of the Millennium. Jesus was chosen to reveal 'the way' to survive this global change for the world to come. This technology and know-how is now enabling us on a global level to master our ascension process into the next dimension.

> Jesus became the vehicle through which humanity could ascend into the fifth dimension and beyond and thereafter into a state of unity and oneness with other worlds and realities. This ascension process is re-connecting us into the totality of our DNA system.

DIAGRAM 2.6
Thoth

THE ANCIENT MASTERS OF THE
GLOBAL GRID MATRIX

The ancient magician Thoth stands behind all concepts and teachings of the planetary grid, ever given to Ascended Masters on Earth. Thoth, was a master grid engineer who initially existed in Atlantis, lived through into the first Dynasty of Egypt and was later identified as Hermes Trismegistos in Greece. He was called the Thrice Greatest Hermes, master of geometry and alchemy, creator of the Emerald Tablets - the keys to understanding the magical powers of Gaia's (Earth's) energy body and field.

All Mystery Schools and Golden Ages emerged from Thoth's teachings. The flame of his mastery has passed down to different initiates during different ages on Earth - Isis, Merlin, Mary Magdalene, John the Baptist and Jesus the Christ. In our time he has handed his lineage of power and wisdom to Archangel Michael with his solar initiatory sword. The Hebrew teachings say Michael is the keeper of the secrets of the relations between Heaven and Earth. Melchizedek assists him in this dimension.

LADY NADA

In 2003, it was psychically revealed to me while channelling on location at the sacred site of Tara, in Ireland, that specific teachings and powers (regarding the more crystalline aspects of the Global Grid Matrix) have now been handed onto Lady Nada. This lineage of power and wisdom will now channel directly through her to the Earth and humanity. The frequency will specifically heal grid lines that exist in the Earth that run and sustain themselves more within the **crystal** ley lines of the Earth. The new frequencies she will channel through will also help us to heal the Crystal Kingdom, which will then begin to support the frequency shifts of water all over the Earth. Since the human body sustains 70 percent water, it will begin to heal itself more effectively. *(The specific channelling from Lady Nada is written at the end of this chapter)*.

Archangel Michael, Melchizedek and Lady Nada now hold the *trinity of powers* of the *Global Grid Matrix* on and for the Earth. They are now supporting the Celestial Christ to reveal and channel new sacred information to those who are being initiated as 'grid channellers' on Earth. They are also being assisted by other dimensions - such as the Pleiades, Sirius, Arcturus, Lyra and Orion - to continue to heal, enlighten and align the *Global Grid Matrix* within our Earth and solar system, allowing our dimension to make its transition into the fifth dimension, at this time.

PART 2
DIMENSIONAL SHIFT AND UNIVERSAL REBIRTH

As previously explained, in 1999 a global 'Transference Shift' began that will continue to create radical changes within our body, planet, reality and consciousness, until 2012. Through this vital time of transition we are templating and weaving in different dimensions of the *Global Grid Matrix* to allow us to anchor into a new fifth dimensional reality. We are being universally reborn into a new body and world.

CHIRON

CHIRON - THE HEALING CENTAUR

A Californian astronomer, Charles Kowal, discovered Chiron in 1977. Since its discovery there has been much debate as to what Chiron actually is – a planet, an asteroid or a planetoid. It has now been officially named as a new type of Heavenly body called a *'centaur'*. However, it has been determined that Chiron's physical presence and influence is only temporary. It will not sustain its life force and gravitational pull within our solar system for as long as the other planets. One day it will leave us to enter into a new dimension.

Since the discovery of Chiron, several other centaurs have been discovered. They belong to the Kyper Belt outside our solar system but because of their elliptical orbit they have now entered the orbit of our outer planets. Chiron's orbit is between Saturn (the conservative, conformist planet) and Uranus (the radical, revolutionary planet). It is seen as a 'bridge' between the inner or closer planets and more distant outer planets of our solar system.

THE CHIRON POINT

Chiron also has an access point within the human etheric anatomy, located between or 'bridging' the solar plexus and heart chakras. We can only access this point in the etheric body, through higher consciousness.

1. Chiron has come through physically at this time to activate human and planetary healing. It is a temporary planetary gateway through which we can attune to the consciousness of the *Global Grid Matrix* and the etheric body.

2. The etheric body is the energy blueprint or web sustaining our physical body. By healing the etheric body we can heal inbuilt weakness and genetic disease which exist because of the energy weaknesses within Earth. As the *Global Grid Matrix* of the planet and body is being healed by the Earth and cosmic energies, Chiron helps us weave the higher universal frequencies of the *Global Grid Matrix* into the energetic and physical fabric of our existence.

3. By tuning into the centaur or Chiron consciousness and corresponding energy point within our anatomy, we can access the geometry of the chakras within the etheric body, which allows us to tap into the whole etheric matrix or energy field to realign and repair it.

THE HEALING OF THE GLOBAL GRID MATRIX

The Earth's *Global Grid Matrix* is being healed and perfected through the awakening of the electromagnetic fields of the crystal formation of the Earth and the stellar influxes and frequency shifts resonating from the ever-constant solar flare activity and stellar and planetary alignments.

As the energies of the *Global Grid Matrix* heal and restructure the etheric body and DNA into the correct geometric proportion, they will give the etheric body the internal intelligence and resources to begin to activate *a whole new alchemical process* providing the necessary elements to create or weave in the new anatomy and lightbody. Chiron assists *the body to transfer from a third dimensional template into the Adam Kadmon*, a fifth dimensional template, so the human body and consciousness can ascend into the fifth dimension.

CHIRON AND THE SOLAR SYSTEM

As we begin to master Chiron consciousness and perfect the energetic transition from the solar plexus to the heart chakra, we begin to reach beyond the restrictions of time and space governed by Saturn and Uranus. The physical and intuitive restriction placed on us by the cycle of Saturn is lifted and we begin to release ourselves from the laws of duality or the 'Scales' of redemption, karma, death and reincarnation.

1. The Inner Planets – Ascension Process

The Universe is expanding because gravity is pulling in the *higher frequencies* of matter (compounds of ether) into our reality and dimension. This process is also causing us to shift energetically to ascend. We do this by refining our inner self and intent, breaking through the limitation of Saturn and therefore perfecting our lower chakra system and whole etheric/physical body – creating more of an inner state of perfection. This is orchestrated by the rotation of *the inner solar system and Chiron.*

2. The Outer Planets – Enlightenment Process

The energies that filter through from the *outer planets* of our solar system - Uranus, Neptune and Pluto - allow us to pass through a maze of energetic initiations, transits or rights of passage. They give us the opportunity to create an *enlightenment process by* embodying more *electromagnetic energies for our lightbody* to sustain itself more within form.

> **Enlightenment is a process that must be created *within the body,* not just the mind or consciousness. This is the essence of alchemy and the key to immortality.**

Ultimately, we will become illuminated *in body and consciousness* by utilising the universal energies of the planets, stars, constellations and crystals via the *Global Grid Matrix*. Higher frequencies of the gridding system sustained within the crystals, and all stellar influences from the solar system, are now anchoring through the *Global Grid Matrix* via Chiron the planet and the Chiron point within our chakra system. These energies which are weaving through enable the Earth, and the human body and consciousness to ascend into the next dimension.

PLEIADIANS- THE ORIGIN OF OUR DNA

The Pleiadians were the first lightbeings to inhabit the Earth and evolved through the same process we are now undergoing to enter a new reality, dimension and consciousness. Their DNA mutated as they evolved from and through many galactic worlds until they entered our world when it was still forming. They were able to anchor themselves into the electromagnetic energies of the crystal or mineral formations at the beginning of Earth's existence.

They co-existed within the Crystal Kingdom with the elemental or fairy spirits, learning about the healing elements and energy systems of the Earth. Their etheric body evolved via the internal technology (geometry) of the crystals and resonance of the ley lines of light emanated by the crystals. As the etheric body evolved so did the meridian and chakra system and as the heart chakra opened, their third eye awakened and a new enlightened state of consciousness began to resonate through.

All the while, the Earth was establishing herself within a parallel dimension. The elements evolving in accordance with the laws of Nature, created or formed a new dimension, reality or world that emanated a tranquil and healing environment of perfection. This was called Lemuria.

As the physical world evolved around them, the Pleiadians began to slowly emerge or evolve from the inner caves or dimensions within the Earth to the outer dimensions onto Earth. The planet at this time was truly a Garden of Eden. The Pleiadian beings were nourished by the external elements and cosmic frequencies as their lightbodies began to gently evolve into a soft, ethereal, energetic mass that later solidified into matter.

This was the template of the human body that existed at the time when Lemuria ascended and Atlantis evolved. *The Pleiadians are the template and origin of our existence on Earth,* which explains why and how our DNA mutated into its present state. Initially, we were not made within galactic laboratories by the extra-terrestrials on Earth at the time of Atlantis, but as stated in the Book of Genesis, we were made from the crystals of the Earth. We exist because of a *natural* process of *DNA engineering* created by the internal intelligence and energetic substance of the higher frequencies of the Global Grid Matrix.

CHAKRAS

CHAKRA SYSTEMS OF THE HUMAN BODY

We have seven main chakras spaced along the spine from the base of the spine to the crown of the head. In Sanskrit chakra means 'spinning wheel'. The chakras transmit higher energies from the *Global Grid Matrix* into a very complex meridian system. It is functionally affiliated with the seven principal endocrine glands and therefore with specific organs of the body and specific states of ascending consciousness. The main chakra system feeds the necessary energies and etheric substance from the Universe into the body so the physical form and consciousness can maintain its life force, form and wellbeing in this dimension.

CHAKRA SYSTEM OF EARTH

The Earth also has a chakra system, not arranged in an anatomical sequence, but in an energetic sequence at seven key 'dome centres'.

Earth chakras, like those at the great pyramid of Giza in Egypt, or Glastonbury Tor in England, are a huge energy vortex, like a two-way grid door - several miles in immediate diameter and extending much further than the area of influence. The other locations are the Gobi Desert, Mongolia; Mt Regions of Eastern Tibet; Avebury, England; Tara, Ireland; Uluru, Australia; Machu Picchu, Peru and Mt Shasta, California.

These major chakra points or vortices weave-in the universal energies from the *Global Grid Matrix*. They are located at the intersections of the 22 main crystal ' grid lines of force' within the Earth, which connect up to create the etheric energy system (grid) of the planet. This is like the etheric energy system of human anatomy.

If the Earth's chakras lost their ability to re-energise the specific grid lines and connection points of the *Global Grid Matrix* within the Earth, the anatomy and consciousness of the Human Race would not sustain itself within this dimension. We simply would not and could not exist.

DIAGRAM 2.7
Earth Chakras as Mapped on the Human Body

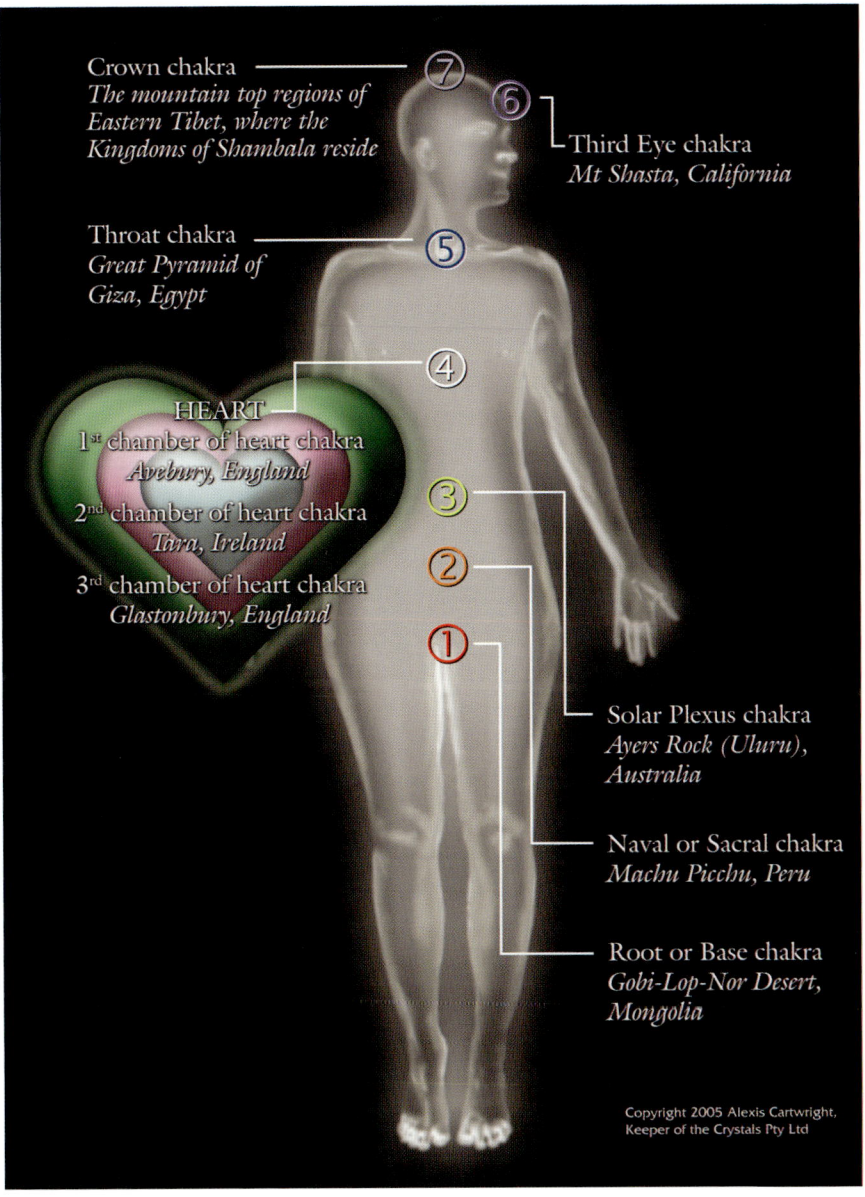

Crown chakra
*The mountain top regions of
Eastern Tibet, where the
Kingdoms of Shambala reside*

Third Eye chakra
Mt Shasta, California

Throat chakra
*Great Pyramid of
Giza, Egypt*

HEART
1st chamber of heart chakra
Avebury, England

2nd chamber of heart chakra
Tara, Ireland

3rd chamber of heart chakra
Glastonbury, England

Solar Plexus chakra
*Ayers Rock (Uluru),
Australia*

Naval or Sacral chakra
Machu Picchu, Peru

Root or Base chakra
*Gobi-Lop-Nor Desert,
Mongolia*

THE FIVE HIGHER CHAKRA SYSTEMS BEYOND THE SEVEN MAIN FUNDAMENTAL CHAKRAS

Another chakra system consisting of five vortices on a higher frequency again, interlocks with the seven major chakras. These five chakras anchor-in the lightbody by weaving through the levels and layers of the electromagnetic field into the etheric/physical body. They have been used less frequently than the other chakras because most of humanity has not reached a level of consciousness to be able to access them – like the Ascended Masters.

They are positioned in different, higher frequencies above the head, in the heart and below the feet and are named the stellar gateway, causal, soul star, Holy Grail point and earth star chakras. *(Refer to diagram 13.5 in chapter 13 for more information relating to the 11 chakras of the body)*.

Until now, they have done very little in the way of healing the human anatomy because they have not been as vital to the functioning of our physical body as the seven main chakras. However, at this time of transition, they need to be recognised, understood and utilised for their part in the process of anchoring the *new anatomy* we are all in the process of creating.

THE CHALICE AND THE HOLY GRAIL POINT

THE HOLY GRAIL POINT - OPENING THE HEART

The heart is the key through which all emotions are filtered throughout our body; it is the physical organ which allows us to shift consciousness on a cellular level. The physical heart itself is creating a new electromagnetic field to open the heart chakra on a deeper level and is being energetically supported by the *Holy Grail point* within the heart chakra. This energetic point exists within the centre of the heart chakra between the first and second chambers of the chakra itself.

THE TECHNOLOGY OF THE GRAIL POINT AND (2) CHAMBERS OF THE HEART CHAKRA

The first chamber of the heart chakra gives the heart the technology and resources to sustain our physical life force by pumping blood throughout the veins of the body. It also rejuvenates and delegates our *thymus gland* to sustain our immunity and prevent disease from manifesting through and into the physical body.

The Holy Grail point is like a mid-way point which energetically bridges the first and second chakras. When energetically activated it sustains our life force on a deeper level within our body. It does this by opening up the second chamber of the heart which then balances the energy interplay throughout the etheric/physical heart and also heals, repairs and revitalises the electromagnetic aspects of the lightbody system which usually lies more dormant within our body and consciousness. *(Refer to chapter 13 for more information on the first and second chambers of the heart).*

This Holy Grail grid point therefore has the internal resources and know-how to open the **second chamber of the heart chakra.** This then enables the heart chakra to obtain the necessary finer frequencies of crystal light to filter through to revitalise and repair the lightbody system, thereby preventatively caring against lightbody symptoms and viruses coming through and into the physical body. These lightbody symptoms are occurring more frequently because of the energy bombardment from radioactive and solar flare activity, which are side effects of the intense Earth changes at this time.

THE HOLY GRAIL POINT AND CRYSTAL CORE OF THE EARTH

This Grail *grid point* is weaving the necessary frequency shifts from the Earth's **core** into the heart chakra. *(The internal energetic structure and connection of the heart to the Earth's crystal core, is also explained further in chapter 13).*

The crystal core of the Earth is etherically impulsing the heart to change its electromagnetic field. The second chamber of the heart chakra can then open and in turn shift the electromagnetic fields around each cell in the body and then the whole body and consciousness.

This new electromagnetic field of the heart is supported on an energetic level by the electromagnetic energies that resonate from the crystals and grid or ley lines of light which interplay throughout the whole *Global Grid Matrix* and therefore within and around the planet and physical body. This etheric gridding system is supported by the energetic frequencies resonating through and from the *crystals* within the *Earth* itself as well as the stellar activity resonating from the *star gateways* and *constellations* in our solar system.

Grid points within the crystal and stargate systems are like Doorways into higher dimensions that allow energies- cosmic and therefore galactic in origin - to also filter through and into the DNA.

The symbol of the priceless Grail Cup, holding the blood of Christ as the 'key to immortality', is a symbol for the **Sirian** contribution to Earth genetics. The Grail Cup has always been a dream or prize that has eluded us; a quest for salvation *outside* ourselves – yet it lies hidden within us. The Holy Grail point activates Christ Consciousness and the resurrection of the perfected cosmic Christbody.

DIAGRAM 2.8
The Chalice and the Holy Grail Grid Point:
'Key to Immortality'

I interpret the chalice as a symbol representing the 'grid point' hidden behind the heart chakra, called the 'Holy Grail point.'

This point with the assistance of Chiron, helps to clear specific galactic genetic DNA codes and wounding lodged within the etheric and electromagnetic field of the heart chakra and therefore throughout the body.

This is the energetic level where we sustain the pain and distortions that have occurred at certain times in our evolution through our 'Fall from Grace' or 'descension' process.

It is also *the level of patterning* within the heart chakra which identifies/defines the 'Blood line of Christ'.

This blood line is not traced through Christ's genetic Jewish line on Earth but the *genetic essence/coding and patterning of his cosmic body* or lightbody whose resurrection enables ascension into higher levels of consciousness, reality and being.

Those who access this level of patterning belong to the 'Blood line of Christ'.

The Holy Grail Line is a specific aspect of the grid lines of the *Global Grid Matrix*.

It restores the electromagnetic field created by the Holy Grail Grid Point within and around the heart chakra and therefore begins to repair all levels of the energetic and physical heart, so the etheric/physical body and lightbody can respond and restore themselves on a deeper level.

REVIEW

- The Holy Grail point and heart chakra are like a central control box creating the internal technology for the evolution of specific dimensions of the new DNA, anatomy and lightbody.

- The Holy Grail point and heart chakra are also assisting the DNA to re-code itself so the body can rejuvenate and heal old wounding and also revitalise itself at a more rapid rate.

- With the assistance of Chiron, it is helping to clear all etheric wounding in the heart and DNA, not only from the *genetic* line on Earth but also wounding created through the etheric body from *before* our time on Earth.

- It is also clearing global viruses which are manifesting more rapidly on the planet because humanity is being universally forced to clear specific genetic weaknesses and diseases from our body and planet. Viruses create DNA mutation and a mass clearing and purification process so the body and consciousness can evolve and ascend. If we struggle to let go of the old patterning we will manifest more severe symptoms such as cancer, or even more global viruses and diseases, until we allow-in this Divine templating and ascension process.

THE GRAIL LINE SPECIFICALLY HEALS THE GRAIL POINT AND CHAKRA

There is one major grid line of the Earth's *Global Grid Matrix* that specifically needs to be re-energised and realigned to support the much needed healing process of humanity over the next few years.

This *Grail Line* is in the process of re-connecting itself and is vital for the healing and awakening of the *Holy Grail point* and deeper chamber of the heart chakra which will enable the 'heart of humanity' to begin to heal itself on a global level.

The specific grid line of the Earth, that needs to be re-energised and realigned so the Holy Grail point and heart chakra can heal themselves even more, was once known by the ancient Druids as the St Michael's Line. This line starts in the North of Ireland and then runs down through certain locations in Ireland, Scotland and England, ending up at Avebury.

DIAGRAM 2.9
Lady Nada

A CHANNELLED MESSAGE ALEXIS RECEIVED FROM LADY NADA AT TARA IN 2003.

Lady Nada declares, in a frequency that is so pure it is hard to hold in my body, and with a voice that speaks in sounds that echo from beyond an almost impossible point of comprehension.

(Yet her determination persisted until I stood at the sacred site of Tara, Ireland, where this message finally came through).

She reveals that she is now initiating those who are to hold the 'gift', of the 'Blood line of Christ' - that innate ability to create the alchemical healing powers of the 'Holy Grail'.

The Elemental 'Fairy' Kingdom will assist her in these rituals of initiation that she filters down to those who will become global grid, light and Christ channellers on Earth.

She also declares that the Elemental Doorways positioned at the four main grid points on Tara, Ireland, where the four wells stand today, are to open once again. The elemental lightbeings or fairies will help her reactivate certain crystal grid lines or 'dragon lines 'on Earth. This will allow crystallised healing waters to emerge once again, at different locations all around the world.

One of these four grid points at Tara, St Francis Well, will once again flow with water and this will bear testimony to her words.

But first, before this can occur, a main grid line must be healed from Ireland through Scotland, Wales and England (and then I was shown through my third eye, a grid line weaving in a divinely orchestrated silver and crystal light formation).

As I 'tuned in,' I saw the connection points and main grid lines within this weaving formation begin to restore themselves, as the radiant light was spiralling, reconnecting and healing itself.

It was weaving itself from Ireland down through New Grange, Tara and Oshna, and as it extended down into Scotland and England, it connected dots or points of light at numerous, prominent Christian churches, built over earlier megalithic sites.

It then ended its journey near Stonehenge, Bath and Glastonbury where the solar (male) and lunar (female) energy finally enter together into the heart of humanity at that sacred site of Avebury.

Lady Nada declared that I (Alexis) have seen and participated in the healing of these energies within the etheric web of life which sustains itself within the Global Grid Matrix of the Earth.

This will begin to heal the 'Holy Grail point' within the heart of humanity.

Through Lady Nada's request the Elemental Kingdom will once again connect and work with 'chosen grid channellers'.

They will accept them into their kingdom to become master 'grid workers' and will become recognised on Earth as lineage holders of the Lady Nada Line - like Isis, Morgan Le Fay and St Bridget.

Master 'grid channellers' will not only be able to create a Divine healing response, directly within the physical body by channelling through crystal light, but will also be able to create a divine, alchemical healing responses within the Earth and humanity, by shifting the frequency of water itself.

Water sustains 70 of the body so as the 'grid channellers' shift the frequency of water through the healing impact created within the grid lines, global healing impacts will be felt within the whole of humanity.

At the end of this channelling I was told to drink the water from the cup which I held and to my surprise it tasted like 'vanilla'.

This is and will be the sign for others who are to experience this revelation; it will be the sign they have received an initiation by Lady Nada to become a 'global grid channeller' of crystal 'Christ light' and will be of service to the Earth and humanity.

Through channelling these 'ley lines of light' they will connect more to the elemental and angelic planes, feel the purity and power of spirit and come to see miracles taking place within the world around them.

They will have become an instrument for The Light.

IMPORTANT: Completion Ritual

*Before you stop reading this chapter, run your finger from **right to left** across the sacred language below. This procedure will assist you to finalise the energies from this chapter.*

Your action, intent and the sacred vibration of this powerful language, will greatly assist you to fully integrate the information you have just read.

0.618039887 / $1.61803\ 39887$ / $y = mx + b$ / $xy^3 + x^2 + (y\text{-}x)^2 = 6$ / $E = mc^2$ / $y = mx + b$ / $xy^3 + x^2 + (y\text{-}x)^2 = 6$ / $E = mc^2$ / 0.618039887 / $1.61803\ 39887$ / $y = mx + b$ / $xy^3 + x^2 + (y\text{-}x)^2 = 6$ / $E = mc^2$ / 0.618039887 / $1.61803\ 39887$ / $y = mx + b$ / $xy^3 + x^2 + (y\text{-}x)^2 = 6$ / $E = mc^2$ / $y = mx + b$ / $xy^3 + x^2 + (y\text{-}x)^2 = 6$ / $E = mc^2$ / $6789\text{-}3954849 + 40593949$ / $594303 + y = mx + b$ / 30349548 / 54933556 / $y = mx + b$ / $xy^3 + x^2 + (y\text{-}x)^2 = 6$ / $E = mc^2$ / $7354940 + 94837$ / 48372645069

THE LADY NADA TEMPLATE

As featured in chapter 2 of this book (diagram 2.9).

Is now available as a beautiful and powerful quality A4 colour poster. Now you can integrate this profound healing frequency of love and unification into your home or workplace

"The perfect gift for yourself or a loved one."

In 2003 Alexis Cartwright received a channelled message from Lady Nada while visiting the sacred location of Tara, Ireland. This message inspired the creation of the Lady Nada Template, which filters the new Lady Nada / elemental frequencies onto the planet, supporting Lady Nada's role on the planet at this time of change.

Lady Nada revealed through Alexis that she is now initiating those who are to hold the 'gift', of the *Bloodline of Christ* that innate ability to create the alchemical healing powers of the *Holy Grail*. She has enlisted the assistance of the elemental 'fairy' kingdom to perform the rituals of initiation that she filters down to those who will become global grid, light and Christ channellers on Earth. She also declared a re-emergence of the healing waters of the world, preceded by healing of gridlines and the Crystal Kingdom, which will ultimately begin to heal the *Holy Grail Point* within the heart of humanity.

Place your order at www.TRANSFERENCEHEALING.com

IMPORTANT: Commencement Ritual

*Before reading chapter 3, run your finger from **left to right** across the sacred language below.*

Your action, intent and the sacred vibration of this powerful language, will ensure that you are fully open to receiving and integrating the information within.

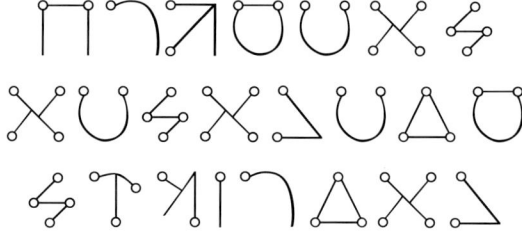

These symbols represent the words "CRYSTAL", "ATLANTIS" and "LEMURIA" written in the ancient Angelic - Language of Light. These symbols attune you to the healing powers of crystals and also help reconnect you to the dimensions of Atlantis and Lemuria.

THE HISTORY AND USE OF CRYSTALS

FROM THE AUTHOR

This is a very complex chapter. I have really exposed myself to share 'out there' information that could overwhelm some readers, so please use your discernment as you read through the material.

It is an opportunity to gain channelled information I have collated from certain psychic readings and channells prior to 1999.

I advise you to see each paragraph as separate and with its own message, with the common thread being the crystals.

There are many separate sections with their own subtitles and although the subjects are diverse, at some point, they all reflect back to crystals.

I have referred to crystals in many different ways, giving intuitive information on how they can be used as spiritual instruments for channelling, healing, spiritual and psychic development and ascension.

I have also included channelled information on Lemuria and Atlantis because of their connection to and use of crystals.

Thank you,

Alexis

CHAPTER OVERVIEW

Crystals were the first form on physical life on Earth. In this chapter you will discover:

- The origin of crystals, how they were birthed physically on Earth, their true value and power, their history and uses.

- The metaphysical, etheric and alchemical healing properties of crystals.

- The gridding abilities of crystals.

- How crystals work as powerful and positive energy healing tools.

- The most effective ways to use crystals for healing.

- Insight into Lemurian Society and how they utilised crystals, their evolution as a genetic species of the Pleiadian Race and the ultimate reason for their downfall.

- The genetic origins of our human existence, the evolution of the humanoid body from the technology of the quartz crystals, through a process of mutation of Pleiadian Race DNA.

- The transition of dimensions from Lemuria to Atlantis.

- The rise and fall of Atlantis, insight into Atlantian society, technology and use of crystals.

- How the Atlantians utilised the technology of quartz crystals to create Merkabah Chambers for levitation and inter-dimensional travel.

CHAPTER OVERVIEW CONT'D

- The true nature of DNA the 'big picture' of evolution past, present and future.

- How different civilisations, races and cultures formed in different locations all over the Earth.

- Multidimensional reality, Earth gridding, the Global Grid Matrix and doorway points within the Earth and Cosmos.

- That the Earth and human body is in a process of rapid change from the third to fifth dimension, the transition will be complete by 2013.

- That in order to complete the transition every human body must anchor a complete 12-strand DNA system so that it can incorporate the fifth element of ether into the physical body.

- The doorway point of the human body and how this 'Doorway' is linked to past life experiences and alien abduction.

- The seven Atlantian Disks and the seventh dimension.

- The 7th Mystery School commencing in 2006.

◆

Crystals existed before time as we recognise it today. They are the refined substance from and of which 'matter', the foundation of our whole physical existence, is built. They contain the power source to co-create, sustain and transform, 'matter' and through the ages have been used as instruments for creation, healing, rejuvenation, consciousness raising, ritual, communication and technology.

CRYSTAL HEALING

Many of today's teachings about crystals originated from Lemuria and Atlantis such as their metaphysical and etheric healing powers and properties through to their innate 'gridding' abilities for healing the body, planet and changing the DNA. Information has been handed down through the ages on how and where to place specific crystals on chakras or meridians to heal physical ailments and unblock distorted energies and emotions.

The *Lemurians* lived in harmony with Nature and used crystals to create an environment that was natural, tranquil, and almost magical in nature.

The *Atlantians*, although spiritually parallel in development, began to use crystals for creating new technology that became the foundation of their civilisation.

Thousands of years later civilisations of Babylon, Egypt, China, and the Stone Age people of Australia and of course the Aztecs and Toltecs all used crystals. However they had a more limited view of the uses of Crystal Healing and crystals in general. Unfortunately, not one of them manifested the *full potential* of crystals.

FORMS OF CRYSTAL HEALING STILL PRACTICED TODAY

* Chakra balancing by 'laying on' or 'gridding' with crystals.

* Vibrational medicine using gem and crystal essences and homeopathic remedies.

* Wearing crystals for *healing* and to aid longevity.

* Wearing crystals *as talismans* or charms for protection, or to aid the gift of prophecy.

* Wearing crystals to *amplify specific qualities* in both humans and animals, for example to enhance courage. (The crystals were surgically implanted into the animals- usually into their heads).

WHY CRYSTAL HEALING WORKS

Scientists now know that disease can be traced to the bio-molecular system, which means our physical bodies can be healed through energy. Healing does not occur on the level of chemical reactions but right down at the level of molecular structure. Healing occurs from inside out - from the etheric to the bio-molecular, through to the cellular and ultimately the anatomical level. When it is brought to the anatomical level, many levels and layers of the anatomy are harmonised.

Crystals are able to encode an energetic healing process into the body because the two are vibrationally compatible - the inner structure or geometry and molecular composition of a crystal are similar to the etheric and molecular composition of our physical body.

Crystals are perfect healers or healing tools as both crystals and our physical bodies respond to and emit vibration, they are both based on the same principle of resonance and vibration. Both the human body and planet itself are created by and formed from the subtle properties and substances of crystals. The body and planet itself are really just substances of mass that are forming crystals. These formations therefore generate their own unique compounds of matter and consciousness

Everything is in a *constant* state of vibration and a healing crystal can project the correct molecular pattern to re-balance the vibrations of any other life forms. They can also protect us by deflecting vibrations that create imbalances, disharmony and disease. When we are sick, our vibration or resonance becomes unstable. Crystals can transfer vibrations to stabilise our energy pattern and therefore bring our body back into a state of balance and wellness.

CLEARING GENETIC WEAKNESS FROM THE DNA AND ETHERIC BODY

Karmic or genetic patternings from past lives lead to most of our current illness. Crystals can release these binding patterns that create repetitive negative behaviour or illness. As the crystal activates the healing of past life pain encoded within the DNA and cellular levels of the body and consciousness a purification process of the etheric body and emotions occurs. Crystals do not manipulate our personality into new behaviour patterns but allow the positive qualities of our inner nature to come through.

HOW CRYSTAL HEALING WORKS

Crystals are made from geometrically precise spirals of silicon and oxygen atoms held together by jointly shared electrons. When pressure is applied to a crystal (when it is squeezed), the electrons nearest the surface are displaced inwards and upwards to be emanated primarily through the point. When the pressure is stopped, the crystal recharges by absorbing free electrons from the air. The easy flow of electrons through the crystal and its ability to resonate with, amplify and transmit our own personal energy demonstrates how a crystal can be a powerful and positive energy tool for working with the body and consciousness.

PURE INTENT AND CONSCIOUSNESS

Crystals cannot heal effectively if they have not been programmed. By directing the energy of the crystal through pure intent, we can activate and channel its energy to heal specific distortion or disease in the body and consciousness.

Crystals are thought amplifiers and become even more powerful instruments when we are focused during a state of meditation or healing. *Energy follows thought or intent.* As our thought form passes through the crystal we connect with the crystal and allow it to resonate correctly and specifically with us, thereby obtaining a personal healing from it. It stabilises our whole energy field and correspondingly activates a healing process on all levels and throughout all layers of our etheric/physical body and consciousness.

> *The purer the power of intent* + *the stronger the thought form* = **a more powerful crystal healing process**

THE CIRCLE OF LIFE

Crystals have played a key role in many cultures throughout the world's history and will continue to do so. The time has come for us to re-learn their true value and use. As we evolve, our life and reality is slowly *returning* to the higher state of being and consciousness originally expressed in past 'Golden Ages' such as Lemuria and Atlantis. Through the Earth changes, we are now encoding a new pure strand of DNA that will enable us to embody the consciousness of our Higher Self and regain access to past life knowledge - including the true value, power and history of crystals.

LEMURIA AND ATLANTIS

LEMURIA

The civilisation of Lemuria preceded that of Atlantis. The Lemurians were an ethereal race of beings whose humanoid bodies were more astral and transparent. They are described as quasi-dimensional – having the ability and consciousness to live within different altered states within several levels of time and space.

CRYSTALS

Their knowledge and belief system ensured that crystals were fully integrated into their lifestyle as a fundamental part of their existence. They used them to amplify their thought patterns and also to amplify their electromagnetic field and lightbody so they could experience lightbody travel and interdimensional reality shifts.

THE GARDEN OF EDEN

When the planet was still forming and was more ethereal in nature, it truly was a Garden of Eden. It was lush with the vital elements needed to heal, grow and evolve. The planet itself was sustained within higher vibrational levels of frequency. The elements of Nature were so ecologically balanced that nothing ever aged, deteriorated or died. Everything within Nature constantly rejuvenated itself.

The Lemurians lived in a state of balance with their environment. They didn't see themselves as separate from Nature. Their architecture and belief system created a society which was in tune and in balance with the whole environment at that time. (This is still the way of indigenous and native cultures who have maintained this knowledge. They now encourage us to become one with Mother Earth, to respect her as a living being and to live in harmony with the natural elements and kingdoms provided by her.)

HEALING

The Lemurians lived within a world and reality of such pure frequency they felt no pain, fear, suffering or death. Their bodies could rejuvenate and resonate internal healing powers. They had an innate ability to absorb the necessary elements from Nature to continually rejuvenate and revitalise their *ethereal* body and consciousness.

They worked with crystals to channel energies and subtle healing vibrations into the etheric/physical body from the natural environment that surrounded them. In this way, if an etheric imbalance created a state of disease, they could instantly receive an energetic healing directly from Nature. They used crystals and the knowledge from the crystals for tissue regeneration and spiritual progression.

PHYSICAL EXISTENCE

Over time and through a natural and alchemical process of evolution, chemical compounds changed into new elemental compositions of physical mass, thus creating Earth's more physical level of existence.

Therefore, the Lemurians correspondingly evolved and slowly transformed and materialised from a more ethereal level of formation into a more physical form. Through this process they lost their direct link to and with the environment. They moved away from their belief system of working so intimately and consistently with crystals and disconnected from their ability to attune to crystals for healing and rejuvenation. This resulted in their downfall and the development of environmentally related diseases. If we look at our own society, we can see clear patterns of how our physical, emotional and spiritual environment creates and shapes the manifestation of general diseases.

LEMURIANS - THE PLEIADIAN RACE

The Lemurians were ethereal lightbeings who came through and into our dimension and Earth, from other galactic realms to begin a new level of evolution. They are cosmically referred to as a genetic species of the Pleiadian Race. They initially lived within and on the Earth over eons of time, as the Earth etherically and physically evolved. During that period of existence their life span was several thousand years in our time perspective and they scarcely heard of disease.

As the Earth began to mineralise and materialise itself more, it shifted energetically into a *descension process*. It began to sustain less electromagnetic frequency and light as the substances became heavier in their elemental compositions. These new substance are what we identify today, as the minerals and properties of 'matter'. During a vital *transition* period when the Earth began to enter into the fourth dimension, where it stayed for a very short period of time, the civilisation of Lemuria began to dissipate. Many Pleiadians sustained their lightbodies and ascended into other planes or different adjoining dimensions and kingdoms. Some entered into the higher and more crystallised, *Elemental* Kingdoms of Sirius while others transferred into the more *galactic* realms and worlds of the fifth dimension within Orion.

The Pleiadians who remained began a natural genetic mutation process that provided the internal technology for the body and consciousness to evolve from their translucent astral form into a more materialised third dimensional humanoid form.

The Pleiadian genetics therefore evolved into *the genetic origins of our human existence.*

THE CREATION OF THE HUMANOID BODY

Lemuria ascended at a time of dramatic global Earth changes. Vegetation and crystal formations altered dramatically during this time of transition due to *the alchemical changes* in the elements resulting from the Earth and cosmic changes. The relevant geometric codes for the Pleiadian DNA to evolve, were woven-in from the internal technology (geometry) of these new Earth and cosmic crystals. This encoding process created a new template for a more *materialised* humanoid body to evolve from the electromagnetic and *translucent humanoid* 'lightbody' of the initial Pleiadian Race.

THE CREATION OF ADAM

The whole body, including many of the organs, evolved *from the technology of the quartz crystals.* This more materialised androgynous *humanoid* body was called Adam, the first born 'Earth Being' of the Pleiadian Race. Adam, the first born body and consciousness, was the temple (individual template) for each lightbody to exist *in physical form.* They could then sustain themselves in *the next dimension and corresponding civilisation* that came to be on Earth - Atlantis.

CRYSTAL SKULLS AND HUMANOID CRYSTAL BODIES

Several crystal skulls have been found in different locations all over the planet. Their creation process is very sophisticated and we do not have the knowledge or technology to reproduce these skulls today.

 **IAGRAM 3.1**
Crystal Skull

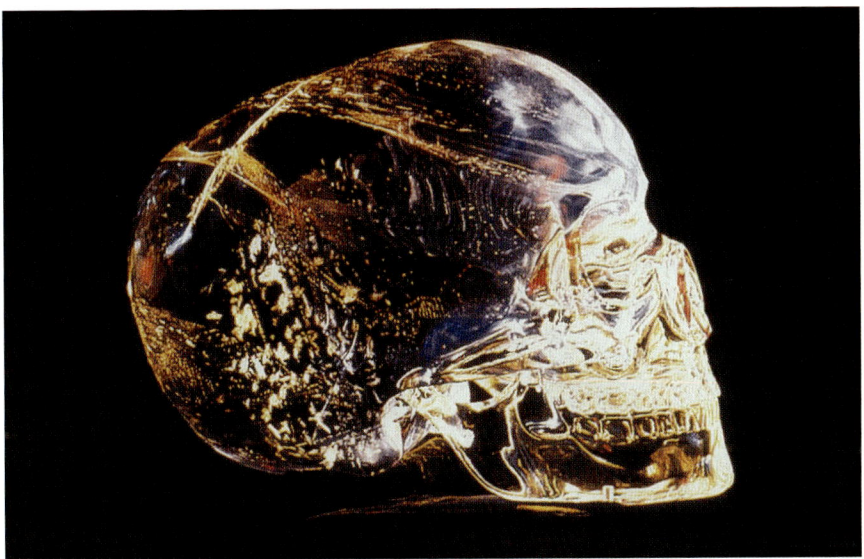

The Mitchell-Hedges Crystal Skull
Photographer: Gale Press. © BBC 1996

CHANNELLING

The skulls that have been found are not the initial pieces that existed on Earth. They were created towards the end of Atlantis, from original pieces that existed at a much earlier time. Originally there were seven fully shaped humanoid crystal bodies, not just crystal skulls.

THE MALE AND FEMALE FORM

The period when these original humanoid crystal bodies were formed and created was during the earlier time of Lemuria when Atlantis was still forming on a fifth dimensional and parallel level.

The crystal bodies were the central device in dividing the androgynous lightbody into the male and female sexes as well as the seven main races that eventually came to exist on Earth. When the crystal bodies had completed there formation process, the lightbody was to be genetically split so that 'Adam and Eve' could come into existence.

Therefore the technology within the skulls of these crystal bodies were used in late Lemuria and early Atlantis to transform the androgynous bodies then existing, into the male and female forms. They were used in Lemuria as a central thought form to aid in dividing the sexes, and in early Atlantis to complete the creation of the seven races of the humanoid body.

The frequency and material compound of the Earth were also critically changing at that time to support the mineralisation process of the lightbody and co-creation process of the divided sexes. The old world known as Lemuria was transferring into another dimension or reality, while the new world- Atlantis was descending and materialising itself more within this dimension.

HOW THE CRYSTAL HUMANOID BODIES WERE CREATED

Quartz was formed by solidifying the geometry of the electromagnetic frequency of sound and light. Pleiadian lightbodies existed ethereally within parallel dimensions to the Earth, in the very early times when Lemuria was still energetically forming. They were able to telepathically attune into parallel dimensions (because they lived in a quasi-dimensional reality) and obtain a conscious understanding of the geometries and ley lines of light that were beginning to manifest through into their reality. These ley lines of light became the etheric dimensions and substance through which crystals were physically birthed within our dimension.

The crystals began to be birthed physically and emerged as the Earth was evolving from ether and light into a more *crystallised* formation of matter. The Pleiadian lightbeings had the ability to tune into the etheric light and technology of the forming crystals. Through highly developed powers of psychic perception and meditation they could filter these imprints of light, ether and technology, into a condensed and understandable form of technology and resources. It was like working with the Doctrine of Signature.

At the beginning of time, the Pleiadians had an innate ability to telepathically talk to the crystals as the crystals were evolving within this new dimension and Earth. The crystals then became a **physical** tool to support the evolutionary process of their etheric/lightbody so they too could be born into this new reality and world. This new planet 'Earth' was the dimension in which the Pleiadians were also evolving through and into. It is important to remember that this was a time of creation and even though the Crystal Kingdom was materialising itself, the Pleiadians still existed in a state more of consciousness and reflection or meditation than physical form. It was only through the materialising of their etheric bodies while being cocooned in the healing and revitalising sensations of the forming crystals that they become more physical.

The Pleiadians were therefore initially more galactic in nature but to evolve into this New Earth and reality, they needed to obtain the necessary dimensions of the lightbody so they could eventually take on a new *humanoid* form or body. For the new body to evolve, their etheric body had to be birthed and created within the quartz crystals. The lightbody at that time of creation reflected the **innocence** and nature of an 'elemental' or 'fairy' like being, because their body at that time had *begun* a whole new gestation process. A new species was being born through the creation and formation process of the Earth and cosmic crystals.

The humanoid crystal bodies to which the skulls belonged came into manifestation at the time of Lemuria as the Pleiadians were attuning to the changing physical formation within and around them. They became *conscious* of the crystallising process of their own etheric body created by the evolving crystals. Even though the technology and resources of the crystal bodies were developed and birthed etherically by the forming crystal and by the planet, they could not have mineralised themselves without the *conscious* support of the Pleiadians that existed at that early time of Lemuria.

> **Therefore the technology of the crystallisation process of the entire human body, including the organs was formed out of quartz. This was a very sophisticated and natural form of genetic engineering, a process that was alchemically created by Nature and the Goddess, not solely by individuals themselves.**

The crystal skulls have been discovered now because we have reached a level of consciousness that allows us to properly release and use the information stored within them. The skulls found today hold the complete technology and resonance to generate the power, energy and technology for creating a complete humanoid crystal body and then transform it into the dimensions of the etheric/physical 'matter' of the humanoid form.

The whole body, including many of the organs, evolved *from the technology of the quartz crystal*. Crystals are now supporting the co-creation process of the new Adam Kadmon body that is evolving as we enter into the fifth dimension. The sexes divided but are re-connecting and re-creating a sense of **unity** within, as we energetically balance the *male* and *female* principles within each of us. (This process of balancing polarity and the principles of the two sexes within is explained further in chapter 6). We are also refining the elemental compounds and nature of our body and consciousness thereby crystallising ourselves so we can once again mineralise more of the lightbody, but in a more completed and perfected form. We are once again at a vital time of transformation like when Lemuria transferred and again when Atlantis fell and are being reborn into a whole new dimensional world and reality.

THE TRANSITION FROM LEMURIA TO ATLANTIS

This *transition of dimensions* happened over eons of time. Many innate healing powers, belief systems and values, as well as natural principles were lost through this *time of transition* from Lemuria into Atlantis. As Atlantis established itself, new knowledge was obtained through crystals. However, the heart still contained the memories and emotions of the tranquil healing reality and dimension of Lemuria and therefore felt a sense of spiritual loss.

ATLANTIS

Atlantis was a society built on technology. The Atlantian's ability to 'tune into' and access sacred knowledge encoded within the geometry of crystals enabled them to develop their intellectual abilities to build the whole foundation of their new civilisation.

Just as our own society has changed and grown through technology so did that of Atlantis. However, their intellectual and intuitive ability was much more advanced because of their divine, energetic connection to crystals. Their whole belief system and technology was built on crystals and their 'power source.' They focused on how to use them to enhance their lifestyle and this more intellectual approach eventually created more 'ego' driven desires.

Technology isn't a negative force when used with the right intentions but the Atlantian's technological changes affected the spiritual principles the Lemurians had lived under. Although they achieved a spiritual level equivalent to the Lemurians, their beliefs and lifestyle were based on organic *technology*.

They mined and quarried crystals for technological and material advancement and extended the powers and use of crystals into building physical formations. As cities were built and realities shifted, they descended from sixth dimensional to fifth dimensional reality. As they focused on establishing a more scientific approach to life, a rift developed between the spiritual and scientific values within the civilisation

Near the end of Atlantis, most of the civilisation had become more disconnected from the spiritual way of living and their intuitive level of consciousness began to deteriorate. They lost more and more of a connection to their innate intuitive and psychic abilities. Ultimately, they descended more into physical matter and became more anchored in 'matter' than in ether. They lost the ability to energetically heal themselves more naturally and to astral project or lightbody travel. They became increasingly dependent on externalising their resources and needed more material instruments or tools to create everything - from maintaining health to creating vehicles for transformation and transportation.

CRYSTAL TECHNOLOGY FOR INTER-DIMENSIONAL TRAVEL

LEMURIAN LIGHTBODY TECHNOLOGY

The Lemurian Race had mastered inter-dimensional travel by using the *internal technology (geometry) of their lightbodies*.

ATLANTIAN MERKABAH CHAMBERS

The Atlantians lost their innate ability to travel through time and space via their own internal energetic resources and therefore mastered the ability to design and create *external* lightbody chambers or Merkabah Chambers for levitation and inter-dimensional travel. These chambers are what we now identify as physical spacecraft.

They did this by accessing and amplifying the internal geometric technology of *quartz crystals*. They used *crystal technology* to create the correct geometric co-ordinates within the lightbody travel chambers to enter through the energetic Doorway of the stellar constellation of Orion. This enabled them to interact with other realities and worlds existing within and beyond a fifth dimensional frequency, including what we now call the higher 'galactic realms'. In this way they explored other worlds and realities and through contact with them advanced their own culture.

THE MANIFESTATION OF DISEASE

At the time of the collapse of Atlantis, the life span of its people had dropped from 800 years to 200 years in our time perspective.

As Atlantis descended, disease began to enter the civilisation. They created what we now refer to as 'orthodox medicine,' by *alchemically manipulating* the natural elements rather than using the spiritual technology of crystals to absorb the energies and elements from the natural environment. Cutting themselves off from the Earth's natural and spiritual healing forces created even more stress.

Their desire to explore new worlds led them into lower dimensional realities where they began researching different compounds and elements from within the 'outer worlds' and also researched and developed a genetic engineering process to begin new races on these struggling planets. Entering these domains below the fifth dimension went against Universal Law. They began to contaminate themselves etherically and this impacted the whole civilisation, ultimately creating a distortion in the energy field and gridding of planet Earth.

UNIVERSAL BALANCE

Gurudas (author of "Gem Elixirs and Vibrational Healing" Vol.1 and 2) compares this scenario in Atlantis to the scenario now being played out in our world. Whilst there are some obvious differences, the similarities between our society and Atlantian society are sobering. We have also endeavoured *to replace natural resources with technology* - which was one factor in Atlantis' decay. However, at *this* present time of Earth changes and dimensional transition we have the opportunity to unify knowledge of science and spirit and recreate a state of balance within ourselves by attuning to the

Divine healing powers and universal knowledge of Nature and the Universe once more.

> **The unification of science and spirit will create such a profound shift in our perception and consciousness that we will begin to live in the pure, high frequency of *Christ Consciousness*. This is our next evolutionary step.**

EARTH GRIDDING AND CRYSTAL POWER

The Atlantian architects designed buildings in perfect alignment with the geometry and energy of the Earth's crystal grid lines. They intuitively knew how and where to build a unit or home to resonate positively with the geometric proportions of the grid or ley line.

Crystals were also placed in the walls to create and sustain specific geometric electromagnetic energy fields in certain rooms of each home. This created and maintained a purer frequency and therefore a more therapeutic environment to live in. (The Transference Healing Master Christ Template Set has been channelled through to once again create and sustain a balanced and more pure energetic space within our home environment. *Refer to page 197 for more information on this product.*)

Smaller crystals were integrated into the very foundations of Atlantian homes to create a process of natural lighting and climate control within their living environment which automatically adjusted throughout the day.

The crystals were in a constant state of resonance, receiving and generating energy to create a continual source of 'electrical' power. This was a much more advanced way of generating electrical energy which reflected a more natural form of lighting to help support a state of wellness within the body and consciousness of the occupants.

A PERSONAL PAST LIFE READING

PRIESTESS POWER AND KNOWLEDGE OF EARTH GRIDDING

In one particular reading, I saw myself in Atlantis as a priestess. My work involved maintaining a direct connection with crystals. I learnt from the crystals and worked at mastering their teachings. To achieve this I had to sustain my connection to the Goddess and maintain a lineage of teachings in regard to crystal knowledge and the gridding of the Earth. These teachings were part of the later teachings of the Egyptian Mystery School of the Goddess Isis.

In that incarnation I mastered the innate ability to retrieve sacred knowledge and information from within the crystals and the understanding of the gridding of the Earth that was formed through crystals. I also tapped into and channelled crystal generated power or energy. With clear intent, I could send the energy of specific crystals through the etheric grid or ley lines into the gridding of the houses in a particular location to help repair any distortion that might have come through in the energy field of that specific area. This was possible because the houses were built in alignment with the Earth grid and energetically sustained the correct geometric dimensions and proportions by the crystals that were built into them.

GIFTS AND TALENTS

In that lifetime in Atlantis I was recognised as a *grid master, crystal channeller and healer* creating a self-healing and ascension process on and for the Earth. I mastered an ability to tap into the etheric body and heal energetic imbalances so the etheric/physical body could heal itself rapidly. The lineage of teachings and services that I practiced in Atlantis ranged from being able to reconstruct the lightbody through crystal power and geometry through to channelling cosmic grid line information for space-time travel.

It was partly because of this past life in Atlantis and another significant life in Egypt that I am now able to obtain a more in-depth understanding of the gridding system of the human body, planet and solar system.

The past life 'gifts and talents' from these specific incarnations have enabled me to channel the procedures of Transference Healing to once again create a self-healing and ascension process on Earth, during this present time of transition. *The Transference Healing procedures weave through the Earth and cosmic energies to create the crystal geometry of the etheric templates which channel the Transference Healing Ray.*

THE INCARNATION OF LIGHTBODIES

CHANNELLING

In the very beginning, when the Earth was forming, before the time of Lemuria, geometric symbols were embedded within the crystals to maintain and sustain the structural form of all life forms that *were to evolve* - right down to the genetic coding of the 'human being'.

The forming quartz crystals resonated signals or vibrations throughout the universes, sounds that expressed the true nature of a new and evolving planet. Holographic sounds and images created by geometric ley lines of light resonated and reflected from the crystals. This telepathic form of communication is very much like the ' language of light' or in our world, the frequencies emanating as solar radar waves but are of a much higher and purer level of frequency. Dolphins use this crystal form of communication and can reach and speak to each other over hundred of miles of ocean. Crystals however, can communicate inter-dimensionally and can reach out and beyond space and time itself.

Telepathic images reached out into other dimensions reflecting the healing nature of this newly evolving planet. The elements sustaining the Earth and cosmic energies of this new planet and adjoining solar system, were to be a new dimension and healing *haven for the Cosmos*. This dimension was to create a reality and realm through which cosmic lightbeings could take a new and vital step in their physical and spiritual evolutionary process.

Through readings, I have seen lightbeings entering the Earth at the time it was creating itself like stars falling from the sky. These lightbeings upon entering the lush, tranquil and healing environment of its energetic nature could experience the healing sensation of its elements. It sustained the necessary technology, minerals and properties to template and begin an automatic *transference* process of reshaping their original lightbodies into the humanoid lightbody of the Homo-sapiens – or the Human Code of Form. These lightbodies still emanated as translucent lightbeings but with the geometric proportions of the human skeletal and structural system of two arms, legs, body and head.

'Cosmic' entities travelled in their lightbodies from different realms and when they entered the Earth's dimension, slowly became conscious of the Earth and its life force and healing properties. As they entered into this new dimension, they felt like they were waking up from a deep dream state and although they remembered a little of their previous journey and existence, they were slowly becoming conscious of the new environment around them. The Australian aborigines refer to this time as the 'Dreamtime' *(see diagram 3.2)*.

They energetically felt the sensations the planet and its adjoining solar system created for them and the healing and tranquil resonance of its elements. They became embedded into the energetic fabric of the astral planes of the Earth and its crystals, through which they began their *etheric* gestation process into a humanoid lightbody and a **new** gestation process that created the foundations of a new gene or race of Pleiadians. These Pleiadians lived within the evolving Earth and its Elemental Kingdom, for eons of time. They not only existed within the crystals but eventually all elements that were being created in and on the Earth, such as the trees, streams and so on. As they lived within the elements, their lightbodies, consciousness and life force supported the creation process of the life force of the planet, at the time of Lemuria. The Pleiadian lightbodies lived and evolved with the planet and through Earth and cosmic changes to eventually evolve and become the genetic root race of the Human Race.

(The inner life force and consciousness of the elemental 'Pleiadian' beings can be seen in the new Transference Healing 'Animal Magic' Deck. *Refer to page 355 for more information on this product*).

DIAGRAM 3.2
Aboriginal Drawing Depicting the Translucent Lightbody

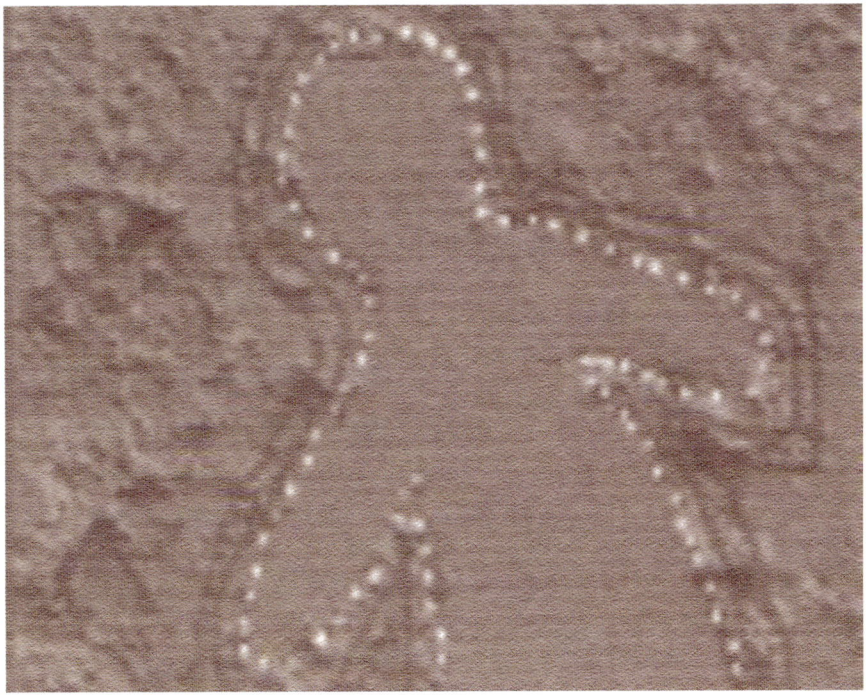

Australian aborigines who are still connected to the Dreamtime can access this early memory of the lightbodies first forming when entering the Earth plane at the earliest time on Earth, when Lemuria was coming into manifestation. They have drawn them on rocks located at sacred sites at different locations in Australia (diagram 3.1).

READING

This insight came from a channelled reading for a client. I saw him as 'energy' and incarnating into the Earth realm during the early time of Lemuria. Previous to this incarnation, he existed in a more astral realm within a dimension that was similar to our ocean, but more like ether than water. (These 'alien or extra-terrestrial realms' are referred to in chapter 13 as the struggling worlds which exist within the 2.8 to 4.9 dimensional frequency levels and realities - out beyond the Pleiadian dimensions.)

His body formation looked very much like a jellyfish but his consciousness in that 'galactic' existence was more advanced than our marine life today - or even the Animal Kingdom today- and parallel to the human intellect of our planet now. He emanated a different consciousness than what we do now - more like that of the reptilian dimensions. However, as soon as his lightbody energetically incarnated into the ethereal planes of the Earth and its crystals, he automatically took on the formation of a non-materialised humanoid lightbeing. It was from the inner technology of the crystals and changing elements that he evolved the etheric/lightbody but also through filtering in the elemental compounds within and of the planet 'Earth' the physical body began to mould and create itself. Through that process he became 'human or humane' in body and consciousness.

He could relate to this reading because he was an artist and previous to the reading had drawn an abstract picture of the melding of different life forms within the ocean. Some of these 'unique life forms' looked like different formations of jellyfish. To him this reading didn't seem unusual but rather inspired his creativity and gave him a deeper spiritual understanding of his art.

THE TRUE NATURE OF THE DNA

CHANNELLING

This reading confirmed my belief in an aspect of 'Darwin's theory'; that stated we evolved from the Animal Kingdom, specifically the apes. I believe however, that this theory is only a small limited aspect of the truth and the so called 'big picture'. I feel we are a more highly evolved aspect of the Animal Kingdom, because our emotions and consciousness hold different attributes of the *inner nature* of **all** animals themselves, just as we hold different attributes of the *inner nature* of all elements within the Earth and Cosmos.

We have genetically and physically evolved through the elements and Nature of the Earth. While doing so we have filtered in the *consciousness* of **all** the kingdoms into our DNA. We have mutated our DNA and consciousness through integrating energetically, the consciousness of all that lived and lives on and within the planet. We are at a different level of evolution in consciousness and physical form, from each of the animals and elements on Earth, because of our **collective** and **re-connective genetic mutation process of evaluation.**

Not only did we mutate the elements and attributes of the inner nature of the Earth and its animal, mineral, plant and cosmic elements, but our DNA is also a *genetic mutation* of and from many kingdoms and their elemental compounds, that existed in previous *galactic* realities and worlds, before the Earth was created. So you see how complex the human genetic DNA system is.

> **The body, Soul and consciousness of the human being, is therefore a manifestation and expression of the mutation of many genes that hold and emanate specific aspects of Nature.**

Through the genetic mutation process of our DNA, the human body and consciousness can master more effectively and become a more *evolved* species in body and consciousness, a species that can energetically support all kingdoms existing within 'struggling' and still evolving, parallel worlds and realities.

Through the genetic re-connection, mutation and evolutionary process of the human DNA, the human being is becoming more perfected in its humane attributes. So to heal the planet or planets we need to look within and 'heal thyself'. This is one of the most profound teachings of the Christ, the teachings that enable us to not only *master* the elements of Nature, **alchemy** but while doing so, *master* the forces of Nature and become 'Christ-like in body and consciousness. *(This is explained further in following chapters)*.

THE GENETIC MUTATION OF THE DNA

SUMMARY

The Pleiadian Race and then the Human Race initially originated on Earth, from the genetic mutation of many other galactic realms and life forms *(explained further in chapters 13 and 14)*. When the initial lightbodies entered the Earth plane, they were automatically transformed into humanoid lightbeings via a geometric template created by *the crystal formation* of the planet. This humanoid *physical* form was eventually created from an illuminated, translucent and *astral* substance.

The DNA of the Pleiadian Race continued to mutate through the incarnation of many species until the foundation of our whole DNA system had been created. This genetic mutation process is at the root of our whole civilisation. We are still perfecting aspects of many imbalances within the DNA from previous incarnations on and off the planet and this will continue until we heal the wounding from the past and evolve into a *pure* template of body, consciousness and light.

FOCAL POINTS FOR PHYSICAL REALITY

BIOLOGICAL LIFE

As previously stated, crystals were the first form of physical life on Earth. They are the refined substances from and of which 'matter' and the whole physical foundation of our existence is built. Crystals have the power to co-create, transform and sustain 'matter'. Existing in perpetual resonance, they provide the focal point our Soul needs to ground and sustain the 'self' on a physical plane such as Earth.

When we have properly investigated other planets, we will find that certain crystal structures will not be found if the planet is devoid of biological life. This confirms the theory that *we could not sustain our life force here without the crystals.*

They are an instrument of universal energy to ground our 'Soul' into a physical form or body and also allow us to tap into higher dimensions to gain much needed energetic resources and spiritual information. Crystals sustain, stabilise and balance our life force on all planes across all seven parallel dimensions, so we can go on growing and learning until we have unified all of these aspects of ourselves, thereby returning to our original state of Unity. When we return to this evolved state of 'oneness' we will be able to understand the nature and consciousness of the universes and embody the principles of *alchemy to create* the necessary elements for physical life.

ALCHEMY

CREATING THE HUMAN BODY AND THE FIFTH ELEMENT

We know that space is not empty, it contains many gases. The vibrations resonating from all life forms create an electrode (magnetic field) and as this emanates into the air it activates the ether in the atmosphere which feeds or transfers nutrients to our etheric body.

Crystals can create a rapid *alchemical* healing process by emanating an electromagnetic charge to absorb the *correct* geometric proportions of ether into the etheric/physical anatomy so matter can both restore itself into wellness and also resonate into higher frequencies to *create the lightbody*. Crystals can therefore provide the *correct geometric proportions of light and elements* necessary for a *pure* healing and ascension process.

CRYSTAL ESSENCES IN THE LIGHTBODY KIT

I have programmed the crystal essences in the Lightbody Kit, with guidance from the Celestial Christ, to *harmonise and heal* particular areas of the body and help the *transformation of our body and consciousness* into the next dimension. These 77 essences of crystals, colours, rays, sounds and geometric symbols also create the electromagnetic properties necessary to transform the physical body into the lightbody – 'matter into light.' *Refer to page 507 for more information on this product.*

MULTIDIMENSIONAL REALITY AND EARTH GRIDDING

At the time of the Earth changes, when Lemuria transcended and Atlantis fell, the land shifted and continents formed. The crystallised and magnetic grids of Earth formed geometries that created energy vortices, sustaining and maintaining specific plant and animal life, climatic conditions, ecological balance and astrological/cosmic interaction.

Civilisations, races and cultures formed in different locations all over the Earth. Different races and cultural belief systems were not only established through migration and environmental influences on Earth but also because specific dimensions energetically influenced them. *Specific star constellations* and their astrological, energetic impact affected not only the health and karmic, genetic imprints of different civilisations and races, but embedded deep belief systems and levels of consciousness. In this way, every civilisation, society or indigenous culture established its own colour, race and unique life style and belief system.

Certain species still energetically support the evolution of genetic mutation by connecting through the grid points of the Global Grid Matrix at specific locations on Earth which link up to *specific, corresponding,* cosmic grid points aligned with star formations or systems.

These formations create and sustain stellar gateways or connecting corridors into adjoining worlds within different frequencies and dimensions of space. For example a grid line from Egypt connecting precisely to the star Sirius in the Belt of Orion then creates a Doorway through Orion into specific galactic and spiritual realms within both Orion and Sirius. The vibration or energies created from grid points within the Earth and Cosmos connect to these specific star constellations creating a universal pull and connection to energetic Doorways into different dimensions and their existing realities.

> **From deep within our consciousness we communicate from and through Earth to the stars and beyond, into other realms and to intelligent life forms from different parts of the Multidimensional Universe.**

DOORWAY POINTS WITHIN THE EARTH AND COSMOS

SACRED SPACES

The Earth has sustained all *'matter'* within different levels of frequency within a third dimensional hologram, for the last 12,000 years. Specific grid points on the Earth where ancient and mysterious formations have been naturally or magnetically created, like Sedona, the Pyramids and Stonehenge are areas of powerful magnetic gridding within the Earth. They open to specific points in space, directly connecting to specific planets and galactic civilisations and to elemental and angelic realms. By providing inter-dimensional access the powerful energy vortices that resonate from these locations can support the evolutionary process of the human body, mind and spirit.

> ## I call these sacred sites, spaces, vortices or grid connection points on Earth, 'doorway points'.

Magical and miraculous experiences can occur at these frequency points such as:

+ Awakening and enhancing of intuitive and psychic abilities.

+ Accessing higher consciousness to solve problems.

+ Creating a profound energy shift for healing and ascension.

+ Opening communication with other realms and with Ascended Masters.

+ Creating 'Doorway' experiences of going backwards and forwards in time.

+ Creating a time or reality shift that not only takes us through time but connects us in consciousness through and into another parallel dimension.

EARTH AND COSMIC CHANGES

The Doorway Grid Points are a vital part of our encoding and ascension process into higher consciousness. By encoding the 12-strand DNA system, we are genetically mutating and ascending into higher consciousness. The doorway points provide access to the knowledge, codes and characteristics of other dimensions and also transmit necessary Earth and cosmic energies into the planetary grid and human anatomy to create healing and transformation.

GLOBAL GRID MATRIX

At this time of global transition from 1999-2012 the Earth's grid is shifting and the entire planet and humanity is therefore shifting frequency from the third to fifth dimension. The fifth dimension is the gateway to explore other worlds and realities that were also created through the Christ template, eons ago.

Consequently, profound changes are occurring within the etheric templates of the crystals, the Global Grid Matrix and humanity which are sustained in our dimension by the crystals. New Doorways and alignments continue to orchestrate this process. Some of us are already experiencing multidimensional realities and have literally begun to 'walk between the worlds'.

FIFTH DIMENSIONAL HOLOGRAPHIC REALITY

Everything is in a process of rapid change to allow the new fifth dimensional holographic reality to manifest. Our *complete* 12-strand DNA system must be anchored into the body before 2012 to allow us to make this transition into the fifth dimension in 2013. *This inter-dimensional shift is explained further in chapter 4.*

ORION AND THE 12-STRAND DNA SYSTEM

By 2012 we will complete the 12-strand DNA transformation and *in 2013 we will completely enter into the outer realms of the galactic worlds of Orion.* Slowly, as we shift into higher consciousness over time, the psyche of humanity will become conscious of these other worlds and realities. We will have entered the fifth dimension in 2013 and begin a new journey of self-discovery. This journey will continue over the next 1,000 years.

ETHER

At this time of transition, we are perfecting our 12-strand DNA so we can begin to create and incorporate the fifth element, *ether* into our physical body. We are already creating and incorporating more *ether* within the very foundation of our physical body and existence. As the *electromagnetic or lightbody* resonates through, it will alchemically change the frequency and alchemical compounds of every fragment of living matter.

> **Right now we are in the process of being recreated and reborn into a new template of existence while still in our physical body.**

DOORWAY POINT WITHIN THE HUMAN BODY

Within our etheric body we have an energetic 'Diamond Doorway,' in the crown chakra just above the head, that allows us to go backwards and forwards in time.

This 'Doorway' can sometimes energetically open in such a way that it brings through into consciousness experiences, of etheric or physical surgery experienced during previous lives or times of existence, that sometimes remain stored in the DNA and cellular levels of the body. This only happens to a minority of people and can happen unexpectedly. However, it can only happen with consent from the Higher Self.

PAST LIVES AND ALIEN ABDUCTION

When this 'Doorway' opens, the old, painful memories that 'tear' the etheric body and create unusual symptoms can feel like the experience of an 'alien abduction' and surgical process being performed within another space realm. So, *some experiences attributed to 'alien abduction' are in fact the result of the 'Doorway' being energetically opened.*

Alien abduction is an aspect of multidimensional reality that creates great fear. It is important to address this issue to support those who sometimes suffer quietly and feel very alone in this experience and to help clear the fear of alien contact or encounters.

Transference Healing procedures can clear and heal this dimension of the 'patterning'. The opened 'Doorway' allows us to re-connect to and clear negative experiences from the past or sometimes even create and feel a positive etheric surgery process from the higher realms. There is also an essence in the Lightbody Kit called the **Cosmic Shield of Connection and Protection Essence** which clears memories of painful etheric surgery from the past. It also closes the 'Doorway' in the top diamond of the etheric body so the person no longer has to experience this strange phenomenon. This essence not only clears the ongoing experiences that some have regarding 'alien abduction' but also helps heal etheric distortion in the physical body. It enables the physical body to rejuvenate and heal ongoing and sometimes unusual symptoms that haven't been able to clear. At this time of transition, this essence also clears the *lightbody symptoms* that are coming through because of the Earth changes.

DOORWAY TECHNOLOGY / COMMUNICATION DEVICES

THE CRYSTAL SKULL

In the year 2000, I was given an opportunity to communicate with a naturally formed crystal skull. When I 'tuned into' it, I noticed specific emanations resonating through. It said it was an 'instrument' through which certain interdimensional lightbeings could communicate with grid masters who were able to attune to its frequency to receive downloads of specific information. At the time of transmission I communicated with both the angelic and galactic lightbeings.

It was like looking into a crystal ball. I was able to see and communicate with other beings to receive specific information and at the same time receive a more in-depth understanding of crystals and the part they play in creating the energetic make-up of the lightbody. The crystal skull allowed my brain and mind to comprehend knowledge from other dimensions that would normally be very difficult to absorb physically.

GALACTIC MESSAGES FROM
THE CRYSTAL SKULL

These lightbeings were communicating from within the realms of Orion and were transmitting channelled information to *grid masters*, foretelling Earth changes that were to come.

- They downloaded *a great amount of insight on the Earth changes* - how they would affect our body and how the *Earth and cosmic energies* were changing our body, consciousness and planet.

- They showed me how the Earth is connected to the Orion Belt and revealed that we are actually sustained within a lower dimensional frequency, outside of the inner, circle of planetary 'galactic worlds' that coexist within the fifth dimensional frequency of Orion.

- *They gave me information on Earth gridding - saying* as the energies on the planet begin to change more, they would give me certain information on the Global Grid Matrix. They said they would be working in conjunction with Sirius to give information on the Earth changes and show me how *to activate certain 'grid points' on the Earth* to help with a global healing and ascension process.

* Specifically, they would support me by giving me more in-depth information and abilities to channel in the relevant energies to *support the creation of the new lightbody.*

* They revealed that the body and lightbody could not unite into a state of oneness until the Earth had templated relevant energies from Orion and Sirius.

* *They also transmitted codes into my DNA,* which in time would reveal specific information about the future. These codes were like 'crystal implants' or receptors resonating information only when activated by the lightbeings – and a connection could only be reactivated if I could anchor enough light for the crystals to resonate as receptors.

MESSAGES RELATING TO THE ATLANTIAN DISCS AND THE SEVENTH DIMENSION

The lightbeings also told me they had channelled specific information to grid masters in Atlantis on how to make seven crystal and metal discs. The discs allowed the seven main chakras to filter and weave through necessary energies from the 'Earth and cosmic' Global Grid Matrix, for the body to ascend into *the seventh dimension.*

These discs were channelled through and onto Earth to allow individuals to master lightbody travel from Earth into higher dimensions via the Merkabah. Thoth mastered the power, information and technology of these discs before they were given to Earth during the time of Atlantis.

'The Merkabah is the vehicle in which the lightbody travels through space and into parallel dimensions and co-existing worlds. The lightbody and co-existing Merkabah technology therefore give us the resources to partially co-exist within - and lightbody travel into - parallel dimensions and co-existing worlds, within the Earth and Cosmos.'

Those who knew how to work with these discs could reach beyond the limitation of gravity, time and space by transferring the lightbody, via its internal Merkabah technology into a more translucent, ethereal and crystallised form of matter.

They could then physically access the necessary energies to allow the full manifestation and *perfect formation* of the lightbody, so they could begin to access the higher dimensions of the Christ Realm.

These discs were tools allowing the physical body to anchor in specific grid energies, crystal energies and stellar templates to allow the body to master ascension.

They revealed that all Earth changes that would come to pass were part of the Earth's transition and ascension process.

The Earth would evolve *from within itself* so it could eventually exist within the more ethereal existence of the fifth dimension and then ultimately over 1,000 years slowly shift its frequencies so that it come to exist within the seventh dimension in 3013.

They also revealed that, in time, more information would be given through me so the technology of the discs could be re-channelled onto the planet. In 2003 more information began to filter through.

SEVEN ATLANTIAN DISCS

During a Melchizedek 'trance channelling' for a graduate (Diamond Pyramid of Light Conference, Paradise Island, Bahamas at the time of the Harmonic Concordance, 8 November 2003), I was shown that the **seven** discs that had been channelled, created and then used in Atlantis, still exist under the floor of the Atlantic Ocean. The Graduate was given insight and information on a connection he once had to one of these particular discs during an incarnation in Atlantis. Information was also given on how he would come to understand and work once again with this disc and its crystal technology. This innate ability would come through for him as he healed and reconnected to that aspect of himself through his own Mastership and ascension process on Earth. I was also told telepathically during that channelling that the time had come for me to reveal and channel more specific information from and about them for humanity. Therefore the new information coming through will be taught in the 'Thoth' teachings that will be an aspect of the teachings held within the '7th Mystery School' that will commence in 2006. *For more information on the Mystery School, refer to page 301.*

ANGELIC MESSAGES FROM THE CRYSTAL SKULL

These spiritual beings, who emanated, manifested and transmitted universal information, through the crystallised properties of the skull also revealed that deep *within* our etheric body we have a dormant energy system. When activated it allows Sirian and Arcturian codes to awaken and filter through specific energies, and pure frequencies from these dimensions. These energies allow not only the *perfection* of, but also a more *crystallised manifestation* of the lightbody and ultimately the *Christbody* to come through.

 The angelic Arcturian beings revealed to me, the *new* dimensions of the global gridding system or matrix that I have channelled through and called in Transference Healing 'The Crystal Cross Christ Matrix'. This template supports the filtering process of the necessary energies, crystal technology and pure inter-dimensional frequencies so that the lightbody and the Christbody can begin to co-create themselves more within our physical body and consciousness. *(For more information on the 'Crystal Cross Christ Matrix', refer to page 49).*

ASCENDING MASTERS AND MYSTERY SCHOOL TEACHINGS ON EARTH

Through the information given by these Arcturian Archangels and an initiation of spiritual empowerment that occurred at that time, I was given the sacred power and authority to initiate those who are becoming *'Ascending Masters'* on Earth. This process will be given more *directly* through the **Mystery School teachings** I channel through, which are also taught in the advance level teachings of Transference Healing.

The necessary skills, procedures and energies can automatically channel through me now, in the moment, to slowly, alchemically create the Christbody for those people who are to become 'Ascending Masters' on Earth. *Those who anchor in the Christbody will become the principal masters on Earth and a direct channel for the Celestial Christ and the Spiritual Hierarchy* who will intuitively guide them to support the ascension process of the Earth and humanity into the next dimension.

They will be the master channellers, healers and grid-workers of the future. They will create the new foundations of our health system and belief system at this time of transition and will be key catalysts in influencing the personal and spiritual growth and ascension process of Earth and humanity.

REVIEW

- ◆ The planet and humanity are now entering the fifth dimension at this time of global transition from 1999–2012. The fifth dimension is the gateway to explore other worlds and realities that were also created through the Christ template, eons ago.

These worlds now exist in higher frequencies and dimensions of light, in a parallel space-time to Earth.

* At the same time, the masters are being awakened on a parallel level to the rest of humanity and are being encouraged to enter into the sixth to seventh dimension while on Earth. Through this process they can access higher levels of consciousness and receive sacred information to support the changes on Earth. As they master their own personal ascension process through encoding and embodying their light/Christ and Merkabah bodies, they will receive direct assistance from the higher galactic and angelic planes and channel through the necessary energies to support the changes in their body/consciousness and the planet itself.

* These 'spiritual initiates' are in service to the planet and humanity as they become the 'Ascending Masters' on Earth. Spiritual growth and empowerment will give them absolute freedom to explore and learn from the wonders of other realities and worlds once again.

* Time and gravity will no longer restrict those who master the Christbody. They will assist the rest of humanity and Earth to enter the energetic portal of Orion and a new level of existence - one of a higher, fifth dimensional frequency and consciousness.

IMPORTANT: Completion Ritual

*Before you stop reading this chapter, run your finger from **right to left** across the sacred language below. This procedure will assist you to finalise the energies from this chapter.*

Your action, intent and the sacred vibration of this powerful language, will greatly assist you to fully integrate the information you have just read.

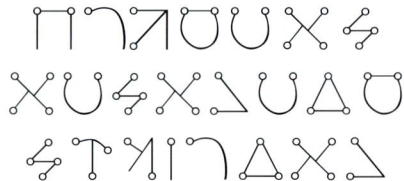

THE MASTER CHRIST·TEMPLATE

This sacred symbol is the template that supports and co-creates the healing and ascension power of Transference Healing®. It templates, grids, filters and weaves the Christ frequencies from the heavens to Earth, so that Earth can be supported spiritually and the Earth and humanity can transcend into higher dimensions via the Earth and cosmic changes currently taking place.

This template energetically supports the *unification* of all belief systems, dimensions, mystery schools and golden ages and creates the '*resurrection of the 7th Golden Age*' on Earth. It also initiates a *self-mastery process* so that one can begin to template a Divine connection to, and co-exist with, the spiritual guides, worlds and realities that are connected with and are part of the Christ light.

* Note this template is sold either individually or as part of the Master Christ Template Set of five (see page 197). It can be placed in any room within your home or workplace.

This sacred symbol weaves and filters through the Christ light (via its celtic crystal cross). It then seals and anchors the Christ light into our Earth and Cosmos (via the Star of David). The cross channels the Christ light and its inter-dimensional frequencies, kingdoms/worlds, realities and consciousness into our dimension via the Ankh, Chalice, Eye of Horus, Star , Om and Moon. All these sacred symbols are gold sealed 'within and with' the Star of David creating the *Master Christ Template*.

This deep purple template has been overlaid with fine gold leaf, to reflect its magnetic and electromagnetic energies and has a detailed explanation on its reverse-side.

Place your order at www.TRANSFERENCEHEALING.com

IMPORTANT: Commencement Ritual

*Before reading chapter 4, run your finger from **left to right** across the sacred language below.*

Your action, intent and the sacred vibration of this powerful language, will ensure that you are fully open to receiving and integrating the information within.

♈ ♉ ♊ ♋ ♌ ♍ ♎ ♏ ♐ ♑ ♒ ♓ ☉ ☽ ♀ ♂ ☿ ♃ ♄ ♅ ♆ ♇ ⚷

25 cosmic and astrological symbols are diagrammed above. They include the 12 symbols of the Zodiac signs (Aries, Taurus, Gemini, Cancer, Leo, Virgo, Libra, Scorpio, Sagittarius, Capricorn, Aquarius, Pieces) and also 13 planets (Venus, Mars, Mercury, Jupiter, Saturn, Uranus, Neptune, Chiron, Sun and Moon).

These symbols create an energetic alignment process with certain cosmic and astrological influences that filter through from the universe, thereby supporting your healing and ascension process.

REVELATIONS OF THE CHRIST

CHAPTER OVERVIEW

In this chapter you will discover:

♦ The 'Book of Revelations' is the last testament of the Bible, and is the most mystical. It is presented by St John the Divine and predicts changes and catastrophes for the Earth around the change of Millennium during the transition to the New Golden Age and that it is considered a great work of both Pagan and Christian inspiration.

♦ Alexis has seen that John is actually foretelling a time of *bodily transformation* on a global scale, created by the energetic return and awakening of the Christbody and Consciousness onto the planet. Further that hidden within this *esoteric* book is the *key* to understanding the energetic makeup of the body; its integration with the planet; the causes and effects on our health and the outcome for the Earth, through and after this time of transition from 1999-2012.

♦ The 'Book of Revelations' contains the esoteric knowledge of an ancient form of healing and energetic technology that Christ mastered when on Earth.

♦ The 'Grand Cross' astrological alignment on 11 August 1999 signified the 'Second Coming of Christ' and the rebirth of humanity's physical body and consciousness into the next dimension. It marked the beginning of the energetic activation of the 'resurrection' of the *whole of humanity* to take the next vital step in their physical/spiritual evolution.

♦ The 'Grand Square' astrological alignment of 5 May 2000 signified the rebirth of planet Earth into the next dimension.

- The 'Grand Square' is energetically working with the Grand Cross to create a 'time of transition' from 1999 – 2012 from the third to the fifth dimension.

- The four fixed signs of the Zodiac – Aquarius the angel, Leo the lion, Taurus the bull and Scorpio the eagle - activated by the Grand Cross, are associated with the *'Four Beasts of the Apocalypse'* - the sign of the 'end of time' prophesised in the' Book of Revelations'. They are also the four symbols at the four corners of the Wheel of Fortune card in the 'Rider Waite Tarot'. The archetypes of these four zodiacal points are impacting the body and consciousness on a global level. They are activating a global healing shift within specific dimensions of the etheric/physical body so the body can ascend into higher consciousness. You will discover how each archetypal energy is directly affecting the human body at this time.

- Transference Healing is the *energetic key* to receiving the healing properties spoken of in the 'Book of Revelations'. It has become a channel for this universal 'Christ' healing process, now energetically filtering through to humanity and the planet.

- A procession is an Earth cycle whereby the Earth moves slowly backwards through the entire Zodiac. It takes approximately 25,000 to 26,000 years for the Earth to move back through the entire Zodiac. Our solar system takes about 2,100 years to pass through each one of the 12 signs of the Zodiac. After the 2,100 years we move out of one Age and into another. We are currently shifting out of the Age of Pisces into the Age of Aquarius, there is much speculation and debate as to the exact timing and length of time for this shift to occur and the New Millennium and New World to commence. This chapter looks in some detail at the prophecy, research findings and astrological events currently available to assist in this determination.

- Alexis states her proposal for the timing of the shift into the new world. She states that she believes the 'Grand Cross' of 11 August 1999 was the principal turning point for our shift into the new millennium, Age of Aquarius and next dimension. That we have now left the third dimension where we have existed since the fall of Atlantis around 12,000 BC. From 1999-2012 we will be suspended within the brief transition of the fourth dimension 'the time of no time'. In 2012 we will enter the fifth dimension where we will exist from the next 1,000 years. The fifth dimension will allow more freedom and less restriction on all levels.

- The Divine intervention of the Celestial Christ (through the cosmic appearance of the astrological templates) enables humanity to receive and co-create a *natural and pure ascension process* that is of *The Light* and not of man. Now that this Divine ascension process is occurring through these astrological templates, we can 'tune in' and comprehend the mysteries of Nature by connecting directly to the Celestial Christ through our own individual and universal ascension process. All mysteries of time, space, our genetic lineage and the meaning of the 'Alpha & Omega' will be understood as we ascend through the templating process of the Celestial Christ and the healing Nature of the Goddess.

◆

THE BOOK OF REVELATIONS

> *Blessed is he that readeth, and they that hear the words of this prophecy, and keep those things which are written therein; for the time is at hand.*
>
> *Revelation of John the Divine 1:3*

The 'Book of Revelations', the last testament in the Bible, is known as the 'Book of Prophecy.' It was presented by St. John the Divine and is the most mystical of all the Bible testaments. It is highly suggestive of Earth catastrophes at a time of redemption and judgment; signs that are slowly showing relevance in our current age.

PROPHECIES

The 'Book of Revelations' predicts changes and catastrophes the Earth is to experience around the change of the Millennium - during the transition into the New Golden Age.

Similar prophecies and predictions of worldwide catastrophe have existed among the people of all continents including the Sumerians, Babylonians, Persians, Egyptians, Hebrews, Hindus, Scandinavians, Greeks, native North and South Americans, Eskimos and the Fiji Islanders.

The Hopi Indians for example, believe that at the time of the New Millennium the world will pass into the 'Fifth World' of the Native Americans. Nostradamus - the 16th Century French Astrologer and more recently, Edgar Cayce - the 20th Century American seer, known as the 'Sleeping Prophet,' also foresaw and prophesied that the Earth's polar axis would 'turn in the winter of 1998'.

THE ORIGINS OF THE 'BOOK OF REVELATIONS'

The proximity of the two spiritual centres of Ephesus and Patmos in the Eastern Aegean, has led to suggestions that the 'Book of Revelations' is simultaneously a great work of both Pagan and Christian inspiration.

Ephesus, on the Turkish coast, was home of the temple of Diana, a sacred city of *the Mystery religions* and focus of the secret doctrine. It was a laboratory where the essence of the Mystery cults and various eastern religions from Chaldea, Egypt, Persia, India etc, was distilled.

Patmos is the island where the Virgin Mary is reputed to have spent her last days and where John the Divine was buried in a sacred tomb under the nearby mountains. It is where he was said to have written the apocalyptic 'Book of Revelations.'

This Pagan/Christian paradox has elicited great controversy concerning the origin and meaning of the 'Book of Revelations'. Consequently, it has been interpreted in a multitude of ways and its passages quoted and applied to events throughout history.

It is accepted as a sacred *Christian* book encoding in symbolism, the occult teachings from the Egyptian and Greek Mystery cults or schools which are hidden within Christianity. Because a combination of these Mystery School teachings is encoded within this prophetic book, it contains the power to re-establish the foundation and secret 'esoteric' teachings of *Mystic Christianity* back onto the planet. Only when the 'Book of Revelations,' has truly been understood will people be able to re-learn, through the Divine messages encoded within it, the sacred knowledge acquired by the 'elect' who once attended the ancient Mystery Schools established on the planet, from the time of Atlantis.

For thousands of years, people of all cultures and religions, since the early time of Egypt, have been preparing themselves for, and prophesying about, the 'end of time' or 'end of the world' as we know it. This book reveals the true meaning and outcome of the changes that are occurring within our planet, body and consciousness and gives a spiritual and technological understanding of the transition and ascension process that is now occurring, as we all begin to be universally reborn into the next dimension.

MY PERSONAL REVELATION

St. John predicted dramatic and bizarre images of the 'end of time' – the Alpha/Omega (the beginning and the end). However, I see that he is also foretelling a time of *bodily transformation* on a global scale, created by the energetic return and awakening of the Christbody and Consciousness onto the planet. I am in the process of channelling and writing a 'New Age' perspective on the 'Book of Revelations.' I believe that hidden within this *esoteric* book is the *key* to understanding the energetic makeup of the body; its integration with the planet; the causes and effects on our health and the outcome for the Earth, through and after this time of transition from 1999-2012.

At this time, humanity and the Earth are being physically reborn into a new dimension. We are undergoing an interdimensional shift in physical body and consciousness from the third dimension to the fifth dimension. 'Matter' as we know it, is changing. Specifically, the compounds of the four elements within the planet and body are changing to sustain more of the fifth element *ether* and this process will enable the body to transform into a higher frequency of 'matter' - by slowly anchoring in more light.

TWO SIGNS OF THE NEW MILLENNIUM AND SHIFT INTO THE NEW WORLD

1. THE 'GRAND CROSS' ASTROLOGICAL ALIGNMENT, 11 AUGUST 1999

This alignment signified the 'Second Coming of Christ' and the rebirth of *humanity's physical body and consciousness* into the next dimension. This Grand Cross aspect was in the fixed signs of the Zodiac – Leo, Aquarius, Taurus and Scorpio. It was associated with the last *total* solar eclipse (Sun/Moon conjunction) for the 20th Century '*heralding* new beginnings being brought about by radical changes'.

This Grand Cross marked the beginning of the energetic activation of the 'resurrection' of the *whole of humanity* to take the next vital step in their physical/spiritual evolution.

It also began the nine month gestation period leading up to 5 May 2000, Taurus alignment when the '*Earth*' along with humanity began a process of being templated and reborn into a new evolutionary process.

DIAGRAM 4.1
The Astrological Template of the Grand Cross

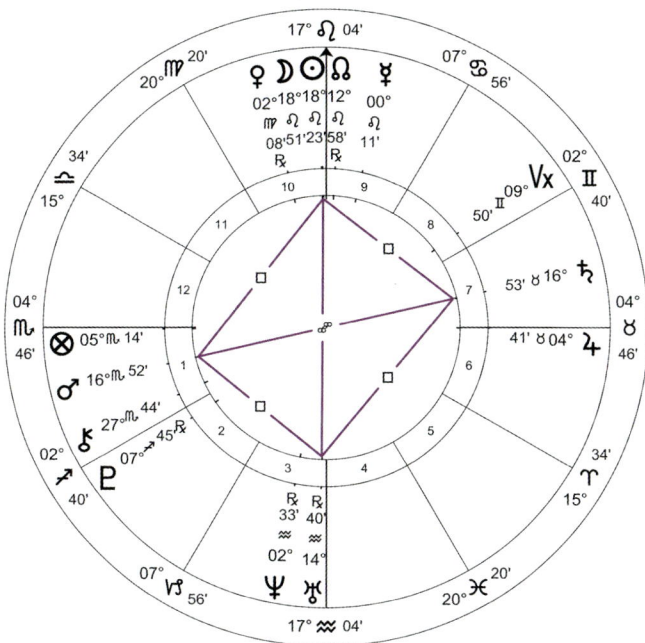

The Sun/Moon conjunction (also known as a solar eclipse) formed a Grand Cross with Mars, Saturn and Uranus. The Sun and Moon conjunction in Leo opposes Uranus in Aquarius. Mars in Scorpio opposes Saturn in Taurus. All planets square are at 90 degrees to each other. At the same time Mercury in Leo opposes Neptune in Aquarius. They both square Jupiter in Taurus. This is a fixed "Grand Cross" T-square. A total of eight out of ten planets are in fixed signs.

2. THE 'GRAND SQUARE' ASTROLOGICAL ALIGNMENT, 5 MAY 2000

This alignment signified the 'rebirth' of *planet Earth* into the next dimension. It has four points in the same *fixed-sign polarities* as the **Grand Cross,** 11 August 1999 – Leo, Aquarius, Taurus and Scorpio.

The Grand Square is energetically working with the Grand Cross to create the time of transition from 1999-2012. *It frames and sustains the template of the Grand Cross-within our third dimension.* It is as if the *Grand Square* is energetically creating a *temporary* reality shift into fourth dimensional space/time that will be sustained until 2012 - a period of only 12 years. This will allow the astrological energies of the *Grand Cross* to create the necessary healing and *physical* ascension process for the Earth to shift all matter into a higher frequency.

DIAGRAM 4.2
The Astrological Template of the Grand Square

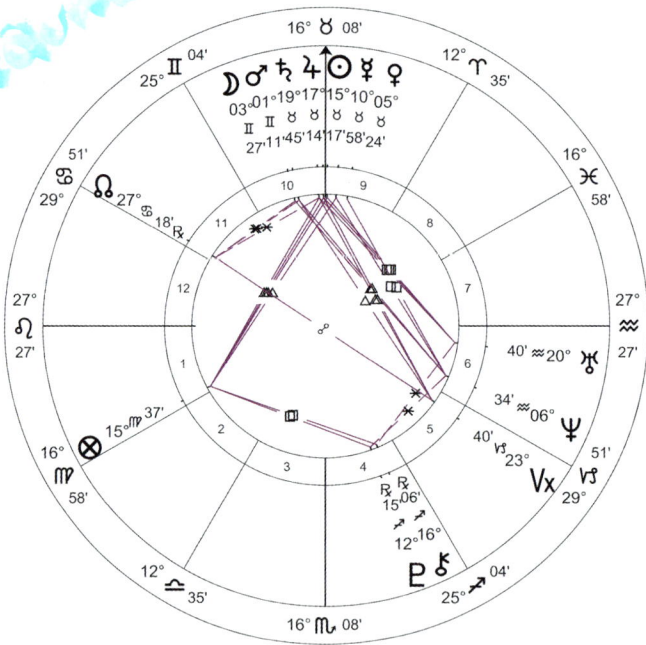

The April/May 2000 Taurus Stellium (Sun, Moon and five planets in Taurus) was activated by the transits of the original fixed 'Grand Cross' configuration of the 11 August 1999 solar eclipse.

THE ARCHETYPES OF THE TRANSITION

The four fixed signs of the Zodiac – Aquarius the angel, Leo the lion, Taurus the bull and Scorpio the eagle - activated by the Grand Cross, are associated with the *'Four Beasts of the Apocalypse'* - the sign of the 'end of time' prophesised in the' Book of Revelations'. They are also the four symbols at the four corners of the Wheel of Fortune card in the 'Rider Waite Tarot'. This tarot card is the expression of *the energies* of the Grand Cross activation of 1999, which was and has created a universal re-birthing process within humanity by triggering the Earth and Universe into a *time of transition.*

DIAGRAM 4.3
The Rider Waite Tarot - Wheel of Fortune Card

This card was a part of the Rider-Waite-Smith Tarot Card Deck published in 1912 by William Rider & Son. The deck was a collaborative effort between Pamela Colman Smith (artist) and Dr. Arthur Edward Waite, who were both members of the Order of the Golden Dawn.

The planets involved in this *Grand Cross* formation are in the four Zodiac signs of Aquarius *the angel*, Leo *the lion,* Scorpio *the eagle* and Taurus *the bull.*

The archetypes of these four zodiacal points are impacting the body and consciousness on a global level. They are activating a global healing shift within specific dimensions of the etheric/physical body so the body can ascend into higher consciousness.

> **The two astrological templates - the Grand Cross and Grand Square – resonate archetypal energies which enable interdimensional energies from the Earth and Cosmos to filter through into the etheric/physical body and planet to create our new body, world, reality and dimension.**

Below is a brief description of some of the main dimensions of the body and consciousness that will be impacted by the energies from these four planetary grid points, until 2012.

TAURUS

Planetary ruler- Venus; Symbol - Bull; Key word - Communication

The bull with wings on the bottom left-hand side of diagram 4.3 (and appearing above) represents the planet Venus and also the conjunction of Saturn in Taurus, in the Grand Cross Alignment. Taurus and its ruling planet Venus primarily resonate with and influence the fifth chakra - throat, inner ear and thyroid, and also enhance all levels of communication.

DIAGRAM 4.4
The Dimensions of the Anatomy Affected by the Astrological Influence of the Planet/Venus - at the Time of the Grand Cross

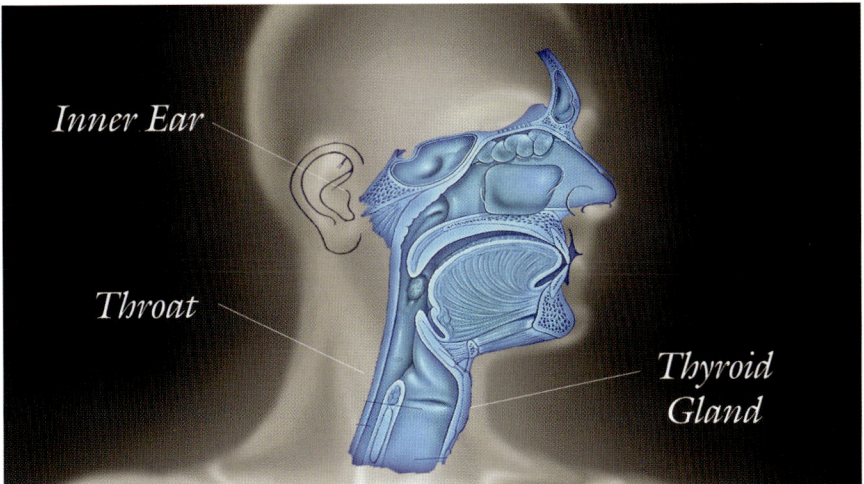

Copyright 2005 Alexis Cartwright, Keeper of the Crystals Pty Ltd.

The fifth chakra and corresponding dimensions of the body are being pushed beyond their limits to open. Many neurological imbalances and emotional disorders - learning difficulties, forms of depression etc. can be related back to this specific area of the body, particularly the throat chakra and inner ear. As we go through a global healing process on this level, many psychological disorders and stress-related diseases will finally begin to shift and heal.

Moving into fourth and fifth dimensional reality is pushing the body's *upper nervous system* to heal and grasp new levels of consciousness. What is happening in the physical world reflects what is happening spiritually. We already have mobile phones, fax machines, computers, and the Internet but as we enter into the fifth dimension and heal this dimension of the body, communication technology will evolve even more rapidly.

As we master new levels of comprehension and communication, we become more *receptive* to communicate more effectively on a universal level. This dimensional level of our healing process is the key or channel to open up and access Christ Consciousness.

As we feel and see beyond the physical reality of our existence, we can connect to and communicate with our Higher Selves, anchor in Christ Consciousness and therefore communicate beyond and with other interdimensional beings. Through this process we can channel and learn from other dimensions, enhance our own process of spiritual growth and correspondingly create a more *spiritually advanced* technological reality to live in.

This cosmic grid point resonating in Taurus/Venus is also anchoring more of the Feminine Principle back onto the planet and into humanity so the powers of *psychic perception* can come back into consciousness. It is also *evolving the emotional body* by opening up a deeper sense of *perception* and *understanding* and a more spiritual sense of awareness.

This planetary aspect also opens the communication channel between *the heart*/ emotional body and *the head* (or brain)/ mental body. It is enabling us to get in touch with what we really feel and to master our emotions so we that we can express our true feelings more effectively, not only to ourselves but also to others thereby enhancing our communication skills and abilities.

This fifth chakra responds to the cosmic grid point symbolised by Taurus the bull which not only resonates with the planet Venus but also connects us to the *Pleiadian* dimensions.

LEO

Planetary ruler- Sun; Symbol- Lion; Key word- Heart/Love

The lion with wings on the bottom right-hand side of diagram 4.3 (and appearing above) represents the Sun and also the Moon conjunction in Leo, in the Grand Cross alignment. Because the Sun is the ruling planet of Leo, it specifically influences the fourth chakra: the heart, thymus gland governing the immune system, lungs and respiratory system.

Cardiac disease is one of the main causes of death today. Healing the heart chakra alleviates pressure through the heart itself and enables us to then counteract cardiac disease. Healing and opening the fourth or heart chakra, also enables us to heal the 'thymus gland' and therefore build general immunity to fight all diseases that are manifesting on the planet and within humanity.

The heart tells the body *how* to feel. By healing this dimension of the body we are releasing all the painful memories stored within our DNA and cellular levels to allow all negative feelings of judgment, hate and fear to be slowly transmuted into the light. This enhances our longevity - a natural cellular rejuvenation to maintain long term health, wellness and life force. The skin also rejuvenates so we can maintain a more *youthful* appearance.

This cosmic grid point resonating in Leo is also shifting the electromagnetic dimensions of the body so that a *deeper chamber of the heart* can open. The heart can begin to feel the emotion of love on a deeper level and therefore allow more love into our life. When this happens we can master our own innate healing abilities from within, anchor-in more dimensions of Christ Consciousness and enhance the feelings of compassion and unconditional love.

DIAGRAM 4.5
The Dimensions of the Anatomy Affected by the Astrological Influence of the Star/Sun - at the Time of the Grand Cross

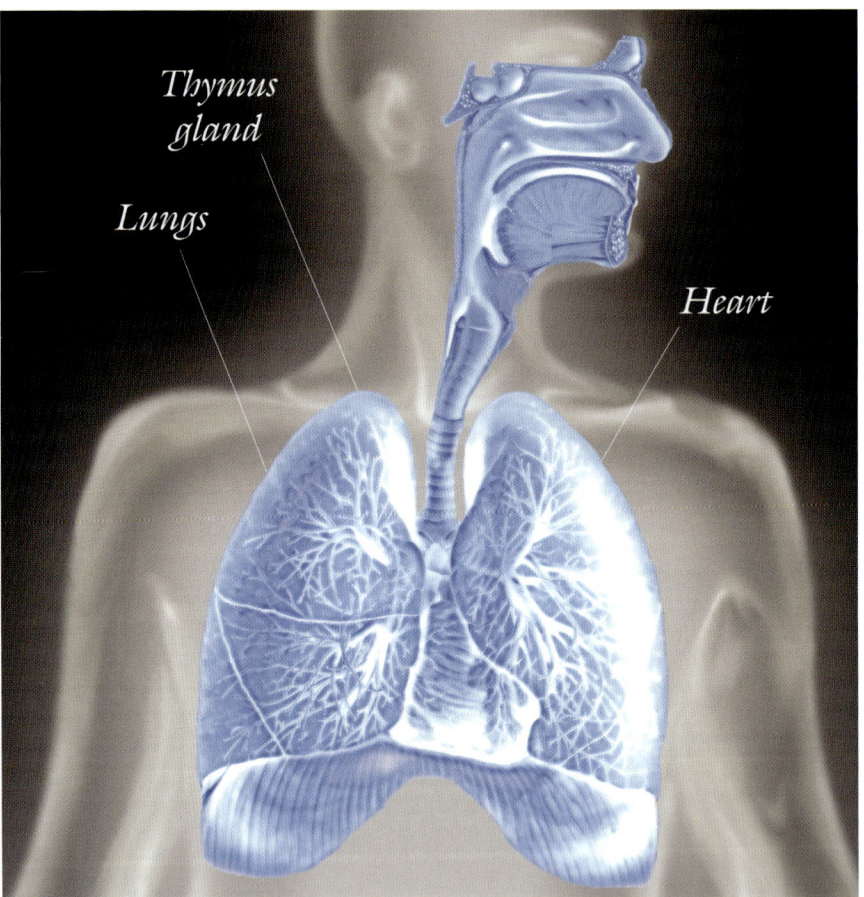

Thymus gland

Lungs

Heart

Copyright 2005 Alexis Cartwright, Keeper of the Crystals Pty Ltd

This fourth chakra responds to the cosmic grid point symbolised by Leo the lion which not only resonates with the Sun but also connects us to the Sirian dimensions.

SCORPIO

**Planetary ruler- Pluto; Symbol- Eagle; Key word-
Transformation**

The Eagle with wings on the top right-hand side of diagram 4.3 (and also appearing above) represents the planet Pluto and also the conjunction of Mars in Scorpio, in the Grand Cross Alignment. Scorpio and its ruling planet Pluto primarily resonate with the first chakra known as the root or base chakra. *The etheric body is vibrationally embedded into the physical body at this point* to maintain overall physical health and wellbeing.

This chakra continually repairs and weaves in the etheric body so the physical anatomy can rejuvenate and heal itself. This chakra responds to the cosmic grid point symbolised by Scorpio, and is not only creating a purification and repair process of the whole etheric body but also the DNA. It is healing *past life wounding* encoded within the DNA, thereby healing general genetic weaknesses of the family line, within the etheric/physical body. The DNA is repairing and re-weaving in the new *pure* 12-strand DNA system.

DIAGRAM 4.6

The Dimensions of the Anatomy Affected by the Astrological Influence of the Planet/Pluto - at the Time of the Grand Cross

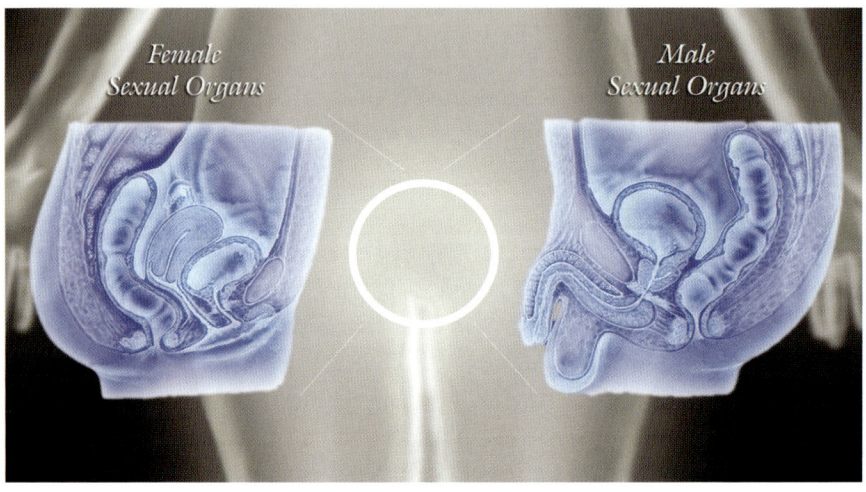

Copyright 2005 Alexis Cartwright, Keeper of the Crystals Pty Ltd

The base chakra is also creating, within its adjoining organs, a *global* healing process around issues concerning sexuality and abuse. Many diseases currently manifesting on the planet are sexually related. These issues and diseases are now going through a universal purification and healing process through the Scorpio aspect of the *Grand Cross*. Sexuality can be a pathway to spirituality and this cosmic grid point and chakra naturally enhances the activation process of the Kundalini that creates initiations into higher states of consciousness. It is also purifying and rejuvenating blood circulation within the heart and throughout the body.

This first chakra responds to the cosmic grid point symbolised by Scorpio the eagle which not only resonates with Pluto and Chiron but also connects us to the dimensions of Orion.

AQUARIUS

Planetary ruler - Uranus; Symbol - the Water Bearer/Angel; Key word - lightbody

The Angel on the top left-hand side of diagram 4.3 (and also appearing above) represents the planet Uranus and also the conjunction of Uranus in Aquarius in the *Grand Cross Alignment*. It symbolises the transformation process of the human body as it becomes energetically and alchemically more *androgynous*. The body and consciousness is integrating into a higher frequency by creating and sustaining more electromagnetic frequencies in the cellular body.

The compounds of the four elements within the body are changing to sustain, more of the fifth element *ether* - to make the body more ethereal again. When there is more *ether* sustaining itself within the body, it begins to transform into the lightbody. The body and consciousness is therefore transforming into a more *divine angelic nature* by anchoring in the androgynous lightbody.

DIAGRAM 4.7
The Dimensions of the Anatomy Affected by the Astrological Influence of the Planet/Uranus - at the Time of the Grand Cross

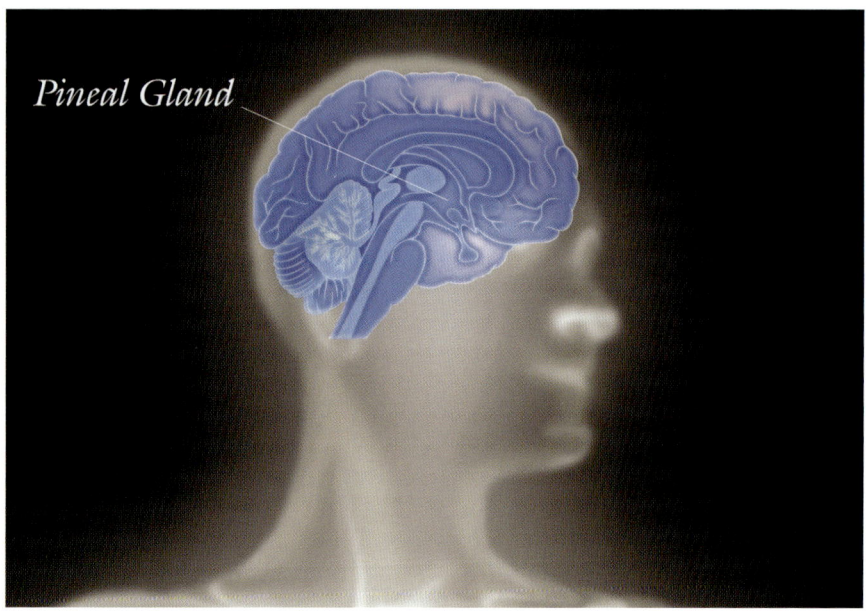

Pineal Gland

Copyright 2005 Alexis Cartwright, Keeper of the Crystals Pty Ltd.

Aquarius and its ruling planet Uranus, primarily govern the sixth chakra and third eye or pineal gland. The pineal gland is still not totally understood by science but is understood esoterically as the third eye - the 'self-healing' gland of the *energetic body*. It is very sensitive to light and transmits specific rays of sunlight and electromagnetic light into depleted organs, nerves and other areas of the body.

This enables the anatomy to receive the necessary energetic resources to heal, rejuvenate and evolve. Through the transmission or transference of' *'light into matter'* the (metaphysical) or emotional state of the body can also heal and evolve. This creates a natural, alchemical, enlightenment process so the body and consciousness can ascend into a higher state of being.

It is through the internal technology of the third eye and pineal gland that higher frequencies of energies and light can weave through to create more dimensions of the lightbody within. The body and consciousness can then *physically* ascend into a higher dimension through the lightbody.

This sixth chakra responds to the cosmic grid point symbolised by the angel of Aquarius which not only resonates with the planet Uranus but also connects us to the *Arcturian* dimensions.

TRANSFERENCE HEALING SELF-HEALING PROCEDURES & PROPERTIES

This Celestial Alignment is impacting the energetic nature or makeup of everything within the Earth-*matter* and the Cosmos-*light*. The *Transference Healing Self-Help Procedures (in chapter 6)* and their corresponding essences, specifically the **Crystal Cross Essence**, supports the integration of these astrological and planetary energies from the Grand Cross Alignment to filter through and into the etheric/physical body.

This Grand Cross astrological phenomenon and corresponding Transference Healing procedures and essences are enabling us to template, heal and shift these particular dimensions of the anatomy (as mentioned above) and therefore create the fundamental changes necessary so that the body and consciousness can begin to:

♦ Filter through specific Earth and cosmic energies and properties necessary to heal and repair the energy system of the etheric field and on a parallel level create the necessary alchemical changes so that the new anatomy or 'Adam Kadmon' body, consciousness and fifth dimensional reality can begin to come into manifestation.

- Support the energies and the initial fundamental changes to occur to create the necessary changes within matter and light itself, so that humanity can create a quantum shift forward in its evolutional process throughout the duration of 1999-2012 and thereby begin the creation process of this new body, consciousness, reality and world that is to come into existence.

THE BOOK OF REVELATIONS - 'NEW AGE' INTERPRETATION

The 'Book of Revelations' foresees the changes of this time of transition as the 'Time of Judgment' - a fearful image of Earth catastrophes. St. John predicted dramatic and bizarre images of the 'end of time' – the Alpha/Omega (the beginning and the end). However, I have been shown by Divine revelation, the key to understanding the subliminal meaning of this process of 'Earth and cosmic change'.

> ## The 'Book of Revelations' contains the esoteric knowledge of an ancient form of healing and energetic technology that Christ mastered when on Earth.

It is foretelling a time of *bodily transformation* on a global scale, created by the energetic return and awakening of the Christbody and Consciousness onto the planet. I believe that hidden within this *esoteric* book is the *key* to understanding the energetic makeup of the body; its integration with the planet; the causes and effects on our health and the outcome for the Earth, through and after this time of transition from 1999-2012.

Transference Healing is the ***energetic key*** to receiving the healing properties spoken of in the 'Book of Revelations'. It has become a channel for this universal 'Christ' healing process, now energetically filtering through to humanity and the planet. It not only maintains our *health* but allows *bodily transformation* and a shift in consciousness so we *can* survive this transition and enter the next dimension without pain, struggle or even physical death.

I have been shown in detail how to re-establish this 'unique' philosophy and form of healing back onto the planet. The procedures of Transference Healing have enabled me to give a more in-depth description of *how* the ascension is influencing our body, health, consciousness and planet.

THE BEGINNING OF THE AGE OF AQUARIUS

PROPHECIES, THEORIES AND DATES
CYCLES WITHIN CYCLES

EARTH'S ORBIT AROUND THE SUN

Our solar system is almost flat (like a CD) and lies within a circular plane called the 'ecliptic'. The 'ecliptic plane' is an *imaginary* plane defined by the Earth's (and most of the other planets') orbit around the Sun.

THE SUN'S PASSAGE THROUGH THE ZODIAC

The constellations are also totally *imaginary*. They are divisions of the sky making it easier for us to recognise and remember the position of the stars. There are now 88 recognised constellations and our astrological Zodiac is a ring of only 12 of these constellations spread or located around the ecliptic plane. The Sun's apparent passage through the Zodiac in the course of a year marks out the months of the year.

As all of the planets except Pluto, orbit very near to the ecliptic plane, they are usually located in the zodiacal constellations. (Capricorn, Aquarius, Pisces, Aries, Taurus, Gemini, Cancer, Leo, Virgo, Libra, Scorpio and Sagittarius - Ophiuchus is the 13th but not included).

PRECESSION OF THE EQUINOXES = PLATONIC YEAR = GREAT YEAR

Precession is the third-discovered Earth cycle, after it's far more obvious daily rotation on its polar axis and annual revolution around the Sun.

Precession is an astronomical phenomenon caused by the gravitational influence or attraction of the Sun and the Moon acting on the Earth's equatorial bulge. As the Earth rotates rapidly on its polar axis this makes it wobble slowly like a spinning top. As the polar axis is not fixed in space, over a very long period of time this wobble moves the polar axis of the Earth *slowly backwards through the entire Zodiac* (with respect to two other astrophysical planes: the ecliptic plane and the galactic plane) and this slow *backward movement* through the Zodiac is called precession.

The Egyptians referred to this astronomical phenomenon as the 'Great Secret of Precession'. They understood its associated geometry, incorporating it into the designs of their great monuments and using it to measure the 12 Zodiacal Ages.

ZODIACAL AGES

It takes approximately 25,000 to 26,000 years for the Earth to move back through the entire Zodiac. So precession is like a star clock that helps us date the 26,000-year cycle of planet Earth through the *complete cycle* of Zodiacal Ages. It measures the length of Zodiacal Ages. Our solar system takes about 2,100 years to pass through each one of the 12 signs of the Zodiac. After 2,100 years we move out of one Age and into another.

The precessional world Ages are a phenomenon that have defined the course of history and have also given rise to much speculation about the 'new Millennium' and the fundamental changes it will bring about for all of humanity.

THE AGE OF AQUARIUS

The dawning of the Age of Aquarius follows the polar axis leaving the Age of Pisces - the sign of two fishes swimming in opposite directions. Jesus Christ lived on Earth during the time of Pisces when the Christian symbol was the fish.

The ancients obviously knew about precession. Throughout the Ages the different animals symbolising each sign were connected with the consciousness of the established religion of the Age. Ram cults developed in Rome, the Middle East and elsewhere during the age of Aries; bull cults such as the Egyptian Apis during the Age of Taurus and the lion/sphinx during Leo. Many believe the zodiacal pointer into the Age of Aquarius will be the shift of focus from the traditional religion of Christianity to a New Age religion 'Mystic Christianity', based on a synthesis of *universal* religious principles which will herald a time of brotherhood and peace.

However, even though we acknowledge the complete astronomical processional cycle is known to be around 25,725 years long, the exact beginning and ending of the constellation of each Age is unclear. Therefore, the exact date for the 'dawning' of the Age of

Aquarius has been the subject of intense speculation and debate. There have been many differences of opinion about the exact timing and length of time for the shift into the Age of Aquarius, 'New Millennium and World' and a great amount of confusion concerning the events it should be based on.

Currently researchers and Lightworkers are looking into the completion of cycles and 'galactic or cosmic alignments' which are unfolding consciousness to shift us into a New World of more galactic awareness. The global shift in energy is affecting time, space and the planetary and human grid and the evolution of consciousness. A new galactic calendar therefore sustains a New Age, Aquarian perspective of time and space.

(New concepts: Gregg Braden – *zero point*, Ken Kalb – *Lightshift;* Lee Carroll - *Kryon*, John Major Jenkins – *galactic centre*; Nick Anthony Fiorenza – '*Holy Cross*'; Jose Arguelles – *Mayan Calendars*, Harmonic Convergence, 13 *Moon Calendar,* '*Day Out of Time*', John Mirehiel - *Harmonic Concordance*'.)

The Mayan Calendars hold a vital key to the concept of 'galactic timing' for the evolution of consciousness. They are based on the universal mathematics of the fourth dimension and believe that once we move into fourth dimensional awareness we will enter a new path of spiritual and mental evolution in tune with the cycles of the Universe – we are now in this prophesied 'time of no time.' The end of their current Great Cycle and the calendar itself is 2012 which also corresponds with the change-over of the current precessional cycle. More conclusive information is given on the Mayan concepts, in following paragraphs.

In '*The Book of World Horoscopes*' Nicholas Campion mentions at least seventy dates ranging over 1500 years which correspond with physical and spiritual happenings supposedly signifying the official 'time of transition' or 'astrological turning point' into the *Age of Aquarius* and the beginning of a New World. Some of these dates are included below and are either esoteric or astrological in nature.

1904 - Aleister Crowley, on April 1904, in Cairo, channelled *'The Book of the Law'* through a discarnate Egyptian entity who proposed the beginning of the *'New Aeon'* would be ruled by Horus, the Solar God of ancient Egypt.

1911 - The Theosophical Society based its calculation for the dawning of the *Age of Aquarius* on Krishnamurti's channelling of Lord Maitreya in 1911.

Madame Blavatsky: predicated a universal Church towards the close of the 20th Century.

1930's - Alice Bailey: in *'The Externalisation of the Hierarchy,'* determined the transition occurred in the 1930s.

1945 - Master Djwhal Khul invoked the powers of light, love and Divine Purpose irrespective of all religions in 'The Great Invocation.'

1946 - Alice Bailey wrote *'the day is dawning when all religions will be regarded as emanating from one great spiritual source'*.

1962 - Willaru Huayta: Peruvian spiritual messenger of the Quechua Nation (part of the ancient Inca confederation) believes the *Age of Aquarius* began in February 1962.

1975 - Dane Rudhyar, transpersonal astrologer and father of karmic astrology: designated 1975 as the time when the Avatar of the New Age would appear. He acknowledged that it might not be the *Second Coming of Christ* anticipated by many, but that the Christ energy could be carried by a series of individuals who would be agents for this message.

1975 - A. Wolben: suggested a range of dates in *'After Nostradamus'* including 1975, 2000, 2023 and 2160. He stated the *transition of World Ages* is never exact and can take hundreds of years because they constitute a modification in collective consciousness.

1997- Carl Jung: inspired by the work of *Nostradamus* supported his contention that the *New Age* would occur between 1997-2000.

1987- Jose Arguelles: Harmonic Convergence, 17 August 1987: announced the forthcoming end of time as we know it and a preparation to move from third-dimensional reality of space into fourth-dimensional reality of time. 'It was the fulfilment of the prophecy of Quetzalcoatl, known as the Thirteen Heavens and Nine Hells. The prophecy stated that following the ninth Hell, humanity would know and experience an unprecedented New Age of Peace. The Hell cycle ended on 16 August 1987. The Mayan calendar *entered* the final 25 year culmination of the Great Cycle of History on 17 August 1987 at the time of the Harmonic Convergence, and is due to end on the Winter Solstice, 2012.

2000 - There are many prophets who agree the millennial year is 2000, among them: Nostradamus, Edgar Cayce, St Malachy, Garabandal, Fatima and other Christian prophets.

The *seer* **Catherine Emmerich** believed Lucifer would be unchained 50 or 60 years before the year 2000. The theory of 'The Divine Plot' by this author, is an astrological model of the historical process expressing multiple, cyclic World Ages. It projects a transition to a *New World Age* in the year 2000.

Margaret Hone who wrote 'The Modern Textbook of Astrology' also gives the year 2000 as a 'symbolic date' for *the New Age*.

2000 - Nick Anthony Fiorenza: "Erection of the Holy Cross: The Sacred Geometry of Global Change" describes the timing of a primary astronomical transition or turning in the natural evolutionary cycle of the Earth (the Precession of the Equinoxes) as the Holy Cross. Hidden within this symbol is a map referring to a unique occurrence of a specific geometric relationship between Earth, the solar system, and our galaxy - an astrophysical event occurring now within Earth's 25,920 year, precessional cycle.

'Although the Holy Cross is a definable and 'mapable' astrophysical transition occurring for Earth and humanity (circa 2000 AD), this event occurs in a spiralling vortex of evolutionary time, and the translation of this event stretches into Earth time over many years through a series of interweaving astronomical cycles. Thus, we are not waiting for some calendrical event to occur; we are in this evolutionary portal moment-by-moment NOW.

The Erection of the Holy Cross is a catalyst for a tremendous acceleration of change on Earth. Earth's pole now leans back toward the galactic plane activating this Holy Cross. It marks the time where we return from 12,000 years of temporal darkness, from our experience in duality consciousness and from the separation of the fallen Feminine and Masculine Principles, to a re-unification in consciousness. The Divine Feminine and Divine Masculine Principles emerge on Earth to demonstrate the Divine Union of the feminine and masculine within ourselves, and our relations with each other and all of life.'

2001 - G Barbarin: stated that according to the principle of the Great Week and the six days of a thousand years of the Adamic Era, there will follow a day of rest, the Millennium, which from the year 2001 will bring a thousand years of peace. While his prophecy echoes the Seventh Day Adventists, it is also similar to the Hebrew Jubilee Year and Nostradamus' Seventh Millennium Theory.

2003- John Mirhiel: Harmonic Concordance, 8 November 2003

Several planets formed the pattern of a six-pointed Star of David around the Earth during a Full Moon Lunar Eclipse. This moment of attunement was called The Harmonic Concordance. John believed 'it opened an energetic 'stargate' for the ascension of Mother Earth, and each of her inhabitants. Many have called this paradigm, the Shift of the Ages. It speaks of the descent of God

Consciousness onto this plane and offers a moment in time for humankind to make a concerted effort to rise up to meet it.

2010 - Peter Lemesurier (in 'The Gospel of the Stars' by Joseph Seiss, 1882) suggests this as an 'official deadline' and entrance into the *Age of Aquarius*. He quotes the French Institute 'Geographique National' for support of his claim.

2012 - END OF THE MAYAN CALENDAR

2012 - Terence (and Dennis) McKenna: founder of Novelty Theory and the software programme 'Timewave Zero,' developed interesting new theories, around the calendar system of the Mayans - while inspired by psychedelic visions. Terence predicted the end of the world would come when our Sun comes into momentary alignment with the galactic centre when levels of planetary novelty will exponentially increase. He presented this as a potentially positive thing - the entry into hyperspace and galactic citizenship

His book 'The *Invisible Landscape*' advances an idea derived from psycho-active drugs and studies of primitive shamanism that our Universe is created by the holographic interaction between two hyper-universes and that the Universe is cyclic and recurrent. Based on extensive computer modelling, he and his brother conclude humanity will experience a *'Resurrection into the Light'* during six days in AD 2012. In the last 135 minutes, eighteen barriers, comparable to the appearance of life, the invention of language or the achievement of immortality, will be experienced - thirteen of them in the last millisecond!

2012- Jose Arguelles discovered a system of natural cycles that encourage peace and unity; called the 13 Moon 28 Day Calendar (based on the ancient Mayan Calendar figured below, 3.8).

This calendar began in 3012 BC. He determined that 21 December 2012, would be the 'Closing of the Cycle' or the 'Great Time Shift.' It would be the end of the 396-year Baktun referred to by the Maya as *the transformation of matter, collapse of global civilisation, Earth's purification and regeneration of the planet, with a following era of information and crystal-solar technology and galactic synchronisation.*

DIAGRAM 4.8
The New Age: 26,000 Tun Cycle

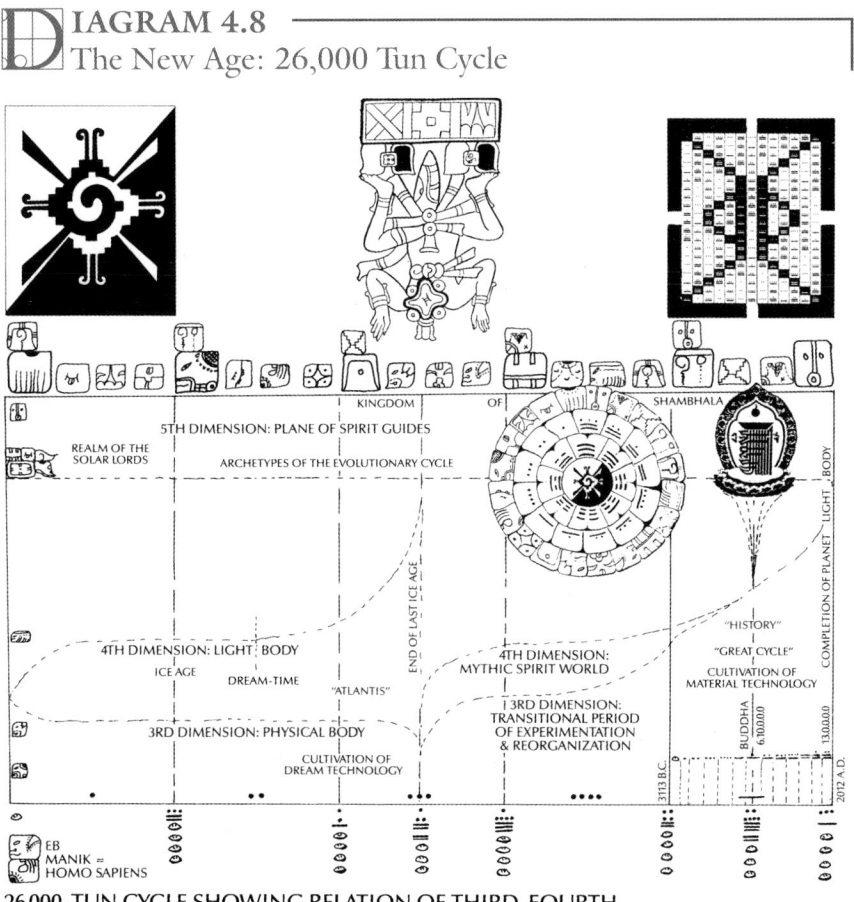

26,000-TUN CYCLE SHOWING RELATION OF THIRD, FOURTH, & FIFTH DIMENSIONS, GREAT CYCLE, AND KINGDOM OF SHAMBHALA

We are experiencing the last decades of a 26,000-year cycle of *Homo-sapiens*, when the lightbody of planet Earth will be complete. The date of completion, AD 2012, is on the right of this diagram. (Arguelles, *The Mayan Factor*).

GALACTIC CENTRE ALIGNMENT

2012 – JOHN MAJOR JENKINS: 'GALACTIC ALIGNMENT'

Reviewed by Willard Van De Bogart

'Over the last century philosophers, archaeoastronomers, and historians of ancient knowledge and wisdom have been deciphering ancient languages, the origins of ancient temples, and the mythology of ancient civilisations to find the source of inspiration and knowledge for the ingenious contributions these ancient civilisations have left on the Earth. Past civilisations are now being newly re-discovered and interpreted for those of us who want to know of our past, our evolution as a species, and the destiny of humanity.'

'Galactic alignment, the transformation of consciousness according to Mayan, Egyptian, and Vedic traditions' - shows that everything the ancients were doing in their civilisations was involved in recognising the significance of the *galactic centre.* Ancient architecture left on Earth, which mirrored the Heavens, encoded the direction to galactic centre in their stone monuments - indicating the ascent to a new spiritual world age. All ancient cultures were aware that alignments to the galactic centre periodically occur and these alignments offer spiritual renewal for humanity - not catastrophe and destruction as is commonly promoted by modern day interpretations.

Terence and Dennis McKenna: in 'Maya Cosmogenesis, 2012' deciphered the ultimate meaning of the Mayan end-date of 21 December 2012, used in the Mayan long count calendrical system. Terence discovered that all of the Mayan priests knew of this end date as the renewal and rebirth of a New World Age resulting *from the solar meridian crossing the galactic equator*, and the Earth aligning itself with the centre of the galaxy.

Alexis Cartwright: After reading these theories and prophesies, I now recognise that all of the *changes* predicted to occur during the transition into the *Age of Aquarius*, are included in the overall concepts I have channelled as the new philosophy, wisdom and teachings of Transference Healing.

TRANSFERENCE HEALING PROPHECY

TRANSITION INTO THE 'AGE OF AQUARIUS'

It is very difficult to determine the exact 'time' of the shift into the New Age of Aquarius, as time as we have known it up until 1999, no longer exists in the same way. The illusion is breaking down; *matter is re-weaving* itself and the world as we know it is *transforming* itself in every way. We are all being suspended and re-created by the elements and energies that are filtering through. Everything within our body and reality is shifting.

Therefore, before explaining the 'time' I propose for the Earth to literally shift into the next dimension, I have given a brief explanation on the time changes occurring within our dimension.

TIME

• We have now left the third dimension where we have existed since the final fall of Atlantis around 12,000 BC.

* From 1999-2012 we will be suspended within the *brief* transition of the **fourth dimension,** a 'time of no time'. As we go through this transition we are rapidly shifting our perception of time. Everything seems to be *speeding up* as we become more and more conscious of our new self and reality and of the new fifth dimensional existence and world that is now being templated and created for us.

* In 2013 we will enter the **fifth dimension** where we will exist for the next 1,000 years. The fifth dimension will allow more freedom and less restriction on all levels.

NON-PHYSICAL AND PHYSICAL WORLDS ON EARTH

As we moved into the fourth dimensional time of transition in 1999, time as we knew it ceased to exist. The ancients prophesised the fourth dimensional transition we are now in as the *'end of time'*, the *'time of no time'* or the *'shift of the ages.'* During this transition from 1999-2012, time as we know it has ceased to exist as we have moved from a *physical* into a *non-physical world*.

Non-physical worlds exist during *times of transition* when the Earth's global consciousness and existence takes a quantum leap into a higher level of physical and spiritual reality. They exist as periods of time *between* physical worlds or holographic realities that come to exist on Earth. The **Non-physical worlds** are contained within different levels and 'degrees of light and consciousness' suspended within *space* (only) within the holograms of the fourth, sixth and eighth dimensions. These dimensions are holographic realms on Earth sustaining more **ether, light, crystal and consciousness** than elemental compounds and denser levels of gravity, matter and form.

Physical worlds are times of *physical incarnation* or formation that have and will come to exist on planet Earth. They are holographic realms on Earth sustaining us in more **gravity, matter** and **form** than ether, light, crystal and consciousness. The **physical worlds** that have and will come to exist on Earth will be contained within different levels and degrees of *'matter'* suspended within *space* and *time* within the hologram of the third, fifth and seventh dimensions.

> **As we go through this shift in time and space and as we enter into the fifth dimension in 2013, we will see everything in a new light. Our consciousness will have expanded and more light and ether will physically sustain our body and planet.**

It has been very difficult for me to give an exact date for the transition into the next Age because there is so much complexity involved in the process, as mentioned above. However, I do feel that the **'Grand Cross'** of 11 August 1999 was the principal turning point for our shift into the new millennium and next dimension.

SUMMARY OF THE INTERDIMENSIONAL SHIFT

'Beyond Doorways' refers to prophesised crystal, Earth, cosmic and interdimensional changes and events occurring between 1999-2012 within our planet, body, consciousness and reality which signify the beginning of the fourth dimension (whose energies are shifting us into the fifth dimension).

• **The Grand Cross and Grand Square Activations**

The Grand Cross alignment signified the activation of a critical celestial event in the co-creation process of the 'new millennium and world'. It is the time of the cosmic intervention and energetic *return of the Celestial Christ on Earth* to create a profound and vital healing and ascension process for Earth and humanity.

The astrological alignment on 11 August 1999 symbolised the ending of the third dimensional world and reality we have existed within for aeons of time and the beginning of the transference and creation of the *New World* we are to exist within.

> **I therefore propose:**
> **the 'Grand Cross' astrological activation of**
> **11 August 1999 is the official *turning point***
> **into the 'Age of Aquarius' and the beginning**
> **of our shift into the fourth and parallel**
> **fifth dimension.**

The Grand Cross had a nine month gestation period - from 11 August 1999 to the time of the **Grand Square** of 5 May 2000 - to complete its energetic or etheric templating process within all levels of *matter* within our universe. This new holographic template provides the energetic resources for us to create the necessary changes within the *foundations* of our body, Earth and reality to exist within a *New World* and dimension.

The energy templating and filtering process of the Celestial Grand Cross is also creating the fifth dimension (on a parallel level), which will officially commence on Earth in 2013 AD and come to pass over the next 1,000 years.

◆ The Star of David Activation: 8 November 2003

This astrological activation was identified by astrologer John Mirehiel who named it the Harmonic Concordance. It is just as significant as the astrological activations of the Grand Cross and Grand Square, and will work with them energetically until 2012.

The Star of David formation resonated an energetic template to create radical changes *specifically* within our *DNA*, so the *New Anatomy or Adam Kadmon* body could begin to materialise itself more within the etheric/physical body. As we physically embody the New Anatomy we begin to create the lightbody and ultimately the Christbody - which will take most of humanity 1,000 years to perfect.

The Star of David began a more conclusive re-programming and filtering of 'cosmic codes' into the DNA so the *androgynous lightbody* could begin to complete its resurrection process over the upcoming years.

The two interlocking triangles of the Star of David symbolise and energetically create the union of the masculine and feminine within, so that Heaven and Earth can unite. Symbolically, this means the spiritual/galactic aspects of the Higher Self can anchor through and materialise within the physical body and consciousness of the Lower Self on Earth. *This union begins the Divine process of ascension.*

DIAGRAM 4.9
The Astrological Template of the Star of David Activation, 8 November 2003

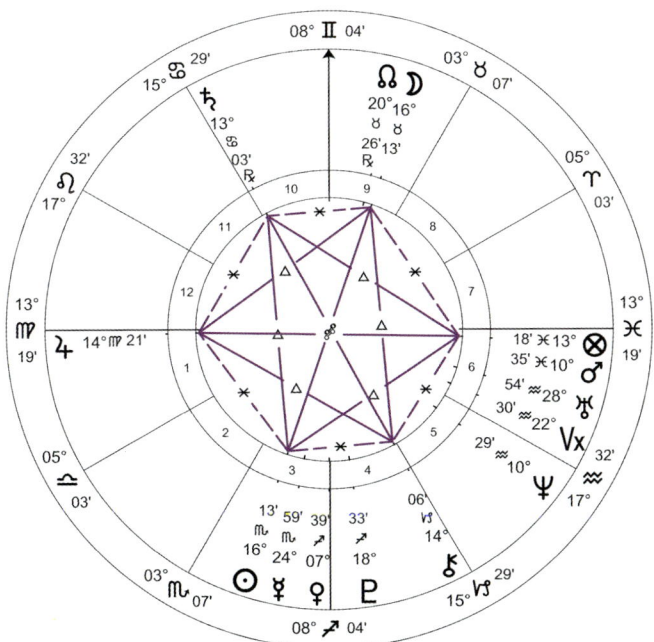

This Grand Sextile aspect is formed by two intersecting Grand Trines which form a pattern known as the 'Star of David.'

In 3D this becomes the universally recognised symbol of the Merkabah or lightbody vehicle of consciousness – a very important symbol for those working with light energies.

Another name for this planetary pattern/symbol is the 'Seal of Solomon' which promises the advent of Divine Wisdom. Other patterns within this Grand Sextile chart include: three Mystic Rectangles, four Kites, and six Minor Grand Trines.

Astrologers will note that there are also three oppositions within the pattern, (four, if the wide Mercury/Moon is included) and a T-Square involving the Sun, Moon and Neptune (effectively bringing Neptune's voice into the pattern).

Further, the square between Venus and Mars along with the oppositions emphasises the male/female, Yin/Yang relationship quality which the oppositions strongly suggest.

*The fact that **a total lunar eclipse is part of the Grand Sextile pattern** greatly adds to its significance. In at least one viewpoint, an eclipse carries the implication of the beginning of some important undertaking or bringing an issue to fruition that had its conception at an earlier time.*

This eclipse could mark one of those milestone events on a global level.

◆ The Star of David and Venus/Sun Eclipse

Just as the Grand Cross activation is energetically supported by the Grand Square over a 12 year period, the Star of David activation is energetically supported by the eight year period between the pair of Venus Transits /Sun eclipses of 8 June 2004 and 6 June 2012.

The Venus Transit, 8 June 2004 symbolises and energetically anchors more of the *Feminine Principle* into the body and consciousness. This will bring through more of the intuitive and spiritual aspects of the self to reinforce an inner balancing process of the Feminine and Masculine Principle. This will in turn support the androgynous lightbody to anchor into the etheric/physical body. After its embodiment we will begin to crystallise the lightbody so we can physically sustain a 'higher frequency and a more pure crystallised formation of elements within our physical body'.

DIAGRAM 4.10
The Astrological Template of the Venus/Transit Sun
Activation, 8 June 2004

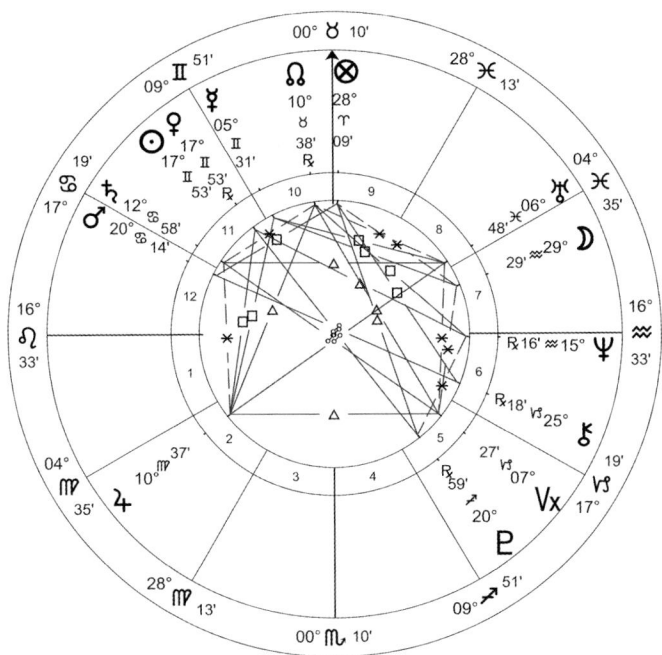

When the planet Venus passes across the disc of the Sun, this is called a Venus Transit.

It is an astronomical event where the planet Venus passes between the Earth and the Sun - a sort of eclipse. Venus transits lasts for 6-7 hours and come in pairs separated by exactly eight Earth years minus two days. As far as human measures go such pairs of transits occur only rarely.

Below is a list of the years of the most recent occurrences, where the second transit in the pair is given within parentheses: 1518 (1526) 1631 (1639) 1761 (1769) 1874 (1882) 2004 (2012).

This transit is a symbol of the unification of the masculine and feminine in the time ahead.

(From Carl-Johan Calleman and Anders Bjarstedt)

GALACTIC EVOLUTION

So at this time of transition from 1999-2012, we can see specific astrological alignments are both creating and energetically anchoring in the parallel fourth and fifth dimensions and new physical/lightbody system. This process is creating the necessary changes within our DNA and etheric/physical body to begin a whole new evolutionary process.

We are in the initial stages of anchoring in light so we can mineralise, crystallise and perfect the integration of our light or cosmic body. This will enable us to sustain our next level of existence within the fifth dimensional holographic world and reality that has already begun its creation within and around us. Over the next 1,000 years we will perfect the resurrection of the totality of the lightbody system thereby anchoring through and living more within the Christbody and Consciousness.

> **We are now embodying the spiritual/galactic aspects of the Higher Self on Earth.**

In 2013 we officially enter the fifth dimension and galactic confederation. We will have anchored within us the *resources* and *internal technology* to create the changes within our body and consciousness to ascend with the planet into a higher dimension that is not so separated from other realities and worlds. It is from this higher fifth dimensional hologram, frequency and reality that we can and will begin to master our re-connection process and participate with the parallel worlds and realities that are part of the *totality* of our DNA.

THE STAR OF BETHLEHEM

Channelled information on the Star of Bethlehem

The Star of David on 8 November 2003 and Venus Transit on 8 June 2004 both resonated similar energies to the 'Star of David' alignment at the time of Jesus' birth, known as the 'Star of Bethlehem.' At that time, *specific* 'cosmic events and stellar gateway activity' occurred to support the anchoring of a coding process within his DNA for the templating and eventual resurrection of the cosmic lightbody.

> *Jesus was born at a specific location and time to enable a unique Earth and cosmic gridding process to occur within his body to support his destiny and purpose on Earth. At the time of his birth, he encoded into his DNA the necessary geometric light frequencies to master the ability to resurrect and materialise the androgynous lightbody/Christbody while in physical incarnation on Earth.*

INCARNATING MASTER

This event heralded and energetically supported the final re-entry of an Ascended Master who had been incarnated at different times on the planet throughout the duration of Lemuria and Atlantis. (The proclamation of a specific incarnating master to fulfil a purpose on Earth is also practiced within the teachings of Buddhism).

Jesus was the incarnated Soul who was to fulfil a long awaited prophecy known only by those of an elite order who sustained, supported and practiced a lineage of sacred teachings that were initially anchored onto the planet by 'The Androgynous Moon God/Goddess - Thoth'.

This order understood the sacred powers and knowledge sustained within the Earth and Nature itself thereby obtaining the healing and ascension powers of alchemy. They also had an in-depth understanding of the energetic forces at play within our Cosmos and created the technology of Astrology, Cosmology and Geometry. This information collated together gave them the ability to build monuments or instruments of power like the pyramids of Egypt. The technology within these 'Temples of Light' sustains beautifully proportioned lightbody chambers to support ones healing and ascension capabilities.

These elite elders maintained a state of preparation for one who was to incarnate and master this linage of sacred celestial teachings, so that he could then create a template for all of humanity to come.

After his birth, Jesus was taken in and educated for his mission. Through dedication and spiritual practices performed within the veil and secrecy of specific Mystery School teachings throughout the Middle East, he came to personally understand and master some of the internal spiritual technology and magical forces and properties sustained within Nature. He mastered innate abilities to co-create the powers of Alchemy by transferring the properties within the Earth/Cosmos or 'matter into light', as well as visionary or 'psychic' powers of intuition and prophecy. These were the innate wisdom and power of the more *lunar* celestial teachings of the long forgotten *Goddess*. *(These teachings are explored further in chapter 7 and unveiled in 'Revelations')*.

REBIRTHING/RESURRECTION

Because of the internal technology encoded and anchored within his DNA and etheric/physical body at the time of his birth, Jesus was born with a higher frequency which ultimately enabled him to overcome the laws of physics, duality, and gravity.

Through mastering the *resurrection* and *mineralisation* of his lightbody throughout his life, Jesus anchored a more celestial energetic template into his body and also onto Earth so the rest of humanity could '*grid in*' a new physical body and corresponding lightbody system. This rebirthing/resurrection process would energetically and physically support the creation/evolution process of humanity's new and more celestial body and consciousness, over the next 3,000 years.

THE WAY, THE TRUTH AND THE LIGHT

Jesus was the *first Soul* to complete a divinely orchestrated evolutionary process by embodying the complete **Christbody** while in a physical or third dimension hologram on Earth. He showed *the way* for other masters to complete the embodiment and perfection process of matter, light and consciousness in their body and consciousness *while incarnated on the planet*. Through Jesus, who became the 'Christ', the masters and then all of humanity could come to understand how to support their own individual healing and ascension process.

The *next wave of masters of ascension* could then complete a stage of evolution by *consciously* and *physically* embodying more light. This would enable them to 'heal thyself' more effectively and ascend into a higher state of consciousness and being on Earth and thereafter - by consciously connecting to and integrating with higher and more evolved parallel galactic worlds and realities. *(The properties, principles and technology to support this Divine ascension process are explained further in chapter 13 and 14)*.

THE ADAM KADMON BODY

The four astrological alignments - the Grand Cross, Grand Square, Star of David and Venus Transit (a 'type' of solar eclipse) - resonate all of the interdimensional energies necessary to weave through and create all new dimensions of the etheric/physcial body and 22-strand DNA system. They will thereby support the creation of the New Anatomy known as the Adam Kadmon body, and on a parallel level the necessary dimensions of the androgynous lightbody/Christbody and Consciousness to also come into *physical* manifestation.

The 'elect' or 'ancient prophets' predicted these 'cosmic emanations' that were to occur at the time of the 'turn of the Millennium'. They also had an intuitive understanding of *how* these astrological phenomena would energetically support the re-creation process of the human body, consciousness and planet. Humanity could then ascend into and through the 'Christ' into the next dimension and eventually beyond, into the higher levels of consciousness and parallel realms, realities or kingdoms. As proclaimed in a verse within the Lords Prayer: 'Thy kingdom come they will be done on Earth, as it is in Heaven'.

A PROPHESY REVEALED

We cannot deny that events described in the literal translation of the 'Book of Revelations' are now beginning to manifest through the changes occurring within our physical body and the environment. However, more of the hidden messages and prophecies are also being 'channelled' through now by those guided to receive and proclaim them. The whole world can now hear the words and take heed of the ancient teachings encoded within the text itself as they see universal truth, being physically and spiritually revealed

> *Sacred knowledge of humanity's re-creation and ascension process has been subliminally preserved or protected within the biblical prophesy of the 'Book of Revelations' waiting to be deciphered at the appropriate time.*

This information was to stay 'hidden' until the turn of the Millennium so Nature could be left alone to create within herself, a perfect and *natural* genetic engineering process to enable the body and planet to survive and achieve the global transition into the next dimension. Science and the rational mind would then be given an opportunity to *understand* the spiritual forces and laws sustained within the technology governing Nature herself - to support our environment and civilisation in the future.

The prophecy of the 'Book of Revelations' foretells that many Earth and cosmic changes will occur at this time, to support the re-creation process of a whole New World and reality. It explains *why* the physical body and Earth is changing and *how* the energetic technology is creating the changes. It also warns that if humanity does not take heed to *consciously* evolve with the world around them, they will suffer the consequences of war, famine, drought, disease, floods, extreme weather and Earth catastrophes such as earthquakes. The massive energetic and geographical changes that are now taking place are energetically forcing and supporting humanity to awaken and evolve at a more rapid pace by living in sync with the laws that govern the universe.

We cannot change the course of this creation or the rapid evolution process that is now occurring - but can only *consciously* learn from and transform through it. Transformation and change are not only felt and obtained within the self, but also extend out into the planet and global consciousness as a whole. Every realisation felt or obtained and every action taken on a personal level, now creates a direct counter reaction from and within the Earth and Cosmos itself.

UNIVERSAL BELIEF SYSTEM

I have been told intuitively that more of humanity will come to listen, understand and learn as the proclamations of 'Revelations' are physically and spiritually revealed by Earth 'channellers' and the Divine intervention of the Earth changes.

Knowledge is power. Everybody will be given an opportunity to personally understand and eventually master the wisdom, technology and hidden forces and powers that exist within Nature and the universe. This will enable and also support the manifestation of a more *universal belief system*. All people within the world at large - from different races, religions, backgrounds and belief systems - will come to see the universal truth and obtain a universal belief system that will give them the internal know-how to heal, ascend and also live in a state of more freedom and manifestation.

As the world ascends into higher levels of frequency and consciousness, and we come to live more by the laws of Nature we will ultimately obtain the ability to self-heal and live in peace and prosperity as a more united nation on our planet. We will also come to live like those who exist within higher levels of consciousness sustained within parallel worlds and realities.

THE CELESTIAL CHRIST

The Divine intervention of the Celestial Christ (through the cosmic appearance of the astrological templates) enables humanity to receive and co-create a *natural and pure ascension process* that is of *The Light* and not of man. It enables us to receive the necessary universal and interdimensional energies to ascend through the *divinely orchestrated,* technological process of Nature and the Goddess.

Now that this Divine ascension process is occurring through these astrological templates, we can 'tune in' and comprehend the mysteries of Nature by connecting directly to the Celestial Christ through our own individual and universal ascension process. All mysteries of time, space, our genetic lineage and the meaning of the 'Alpha & Omega' will be understood as we ascend through the templating process of the Celestial Christ and the healing Nature of the Goddess.

IMPORTANT: Completion Ritual

*Before you stop reading this chapter, run your finger from **right to left** across the sacred language below. This procedure will assist you to finalise the energies from this chapter.*

Your action, intent and the sacred vibration of this powerful language, will greatly assist you to fully integrate the information you have just read.

♈ ♉ ♊ ♋ ♌ ♍ ♎ ♏ ♐ ♑ ♒ ♓ ☉ ☽ ♀ ♂ ☿ ♃ ♄ ♅ ♆ ♇ ⚷

THE TRANSFERENCE HEALING® MASTER CHRIST TEMPLATE LOGO ~ SET

This beautifully crafted set of the five templates *(as seen in chapter 1 and 13)* are the essential healing geometries of the Transference Healing® modality and anchor and encode the Divine healing and ascension powers of the Celestial Christ.

Placed together they create a holographic, energetic **Diamond Pyramid of Light** that etherically resonates through into the very centre of your being and foundation of your living existence, from the Prism of Lyra.

The templates have been overlaid with fine gold and silver leaf, to reflect their magnetic and electromagnetic energies and have detailed explanations on their reverse-sides.

Master Christ Template

The Black Ray OR Earth and Cosmic Star Diamond Templates

Crystal Cross Christ Template

*Note templates must be placed in this correct order within the one room of your home or workplace. The three Black Ray 'Star Diamond Templates' can only be purchased as part of this set of five, while the 'Master Christ' and 'Crystal Cross' Templates can be purchased separately.

Place your order at www.TRANSFERENCEHEALING.com

IMPORTANT: *Commencement Ritual*

*Before reading chapter 5, run your finger from **left to right** across the sacred language below.*

Your action, intent and the sacred vibration of this powerful language, will ensure that you are fully open to receiving and integrating the information within.

$$\text{♓ ♀ ☉ ♌ ♉ ♁ +}$$

These symbols support the balancing of the electromagnetic field of the body by filtering through the light frequencies that reflect through to Earth, because of the wanning and setting cycles of the Sun and Moon. They enable the body and consciousness to maintain a state of balance within the Universe at this vital time of Earth and cosmic changes and thereby support a healthy transition into the next dimension.

CHAPTER
5

THE NEW
DIMENSION

CHAPTER OVERVIEW

The Earth began a global electromagnetic shift in 1999 with the *Grand Cross Activation*. This shift is changing the energetic foundations of our existence – directly affecting the electromagnetic field of the body and planet. We are in a state of transition between the third and fifth dimension, which will be complete by the end of 2012. We are being reborn. In this chapter you will discover:

- That the *master gravity line* which is the master grid line of the Earth (located around the Equator) is slowly changing frequency. This change is altering the axis of the planet and the frequency and gravity pulls of the main magnetic grid lines of the Earth.

- Side effects of this re-alignment are *lightbody symptoms*, changing migratory patterns, extreme weather changes, increased earthquakes, volcanic activity and tidal waves.

- New etheric *energy healing processes* (including Transference Healing) are being channelled through onto the planet to support humanity to filter through the necessary compounds from the Earth and energies from the Cosmos, to make the necessary energetic and alchemical changes within the body to ascend with the planet.

- *Grid Channellers* are also being awakened to support the physical changes the Earth needs to make.

- How the four zodiacal grid points of the Grand Cross Activation hold the internal technology to create the new electromagnetic energy field or grid for the body and planet, as well as creating frequency and energetic changes for our body, planet and solar system allowing the Earth to shift/ascend into a new dimension of space/time.

- The key to mastering this time of transition is to lift our vibration so we can anchor or template through the necessary energies to create the necessary changes within and around ourselves, in line with the changes within our dimension. This will also ensure you are in the 'right place' at any given moment.

- The Earth changes won't be as catastrophic as has been predicted.

- *Scientific evidence* of the Earths' electromagnetic shift and ascension into the fifth dimension includes; the north and south poles of the Sun disappearing transforming it into a homogenous field, dramatic increases in the numbers of M & X Class solar flares and resultant magnetic tidal waves hitting the Earth, the rediscovery of ancient civilisations resulting from a resurgence of 'ancient memories and knowledge', dramatic increases in number and severity of seismic activity including the Asian Tsunami of 2005, unprecedented Ice Cap changes, changing migratory patterns of birds, dolphins and whales (including beaching), multiple Earth *'wobbles'*, a need to recalibrate aeronautical maps for navigation as the magnetic North has changed, a decrease in the speed of rotation of the Earth and the orbit of the Moon around the Earth, and the Earth's gravity field moving towards zero.

- All these changes are part of the transition process the key is to heal ourselves from within. "As we heal ourselves, so we heal our planet."

THE HUMAN AND PLANETARY GRID

As we have determined, the astrological Grand Cross and Grand Square of (August 1999 - May 2000) has been creating the new *electromagnetic* field and corresponding *magnetic* shift in the human and planetary grid. The Earth therefore began a global electromagnetic shift in 1999 which we will continue to feel and integrate until 2012.

This magnetic shift is changing the energetic foundations of our existence - directly affecting the electromagnetic field of the body and planet. It was created when a global magnetic pull of *negative* and *positive* polarity shifts increased in frequency and reversed the polarity of the *grid points* within and from the North and South Poles, as well as the position/frequency of the *gravity field* of the Equator. Therefore the **North's** *negative electrons* and **South's** *positive electrons* are reversing, polarising and creating a change within the negative and positive electrons within each atom of everything within our existence.

The **master gravity line** *which is the master grid line existing within and around the centre of the Earth, around the location of the Equator,* has been slowly changing frequency since 1999 and will continue to do so until 2012. This shift in frequency is slowly altering the axis of the planet and the frequency and gravity pulls of the main magnetic grid lines of the Earth.

Some of the global side effects of this re-alignment process are lightbody symptoms, distortions of the migratory patterns of some of the animal species, through to weather changes and Earth movement.

DIAGRAM 5.1
The Negative and Positive Polarity Shifts of the North and South Pole.

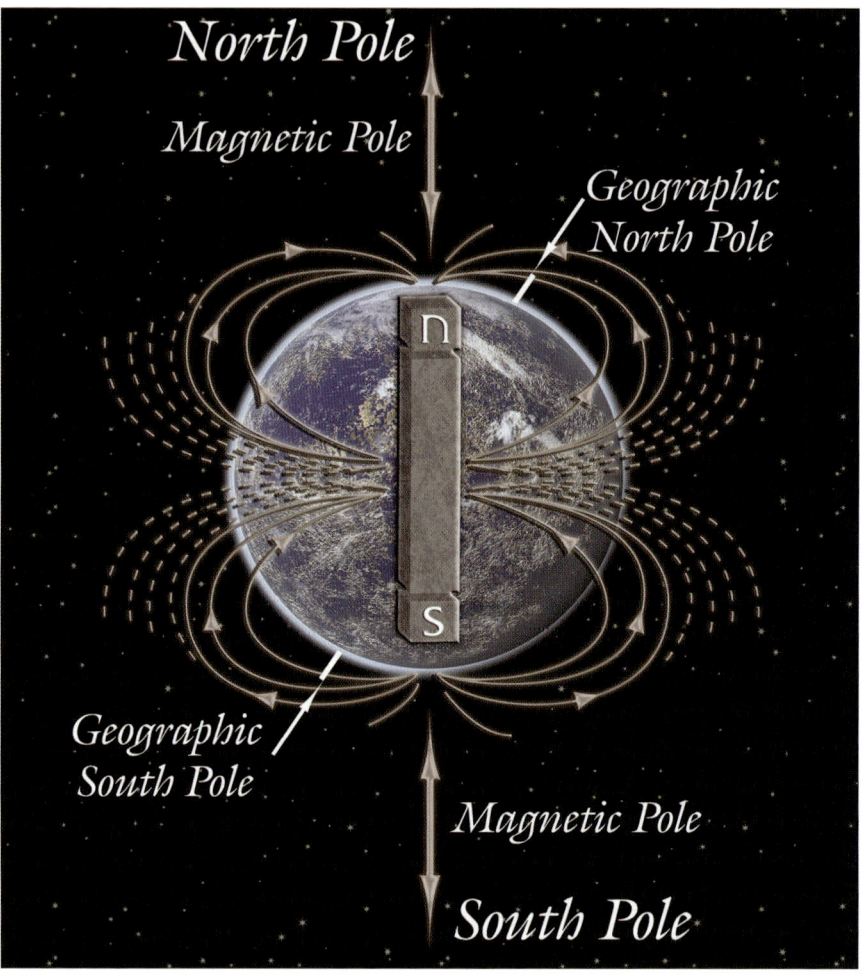

Copyright 2005 Alexis Cartwright, Keeper of the Crystals Pty Ltd.

The human electromagnetic field is also shifting as the Earth changes and the body is adjusting accordingly by realigning itself through the sacrum, gravity line and three main lines of force in the etheric body, as seen in diagram below. This whole process is shifting the gravitational formation of the physical Earth and the human body from a third dimensional form and reality and re-establishing the foundation of the fifth dimensional form and reality within and around us.

DIAGRAM 5.2
The Gravity Line of the Planet

Copyright 2005 Alexis Cartwright, Keeper of the Crystals Pty Ltd.

EARTH/COSMIC CHANGES AND LIGHTBODY SYMPTOMS

The frequency changes within the *electromagnetic* field of the body and planet are shifting as the Earth *magnetics* and cosmic solar flare activity is increasing and creating more *destructive forces* within the body and planet – even more lightbody symptoms, extreme weather changes, earthquakes, volcanic activity and tidal waves will continue to occur between 1999- 2012. These are all side effects occurring because of this global transition.

NEW HEALING PROCEDURES

However, new etheric energy procedures are being *channelled* through and onto the planet to support humanity to filter through these new energetic *compounds* from the Earth and correspondingly the necessary *energies or frequencies* from the Cosmos into the body, so everyone can make the necessary alchemical changes within the body to ascend with the planet. These new healing procedures will release and prevent the side effects occurring within the body and consciousness. Also "grid channellers" are awakening to support the Earth in making the necessary changes in its *gridding* system, which will then support the physical changes the Earth needs to make, so new formations and foundations can be created to assist the Earth's ascension process into the next dimension.

From 1999-2012 we are going through a global death and rebirthing process. As old restrictive patterning and energies are transmuting to release dense levels and layers of matter and consciousness, new energies are being birthed through the Earth and cosmic changes, to create the necessary energetic and alchemical changes within our body, Earth and dimension.

Transference Healing specifically works on all levels to help create the changes necessary within the physical body, consciousness and Earth so we can ascend while in a state of anticipation and bliss, rather than feeling fear and pain, at this vital time of transition and change.

We are being reborn. Without the frequency changes in the electromagnetic field or grid, the body and planet would not be able to sustain a gravity field or have the internal technology to create the new energies and elements necessary for the body and planet to birth a whole new level of existence at this time. All life as we know it would have ended around 1999. However, if we learn how to master these energies we can make this transition into the next dimensions at this time, without struggle.

DIAGRAM 5.3
The Gravity Line and Three Main Lines of Force in the Body

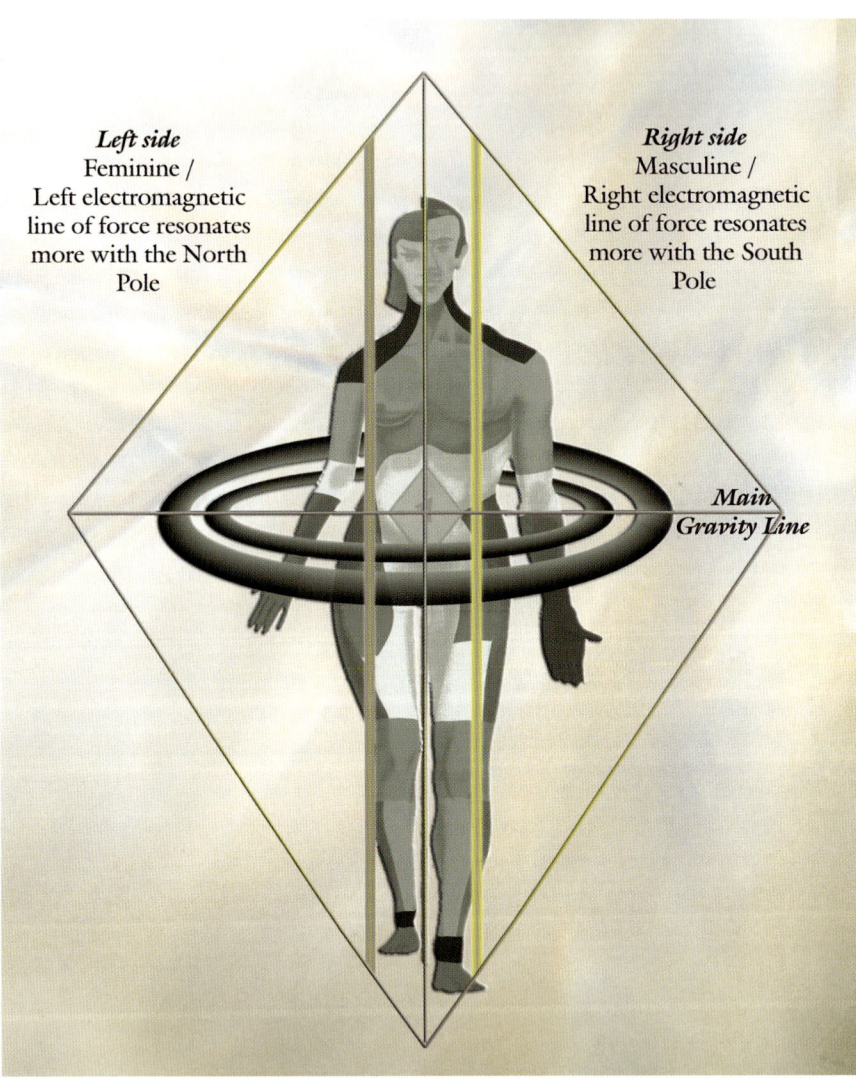

Left side
Feminine /
Left electromagnetic
line of force resonates
more with the North
Pole

Right side
Masculine /
Right electromagnetic
line of force resonates
more with the South
Pole

*Main
Gravity Line*

1. The *gravity line* of the planet runs around the centre of the Earth along the *equator* and sustains the *gravity line* within the body, which runs through the *sacrum* and within and around the naval chakra. The frequency level of the gravity line, of the planet is

shifting and is correspondingly changing the dimensions of the *gravity line* within the body.

2. The *gravity line* of the Global Grid Matrix resonates *etherically* through and around the naval chakra *and* the equator of the planet and looks like one of the rings of the planet Saturn. Saturn itself actually sustains and maintains the gravity pull and magnetic lines of the Earth and its axis, as well as the *lines of force* and the *gravity line* of the body. See diagrams 5.1 and 5.2.

3. Everything within our existence can enter into a new fifth dimensional reality through the gridding process of the two astrological alignments of the Grand Cross and Grand Square. This *energetic gridding process* of the global electromagnetic field of the planet is enabling Earth and humanity to enter and sustain itself within the fourth dimension from 1999-2012, and therefore create the energetic or etheric foundation to, on a parallel level, make the necessary physical changes to 'officially' anchor us into the fifth dimension by the year 2013.

NEW DIMENSION IN SPACE

The four zodiacal grid points of the Grand Cross - and the corresponding star constellations of Taurus, Leo, Scorpio, and Aquarius are creating and resonating the energies to change the polarity of the Earth's axis and the **frequency points** of the North and South Pole. This means the two principal magnetic nodes or grid points at the planet's North and South Pole are also attuning to new frequency points or grid points **within space.**

This is how the Earth is literally shifting into a *new dimension of space/time* because of the gravity changes made from the magnetic and electromagnetic frequency shifts of the Earth's polar axis as well as the two main frequency points, at the North and South Poles of the planet.

The four zodiacal grid points of the Grand Cross therefore holds the internal technology to create the new electromagnetic energies of the Earth and Cosmos and are creating:

- the *new electromagnetic energy field* or *grid* of the body and planet.

- the *(interdimensional) energetic resources* to continue the physical evolution of the new foundations within our physical reality and existence.

- the *frequency and energetic changes* for our body and planet and also the solar system - thereby transferring and creating a whole new dimensional existence. They are weaving through the correct proportion of electromagnetic energies so the body and planet can shift into the higher frequencies and shift the *magnetic grids* and *polar axis* of the body and planet, to change the *gravity force* within our body and Universe so we can ascend.

Consequently, we are shifting and *transferring* beyond our space/time gravity field and existence and this is also supporting us to shift into a higher frequency so we can enter into the next dimension. We are literally relocating our sense of existence in space and are *energetically* entering through the gateway of Orion so we can continue to create the new foundations into a higher dimensional existence. This transference process of gravity, time and space will become clearer to us as we progress through this time of transition from 1999-2012.

THE EARTH AND COSMIC CHANGES

SUMMARY

The key to mastering this time of transition is to lift our vibration so we can anchor or template through the necessary energies to create the necessary changes within and around ourselves, in accordance with the changes occurring within our dimension. Channelled procedures are given in chapter 6 to enable you to 'run energy' on yourself to help you create the changes within the etheric and electromagnetic field of the body, so the *physical body* can create the necessary alchemical changes and ascend.

By shifting our vibration we can also be sure to find ourselves in the 'right place' at any given moment. The Earth changes are creating the necessary energetic and alchemical changes within our *body* so that our body can adapt and ascend into a higher level of frequency and consciousness, as well as creating the necessary energetic and alchemical changes in the *planet* itself, so that it can create the right ecological and geographic environment that is in accordance with the new foundations of our new world.

I believe a lot of these Earth changes won't be as catastrophic as predicted. These changes that are occurring in our world are an expression of the changes occurring in our body. All is in Divine order. I have previously mentioned some of the vibrational impacts occurring in the body and consciousness and the following chapter gives some information on the physical changes that have and are occurring within the planet itself.

SCIENTIFIC EVIDENCE OF THE TRANSITION

1. UNIVERSES WITHIN UNIVERSES

On 14 December **1997**, an explosion was detected from deep space, about 12 million light years from Earth. Calculations indicated that the explosion involved an area about the size of Texas and occurred one thousandth of a second after the 'Big Bang' which is said to have created our universe. To release so much energy, this explosion would have needed all of the known, visible 'matter' in the Universe, an impossible feat given our present understanding of the Universe. Even more amazing is that over 2,000 of these explosions or 'Big Bangs' have occurred since the original one, suggesting that more than 2,000 new universes have been created *within* ours.

Since that first explosion on 14 December 1997, the centre of our galaxy has started pumping huge amounts of energy into the universe. In June 1998 one of these pulses destroyed the 'beeper' satellite and scientists have indicated that if this energy continues to pulse, all of the satellites around Earth will eventually be destroyed.

2. STRANGE OCCURRENCES ON THE SUN

In 1992, our Sun's magnetic North and South Pole were functioning 'normally' by Scientific Standards. However, in December 1994, when NASA's Ulysses Spacecraft arrived at the Sun to measure its magnetic field, it discovered the Sun no longer had a North and South Pole - its magnetic field had transformed into a homogenous field. There was no scientific explanation for the change.

The Soho Satellite studied the Sun for a two-year period and detected two comets entering the Sun's orbit early in June 1998. Although the presence of the comets was not unusual (25 or more asteroids and comets enter the Sun's orbit or graze the Sun each year), the impact these comets had on the Sun's surface attracted attention. Previously, no effects had been noticed when the Sun was struck by a 'cosmic body.' However, on this occasion 30 to 35 solar flares erupted from the Sun's surface.

The eruption of solar flares from the Sun concerns the inhabitants of Earth, since the extra magnetic energy coming onto our planet from just two to three such flares can create magnetic storms and consequently extreme weather conditions as well as emotional upheavals and turmoil. The eruption of up to 30 - 35 flares (or larger M or X Class flares) is likely to have a major impact on Earth and on our bodies, triggering a deep etheric cleansing and renewal of consciousness.

3. THE REDISCOVERY OF ANCIENT CIVILISATIONS

It is also likely that these occurrences in space are acting as a trigger for metaphysical 'eruptions' on Earth. As they affect our energy and that of the planet, we in turn experience a resurgence of 'ancient memories and knowledge.' This explains the many recent discoveries associated with ancient civilisations, such as the:

+ **Underground city in Egypt,** 12 stories deep and up to eight miles in perimeter.

+ **A Secret Book in the Bible,** reported in 'The Bible Code'. It is a computer program which could not be opened until 'the End of Time'. It has now been opened and provides us with further information on ancient Civilisations.

+ **The City of Atlantis off the coast of Bimini**. Aaron Du Val announced this on 23 May 1998. Although discovered three years prior to this date, the information was withheld until its accuracy was established. It has now been proved beyond scientific doubt that this is Atlantis.

4. THE MYSTERIOUS FORMATIONS CREATED BY THE MEASUREMENT OF '19.5 DEGREE LATITUDE'

The measurement of 19.5 degree latitude is where the interlocking tetrahedrons cross the sphere of the Sun. On Earth, these latitudes are where most of the world's sacred sites occur, including the pyramids at Giza. On the surface of Mars, the Cydonia region is where the "Face on Mars" and the pyramidal structures are located, is also on the 19.5 degree latitude. On Jupiter, it is where the orbiting storm, that is its most dominating feature, lies; the so-called "great red spot".

5. EARTH CHANGES

There is a lot of **seismic activity** on Earth resulting from the Earth's magnetic changes and other energetic influences from space. California's Mammoth Lake area and Mount Rainier look likely to have eruptions in the near future, Mount St Helens is experiencing about 170 earthquakes per day and the huge volcano of Pacaya erupted near Guatemala City in June 1998. With an underwater volcano forming off the coast of California, it is being suggested that a major eruption could soon occur, affecting the entire coastline from Guatemala to Washington State.

The Asian Tsunami of 2004

Giant forces that had been building up deep within the Earth for hundreds of years were released suddenly on 26 December 2004, shaking the ground violently and unleashing a series of killer waves that sped across the Indian Ocean. This massive underwater earthquake occurred off the coast of Indonesia's Sumatra Island. It actually rattled the Earth in its orbit and, according to the

U.S. Geological Survey (USGS), was estimated to have released the energy of 23,000 Hiroshima-type atomic bombs. At a magnitude of 9.0 this earthquake was the largest since the 9.2 magnitude 'Good Friday Earthquake' off Alaska in 1964 and actually tied for fourth largest earthquake since 1900.

It is now recorded as one of the deadliest natural disasters in modern history affecting 11 countries, with over 250,000 people deceased or missing and millions more homeless.

Ice Cap Changes

A. Ice Caps are melting off into the ocean specifically in the South Pole area. In 1997 the largest piece of ice ever known (800 square miles) broke off, the result of three active volcanoes erupting under the ice cap. In 2004, there was another large piece that has broken off. It's called Larsen's Ledge B and is about the size of Connecticut. The total size of the Larsen B Ice Shelf is more than all the previous ice that has been lost from Antarctic ice sheets, in the past two decades.

B. Scientists from NASA, US universities and the Centro de Estudios Cientificos in Chile, also report glaciers in West Antarctica are melting at a rate substantially higher than that observed in the 1990's. The loss of ice is 60 percent more than what is accumulated from inland snowfall. The data was collected from satellites and a Chilean aircraft equipped with NASA sensors. The ice loss amounts to a sea-level rise of two millimetres per year.

C. "On May 5th in the year 2000, our Moon, the planets Mercury, Venus, our Sun, Mars, Jupiter and Saturn were aligned with the Earth, significantly increasing the centrifugal momentum exerted on the Earth's crust. On that day, the ever growing ice build ups at the South Pole, upset the Earth's axis -- sending trillions of tons of ice and water sweeping over the surface of our planet." *(As quoted by Richard Noone, National Geographic reporter).*

6. MIGRATORY PATTERNS OF BIRDS, DOLPHINS AND WHALES

The *Earth's geomagnetic field* has been weakening for 2000 years and this has accelerated over the past 20 years. The magnetic lines are undergoing huge changes and shifting in their locations on the planet. This is affecting the migratory patterns of birds, dolphins and whales. The fact that some of these lines now point inland, could explain some of the mass beaching of the Whales which has been occurring more frequently in recent years. These species all use the *geomagnetic* field for their orientation and navigation and are therefore migrating to wrong locations.

7. THE GEOMAGNETIC FIELD

In late September 1994, the Earth's geomagnetic field experienced a *'wobble'* which corrected itself within a few weeks. From June to November 1996, another larger *'wobble'* occurred as the South Pole moved on a daily or even hourly basis; anywhere from two to 17 degrees in a day. After June 1996 the major airports needed new maps in order to land their planes!

If you check the aeronautical maps for any major airport prior to June of 1996 and then compare it to newer ones, you'll find that magnetic North has been changed, which means that the South Pole has moved. In the past few months, the Earth has once again begun to exhibit signs of a magnetic field wobble. This could have potentially devastating consequences for the Earth's geologic stability. We could see earthquakes of unprecedented magnitude. In 1998, the number of earthquakes had doubled from the previous year.

8. GIANT ASTEROID PASSING EARTH

In 1989 a trio of French astronomers discovered and named the giant asteroid Touratis, after the Celtic god well known in France as the comic book hero, Asterix. It is some 4.6 kilometres long and 2.4 kilometres in width and passed only 1,549,719 kilometres away from the Earth, according to the Near Earth object or (NEO) program run by NASA's Jet Propulsion Laboratory (JPL). This is just four times the gap between the Earth and the Moon. It is one of the most studied asteroids of all because its most recent circuit has brought it to Earth. (It took four years to loop around the Sun in a chaotic spin unseen in any other asteroid).

9. SOLAR FLARE ACTIVITY

Many solar flare activities are now occurring and causing tremendous magnetic storms. NASA had announced that it had lost both its Sun satellites, SOHO and GEOS-9 in recent years. Further more, according to Gregg Braden, the solar proton flux which is measured in PUI, rose to about 2500 PUI in the late 1980's. The scientific community was very concerned about this much energy reaching the Earth. A magnetic storm was also measured in July of 1998 that went off the scale. The magnetometer is scaled from one to 200; this storm registered over 200!

10. THE EARTH-MOON

From the essential perspective that the Earth-Moon could represent an interrelated system, the respective spin-orbits should be evaluated to predict the effect of any changes that might result with the passage of time. The spin-orbital rates can be predicted to ultimately change with time due to the spin rate of the Earth. Modern research shows that the spin of the Earth has slowed by a fractional amount throughout the prior 4,000 years. In association with the slowing rotation of the Earth, is the slowing orbit of the Moon. It appears that the orbit of the Moon is growing even wider - and thus is slowing down.

11. THE GRAVITY FIELD OF THE EARTH

The Earth's gravity field is racing towards zero. This has been documented by both Germany and Russia. Russian computer models have suggested that we have now passed the point of no return - the Earth's gravity field is going to zero. The possible results for humans will be agitation and aggression, with incurable insanity as the end result. To protect against this possibility, the Germans have created an electronic belt which creates a balance in the electromagnetic field of the person wearing it. This belt will be distributed to key government personnel in order to keep the government operational in such an eventuality. *(The Transference 'structural procedure' in chapter 6, works with the same affectability as this belt).*

This is all part of *the transition process* and the 'key' is to heal ourselves from within. Our body is the 'key'. By changing, upgrading and healing our physical vibration and body, the Earth will respond accordingly and the structural impact of these Earth changes will be minimised.

> *As we heal ourselves,*
> *so we heal the planet.*

IMPORTANT: Completion Ritual

*Before you stop reading this chapter, run your finger from **right to left** across the sacred language below. This procedure will assist you to finalise the energies from this chapter.*

Your action, intent and the sacred vibration of this powerful language, will greatly assist you to fully integrate the information you have just read.

The TRANSFERENCE HEALING®

MYSTERY SCHOOL JEWELLERY COLLECTION

This exquisite range of silver/crystal jewellery has been created exclusively for Transference Healing®.

Individual pendants made from the highest quality silver-encrusted Black Onyx resonate the power of these sacred symbols affecting both the person wearing the piece as well as their environment and those coming into contact with them.

Symbol pendants available include:

- The Master Christ Template (The Seal of Solomon – The Celestial 7th Star).
- Pentagram (manifestation).
- Om (creation).
- Eye of Horus (knowledge – clairvoyance).
- Ankh (alchemy – health and immortality).
- Scarab (rejuvenation – rebirth).
- Fleur De Lis (majesty).

Also available exclusively from Transference Healing® are an entrancing range of '**Crystal Cross Pendants**' that hold the energy of the Christ Ray for Divine healing. Available in two sizes and various crystals including Clear Quartz, Amethyst, Citrine, Smokey Quartz and Onyx.

"You will feel the profound energy of the new sacred jewellery piece you are wearing, you will see it impacting upon your daily life, you will be amazed at how people will be captivated and drawn to your jewellery often asking for information in relation to it."

For more information on each piece, to view photographs or place an order, visit www.TRANSFERENCEHEALING.com

IMPORTANT: Commencement Ritual

*Before reading chapter 6, run your finger from **left to right** across the sacred language below.*

Your action, intent and the sacred vibration of this powerful language, will ensure that you are fully open to receiving and integrating the information within.

Chakra means 'Wheel' in Sanskrit and it refers to each of the seven main energy centres of the body. Each master Sanskrit symbol is a geometric etheric template or seal that is embedded within the energetic system of each chakra.

These symbols filter universal energies into your physical body, thereby supporting the continual etheric healing and evolutional process of your body and consciousness.

SELF-HELP TECHNIQUES AND TOOLS FOR HEALING AND MAINTAINING THE BODY AND FACILITATING SELF-TRANSFORMATION

CHAPTER OVERVIEW

In this chapter you will discover that:

• We co-exist within the physical and spiritual planes through the emanation of sound and colour resonating from the rotation of the planets of our solar system. Every organ in our body receives the vibrations of sound and colour from the Universe via the main chakras, and these vibrations maintain our organs function and vitality.

• Due to rapid crystal and cosmic shifts we are now receiving new vibrations of silver and gold.

• The *Sun* relates to the *physical plane*, daytime, the external senses, the conscious and rational mind, the left side of the brain and the *masculine line of force, which* resonates down the *right* side of the body. The masculine line of force supports a more magnetic flow of energy throughout the body and sustains the frequency of *gold*.

• The *Moon* relates to the *astral and spiritual planes*, night time, the internal and subconscious mind, inner psyche, the right side of the brain and the feminine *line of force* which resonates down the *left* side of the body. The *feminine* line of force supports a more electrical flow of energy through the body and sustains the frequency of *silver*.

• When we can balance and hold the male and female frequencies and properties of light within our body in perfect proportion, we can co-create and sustain a frequency of the 'Christ Light' within.

• The June 2004 *Sun/Venus crossing* is assisting humanity to bring these male/female energies into balance during this time of transition.

- The body has four electromagnetic lines of force. There are three vertical, vibrational 'lines of force' namely the *left*, *right* and *central* lines of force. The fourth and 'main line of force' is *the gravity line* of the body, which is a horizontal vibrational 'line of force', running around and through the body between the solar plexus and naval chakras.

- Earth and cosmic changes are energetically tearing and breaking these lines of force. Through simple Transference procedures you can alchemically balance and strengthen these lines of force, preventing and / or alleviating all side-effects of imbalance.

- Transference Healing works extensively with the glandular system whose function is *vital* to our overall health and state of mind. Glandular imbalances are creating painful emotions and illnesses ranging from glandular fatigue through to feelings of psychological despair, depression and emotional weakness. The dysfunction of the glandular system on some level usually contributes to many of the lightbody symptoms occurring at this time.

- Changes in our glandular system are supporting our transference process.

- How we are affected by astrological and numerological forces. For example how at *exact moment* of our birth, the Universe provides a template through which we can encode or embed within our body, the more relevant personality traits determining the level of consciousness we will live in during this incarnation on Earth. Likewise throughout our lifetime, the codes of this template unlocks the forces of destiny which enable us to live out karmic relationships and circumstances relevant to our Soul's healing and evolutionary process during this incarnation.

- You will also learn the following basic level fundamental self- healing processes:
  - Structural Procedures; the gravity line, the vertical lines of force, the three harmony alignment points and specific crystal essences.
  - Glandular system procedures: opening the third eye and healing the pineal gland, revitalising the seven master glands, perfecting the glandular and chakra system, balancing the emotional body, severing karmic pain and sub-conscious energy plays, feeling vortex, alien interference, releasing etheric imbalance to awaken Christ Consciousness and relevant essences for each procedure.

◆

THE SOLAR SYSTEM

Pythagoras stated that each planet within our solar system -
including Earth - emanates an individual vibrational sound
or tone when rotating within the solar system. When these
tones are combined together they make the sounds that create the
musical scale. He referred to this cosmic musical scale as the 'Music
of the Spheres'.

AS ABOVE/SO BELOW

We co-exist within the physical and spiritual planes through the
emanation of sound and colour (sound made visible) resonating
from the *rotation* of the planets of our solar system. These universal
emanations of sound and colour are embedded into the very
essence of our being. They are transmitted into 'matter' and our
whole physical existence via the Global Grid Matrix and the Earth
herself and from there into all dimensions of the human etheric/
physical body. Every organ in our body receives the vibrations of
sound and colour from the Universe via the main chakras, and
these vibrations maintain the organs' function and vitality.

However there are now two more recent vibrations that are filtering
through because of the more rapid crystal and cosmic shifts that
are occurring at this time. These two new vibrations relate to the
colour and sound frequencies of silver and gold.

THE SUN AND MOON

INFLUENCES ON THE BODY AND CONSCIOUSNESS

The Sun relates to the **physical plane,** daytime, the external senses, the conscious and rational mind, the left side of the brain and the masculine *line of force* which resonates down the *right* side of the body. The *masculine* line of force supports a more **magnetic** flow of energy throughout the body and **sustains** the frequency of *gold*.

This dimension of the brain and electromagnetic field of the body regulates the *clockwise rotation* of the chakra system through and out of the *front* of the body and anchors through the consciousness of the seven *external* senses. At the moment, most of humanity uses a proportion of only five of these senses - touch, taste, smell, hearing and seeing.

The Moon relates to the **astral and spiritual planes,** night time, the internal and subconscious mind, inner psyche, the right side of the brain and the feminine *line of force* which resonates down the *left* side of the body. The *feminine* line of force supports a more **electrical** flow of energy through the body and **sustains** the frequency of *silver*.

This dimension of the brain and electromagnetic field of the body regulates the *anti-clockwise* rotation of the chakra system through and out of the *back* of the body and anchors through the consciousness of the seven *internal* senses. At the moment, most of humanity uses a proportion of only five of these senses - clairaudience, clairvoyance, clairsentience, instinctual and inner-knowing.

DIAGRAM 6.1
The Electromagnetic Lines of Force and Corresponding
Elements

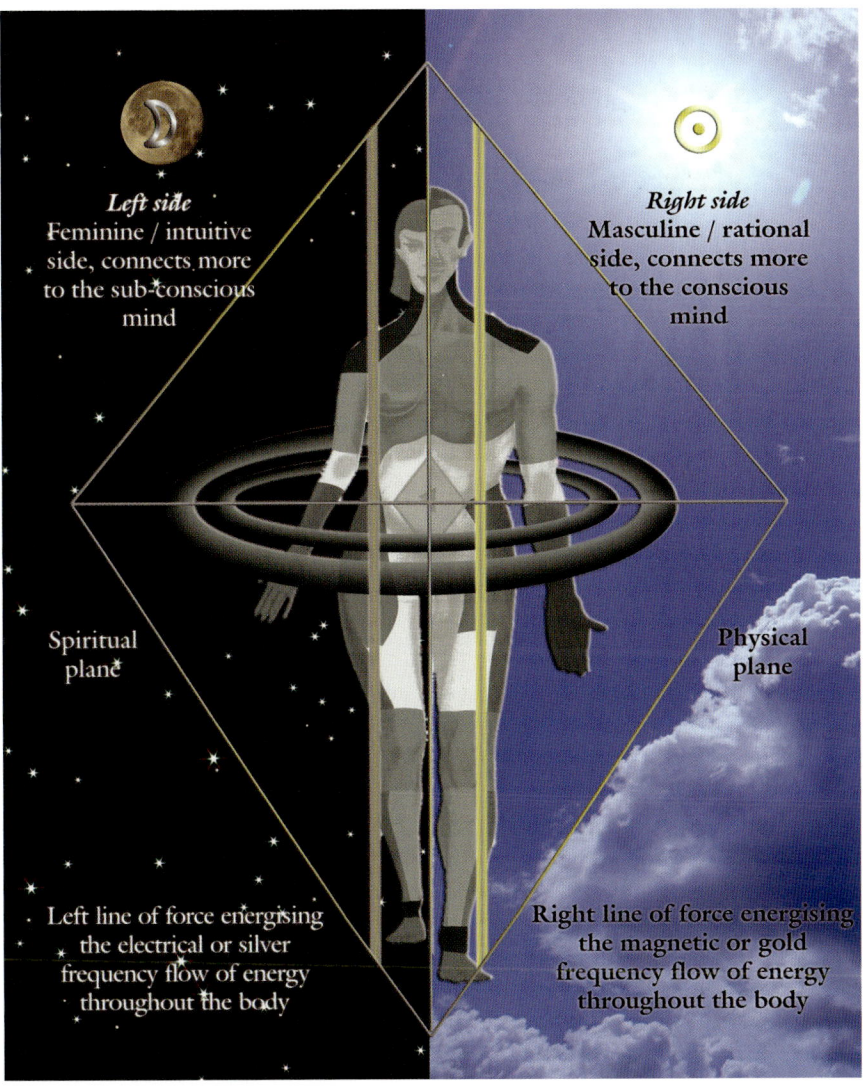

Left side
Feminine / intuitive
side, connects more
to the sub-conscious
mind

Right side
Masculine / rational
side, connects more
to the conscious
mind

Spiritual
plane

Physical
plane

Left line of force energising
the electrical or silver
frequency flow of energy
throughout the body

Right line of force energising
the magnetic or gold
frequency flow of energy
throughout the body

THE SUN /VEnUS ECLIPSE

The Sun/Venus eclipse-like transit on 8 June 2004 astrologically supports the two electromagnetic lines of force coming into a state of **balance** and anchoring more into the etheric/physical body

When we can balance and hold the *silver* and *gold* frequencies and properties of light in the left and right lines of force in our body in perfect proportions to each other, we can co-create and sustain the frequency of the *'Christ Light'* within.

If these two main lines of force are not balanced on a regular basis, we will continue to feel negative impacts from this Sun/Venus eclipse until we can integrate and master these energies as they filter into the body and consciousness. Symptoms and occurrences such as headaches, relationship breakdown, structural pain, psychological and emotional stress, viruses, genetic weakness and lightbody symptoms due to a lack of electromagnetic light filtering through into the cellular levels of the body, will occur.

Venus crossings are extremely rare but tend to come in pairs. The second one will occur in eight years time (and the next not for another 100 years). The energies will continue to balance the *feminine* and *masculine* aspects of our inner nature over the next eight years so we can come into a more *androgynous* state of balance to enable the lightbody to anchor and manifest through.

These energies are also activating a continual shift in the frequency of the brain, central nervous system, master glands and chakra system so our extra-sensory perceptions can continue to awaken and shift humanity into higher consciousness and ultimately Christ consciousness. They are supporting men and women to acknowledge and honour their intuition and to listen and *act* upon it as quickly as it is received, without judgment, analysis or attachment.

TRANSFERENCE HEALING PROCEDURES

I recommend that you perform these procedures in a clear and templated space on a weekly basis. You can do this by dedicating an area or room of your home as your healing space. The Transference 'Master Christ Template Set' *(see page 197 for more information on this tool)* will greatly assist you when running these basic Transference procedures on your body. By placing them in the *Cross* formation shown in diagram 13.6 (page 435), on a wall close to the where you sit in this dedicated room, they will not only support you by creating a more pure and clear environment to work in, but will also filter through the necessary transference frequencies of each procedure into your body and consciousness, to support your healing and ascension process. If you are working on yourself out in the natural environment you could lay a laminated version of the 'Master Christ Template Set' in a *cross* formation on the ground before sitting in a meditative position, to perform the procedures at hand.

It is important that you are aware that these procedures are indeed very basic, only relating to colour, sound and crystal essences. They are offered simply to get you started; they are a **beginning point only**. So if you wish to maintain your wellness throughout our current 'transition' to the fifth dimension while continuing to awaken and grow as effectively as possible, I would recommend that in addition to running these procedures on yourself weekly, you either receive regular Transference Healings from a certified practitioner or empower yourself by becoming a self-healer through learning the Transference Healing Fundamental teachings *(refer to page 485 for more information)*. Either approach will allow you to access the complete spectrum of Transference Healing energies needed at this time. Follow your inner guidance as to determine which approach is the correct path for you.

This picture shows a dedicated healing space and also how the Master Christ Template Set should be used to support healings, being arranged in 'Cross' formation on a wall. © of Kyrona and LIVLIF Healing and Empowerment.

1.0 - THE STRUCTURAL SYSTEM

MAINTAINING STRUCTURAL BALANCE

The gravity line of the body is a horizontal, vibrational 'line of force', running around and through the body between the solar plexus and Navel chakras. Its *exact* location varies from person to person depending on their level of spiritual growth - moving upwards or higher as frequency increases.

A weakness in the *gravity line* can result in underlying Category 1, 2 or 3 conditions (a chiropractic term) which affect the vitality and *structural balancing process* of the whole body.

The *gravity line* is also sustained by three vertical, vibrational 'lines of force' (see diagram 6.1). The horizontal *gravity line* is the fourth 'main line of force'. It centres the sacrum area which then also helps the other three - *left, right* and *central* vertical lines of force sustain more strength and balance within the body.

When all four 'lines of force' are repaired and balanced, they alleviate pressure and prevent imbalances from manifesting throughout the 'central line of force' and spinal chord system, thereby enhancing the functioning of *the central nervous system and brain*.

At this time of transition, these four electromagnetic lines of force' in the body, are energetically 'tearing' and 'breaking' because of the gravity and electromagnetic changes of the Earth, continual shifting of the Earth's axis and the solar flare activity and astrological events which are more frequent at this time.

However, they now have an opportunity to become more *perfected* in their alchemical make up by being energetically strengthened, aligned and balanced by the supporting energies of the four fixed signs of the Zodiac – Leo, Aquarius, Taurus and Scorpio - resonating from the cosmic Grand Cross Activation of 1999.

Through the simple Transference Healing procedures below, the planetary energies of these four signs can be filtered through and down into the etheric/physical body to alchemically balance and strengthen the four main 'lines of force'. This will then help alleviate all side-effects or lightbody symptoms relating to skeletal pain - such as back pain, joint inflammation, subluxation of the vertebrae and even headaches - occurring because of the Earth and cosmic changes.

1.1 STRUCTURAL PROCEDURES

I recommend the following three structural procedures to alleviate pain and re-balance the skeletal area. Run *all three* of these procedures 'a few' times, for 'a few' days.

Silver is used when working with all the 'lines of force' in our body. This is because we need to *balance,* refine or strengthen our *feminine energy*. Since the fall of Atlantis the third dimensional body has been more connected to the masculine, *solar energy* which sustains more gravity and creates more ego driven desires and duality. As we evolve into the fifth dimension and beyond, after 2012, by enhancing the Feminine Principle more within our nature, we will become more centred within the heart than the ego and come more into a state of balance and perfection.

DIAGRAM 6.2
The Gravity Line, Three Lines of Force and the Categories
Harmony Alignment Points Technique

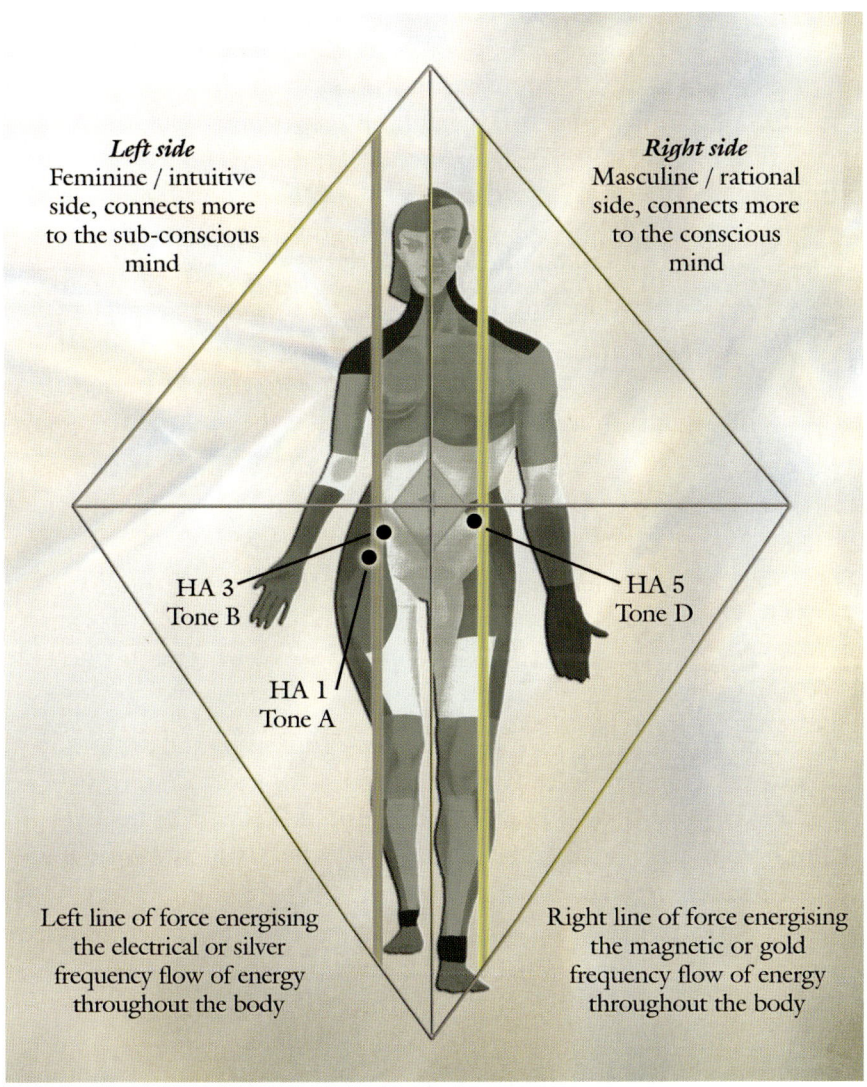

Left side
Feminine / intuitive
side, connects more
to the sub-conscious
mind

Right side
Masculine / rational
side, connects more
to the conscious
mind

HA 3
Tone B

HA 5
Tone D

HA 1
Tone A

Left line of force energising
the electrical or silver
frequency flow of energy
throughout the body

Right line of force energising
the magnetic or gold
frequency flow of energy
throughout the body

Copyright 2005 Alexis Cartwright, Keeper of the Crystals Pty Ltd.

When we become more *balanced* within the masculine and Feminine Principle we will be able to draw on more of the positive attributes of both. This will enable us to maintain a sense of wellness and balance in our etheric, magnetic and electromagnetic field of the body to *refine* our sense of self, while creating a more unconditional and humanitarian nature. As we balance the silver and gold frequencies within, we will be able to filter through a new state of perfection as we anchor through more of the 'Christ Light' within our body and consciousness.

To begin the three procedures visualise a diamond around the body which will remain in place throughout each procedure.

1.1.1 GRAVITY LINE (DIAGRAM 6.2)

Adjust the gravity line energetically by drawing a straight, *silver* 'line of force' across the body.

1. Firstly, place together one 'power finger' (usually the index finger) from each hand in front of the naval centre.
2. Then 'draw' them apart from each other - horizontally along this main *gravity line of force*. Any breaks or weaknesses will be repaired as the fingers draw over the broken or weakened parts.

By revitalising and balancing the *gravity line,* the sacrum area will ultimately begin to create the fundamental support system needed by the structural vertebrae system and also the emotions, to maintain *balance* on all levels within the body and consciousness.

1.1.2 THREE VERTICAL LINES OF FORCE (DIAGRAM 6.2)

Adjust the three vertical lines of force by starting with the 'central line of force' or *immortality line*.

1. Run silver from a 'power finger' up and down the centre of the body.
2. Go to the left (feminine) side of your body, drawing and repairing that line of force.

3.   Go to the right (masculine) side of your body, drawing and
      repairing that line of force.

This procedure maintains balance in the sacrum and preventively
cares against structural imbalances, back pain and curvatures of
the spine.

1.1.3 THREE HARMONY ALIGNMENT POINTS (DIAGRAM 6.3)

**These harmony alignment points balance the three main
Chiropractic Categories.**

Procedure: to create an interdimensional healing response from the
central nervous system to not only revitalise and heal the vertebrae
but also any symptoms created within the body because of a
weakness created by any of the three Chiropractic Categories.

Referring to diagram 6.3, touch each of the three points in the
body and ask for the *tone* of each point to resonate into each of the
three categories to begin a healing process relating to a particular
area of the etheric patterning and corresponding dimensions
within the anatomy.

This procedure clears any weakness in certain organs within the
body, relating to a structural or neurological weakness.

1.1.4 CRYSTAL ESSENCES

There are a variety of crystal essences from the Lightbody Kit
(including the **Structural Alignment Essence** - *see chapter 15,
page 499*) which clear painful symptoms and begin to heal structural
weaknesses from the skeletal, pelvic and also cranial systems of
the body. They alleviate structural weakness, joint and back pain,
cranial tension, distortion and inflammation in the spine, hips and
limbs; revitalise spinal fluids; enhance calcium assimilation; clear
muscle spasms; repair, strengthen and balance etheric, magnetic
or electromagnetic weakness in the main 'lines of force' or field of
the body.

2.0 THE ENDOCRINE OR GLANDULAR SYSTEM

Transference Healing works extensively with the glandular system whose function is *vital* to our overall health and state of mind.

Orthodox medicine still hasn't grasped the total effect of the master glands. They generally do not function on all the necessary levels within our body to create the hormonal and alchemical secretions and changes our body and consciousness need to *continually* develop and grow. If they are not functioning to the best of their ability they can cause a variety of symptoms which can't be medically diagnosed or treated. They are also the source of many psychological imbalances and mental disorders that seem to be manifesting more on the planet because of the Earth changes.

I have come to understand the complexity of how the glands work and interact energetically within the body and consciousness by 'tuning' into and working with the vibrational level of the endocrine/ glandular system. I have channelled through procedures to begin to clear internal weakness, symptoms and diseases manifesting through even more now because of the constant energy impacts of the Earth and cosmic changes.

Glandular imbalances are creating painful emotions and illness ranging from glandular fatigue through to feelings of psychological despair, depression and emotional weakness. The dysfunction of the glandular system on some level usually contributes to many of the lightbody symptoms occurring at this time.

DIAGRAM 6.3
The Seven Master Glands within the Endocrine System

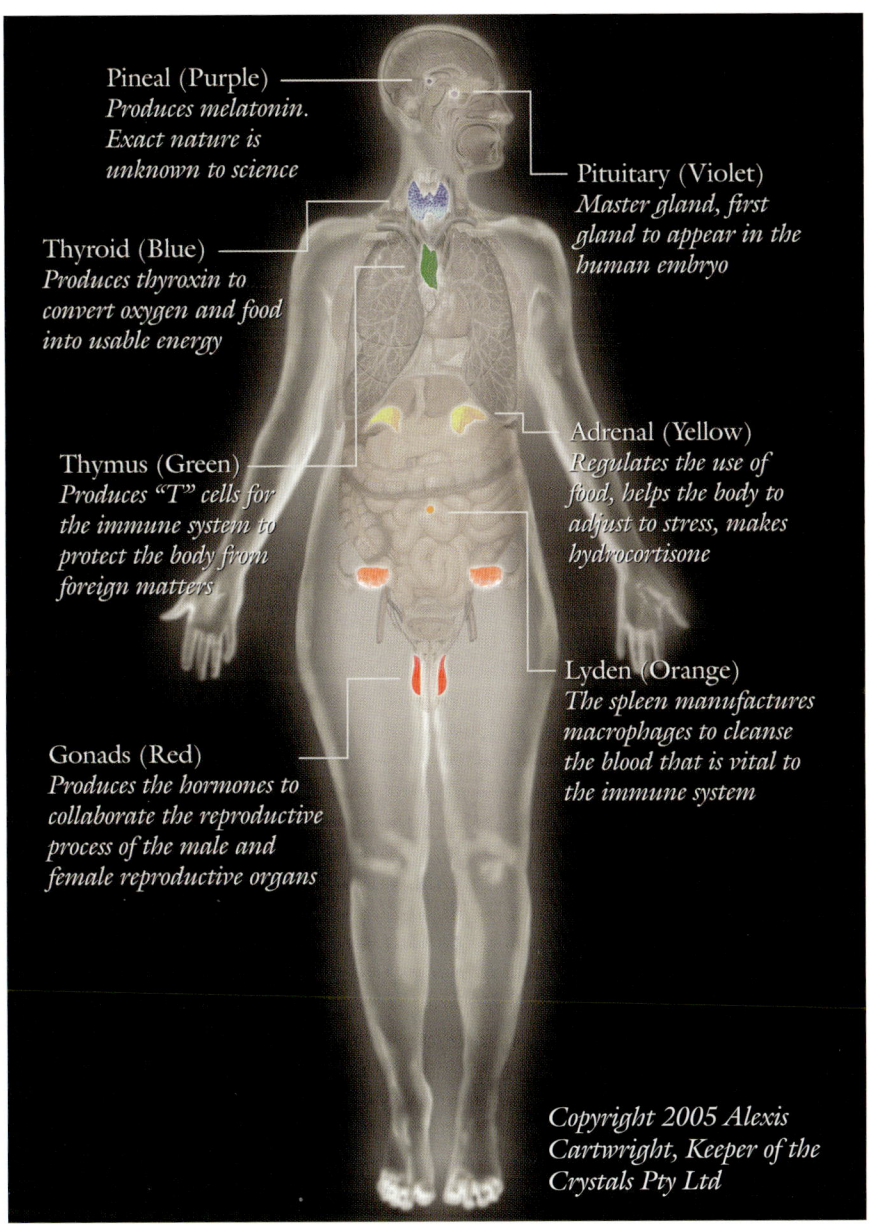

Pineal (Purple)
*Produces melatonin.
Exact nature is
unknown to science*

Pituitary (Violet)
*Master gland, first
gland to appear in the
human embryo*

Thyroid (Blue)
*Produces thyroxin to
convert oxygen and food
into usable energy*

Thymus (Green)
*Produces "T" cells for
the immune system to
protect the body from
foreign matters*

Adrenal (Yellow)
*Regulates the use of
food, helps the body to
adjust to stress, makes
hydrocortisone*

Lyden (Orange)
*The spleen manufactures
macrophages to cleanse
the blood that is vital to
the immune system*

Gonads (Red)
*Produces the hormones to
collaborate the reproductive
process of the male and
female reproductive organs*

*Copyright 2005 Alexis
Cartwright, Keeper of the
Crystals Pty Ltd*

2.1 ASTROLOGICAL AND NUMEROLOGICAL FORCES

THE TIME OF INCARNATION AND GESTATION

At the time of gestation which is further explained in chapter 12, the Global Grid Matrix weaves through into the DNA via the chakra system and glands, the necessary spiritual technology to support the co-creation process of the foetus or new born body that is being formed within the mother's womb. The mother protects, nurtures and provides certain genetic codes for the newborn from her own DNA, while the global grid weaves or encodes into the evolving DNA, the technology and resources to support not only the body's evolutional process but also encodes the necessary technology for the body to work independently from the mother, after leaving the womb when being birthed into the new world or dimension.

It is important to understand that the consciousness of the incoming Soul interconnects with the body from another plane, as the etheric/physical body is evolving within the womb. In this way the Soul is protected at all times while the etheric/physical body is being formed within the third dimensional realm it will incarnate into. There is usually karma between the Soul and the genetic parents it chooses at that time and those memories are also relayed into the DNA throughout the time of the nine month gestation period.

Also at the time of the physical birth into the world at large, a template of astrological and numerological forces which determine the inner nature of the new self and existence on Earth is universally

filtered or woven through the seven main chakras into each
corresponding master gland of the body.

This etheric template of our birth number and astrology - encoding
the degrees and relationships of the Sun, Moon and planets at
the time of birth, is then geometrically embedded into our DNA
(via the chakras and glands), thereby determining the individual
personality traits and also circumstances of fate that will occur for
that person during their time of incarnation on Earth.

ASTROLOGY TEMPLATE

At the *exact moment* of birth, the Universe provides a template
through which we can encode or embed within our body, the more
relevant personality traits determining the level of consciousness
we will live in during this incarnation on Earth. Also, throughout
our lifetime, the codes of this template unlock the forces of destiny
which enable us to live out karmic relationships and circumstances
relevant to our Soul's healing and evolutionary process during this
incarnation.

Therefore we are 'ruled' by the energies and geometric patterns of
the planets under which we are born, living our destiny through
their spheres of influence. However, we can uncover their mystery
through a *Natal Astrology* or *Numerology Reading* which makes it
possible for us to understand and personally identify with the range
of experiences and circumstances these forces provide throughout
our life.

THE GLANDULAR SYSTEM AND THE EMOTIONS

The glandular system determines the overall state and health of
the *emotions* within the body's consciousness. It is responsible for
coordinating (*registering*, filtering and *inter-playing*) the emotional
and psychological strengths, weaknesses and responses from our
DNA, brain and body. The emotional aspects of our personality are

both created and regulated by the hormonal secretions the glandular system creates within our body, which therefore determines how we think and feel.

THE GLANDULAR SYSTEM AND ALCHEMY

The glandular system monitors the clearing/assimilation process by creating the necessary **alchemical changes** for the body and consciousness to evolve beyond the restrictions of the past. It *creates and distributes* the hormonal secretions within the body, which then alchemically rejuvenate and heal the body and consciousness of past pain.

As well as registering *internal* energies from the *DNA*, brain and body, the glands also assimilate the necessary *external, universal* energies *from the Cosmos* to purify and resolve all the emotions produced and carried forward within the body by the glandular system – such as joy, love, anger, fear etc. - *fevers* can be a side effect of the glandular system releasing *fear*.

The glands not only *embed* the necessary external, *universal* energies into the DNA to determine the individual's personality traits in a particular incarnation (overlaying the newly incarnated Soul at that time) but also *transmit external (circumstantial) and internal (anatomical) energies* to create the necessary hormonal secretions needed by the body and consciousness to heal and evolve. This enables us to anchor, assimilate process and clear our *energetic and emotional state of being*, and create the necessary alchemical elements to continue to evolve and grow into a state of wellness and balance.

THE GLANDULAR SYSTEM REGULATES OUR SPIRITUAL TRANSITION

The Soul reflects its influence and force into the physical body and out into the world, through the glandular system. Therefore,

the effectiveness of the glandular system energetically determines
the development and evolution of *consciousness*. The master glands
are the *receptors* for weaving through universal light into the body
and consciousness. Our emotional and conscious state of being
is perfecting itself through the infiltration of the colour spectrum
of light.

2.2 PROCEDURES FOR SPECIFIC DIMENSIONS OF THE ETHERIC/ PHYSICAL BODY

2.2.1 Opening the Third Eye and Healing the Pineal Gland

2.2.2 Revitalising the Seven Master Glands

2.2.3 Perfecting the Glandular and Chakra Systems

2.2.4 Balancing the Emotional Body

2.2.5 Psychic Attack /Energy Plays and Feeling Vortex

2.2.6 'Alien Interference'

2.2.7 Protection and Clearing

2.2.8 Releasing Etheric Imbalances to Awaken Christ
        Consciousness

2.2.1 OPENING THE THIRD EYE AND HEALING THE PINEAL GLAND

The third eye is not only a chakra and energy vortex which
resonates etherically around the forehead and frontal brain area

but also includes the 'pineal gland' situated in the centre of the brain. The pineal gland and third eye activate the glandular system to create a universal *enlightenment* process. It is the area from which clairvoyant abilities are awakened and from which a state of 'enlightenment' is created in the body and consciousness.

DIAGRAM 6.4
The Glands and Third Eye Chakra: Creating a Universal State of Enlightenment

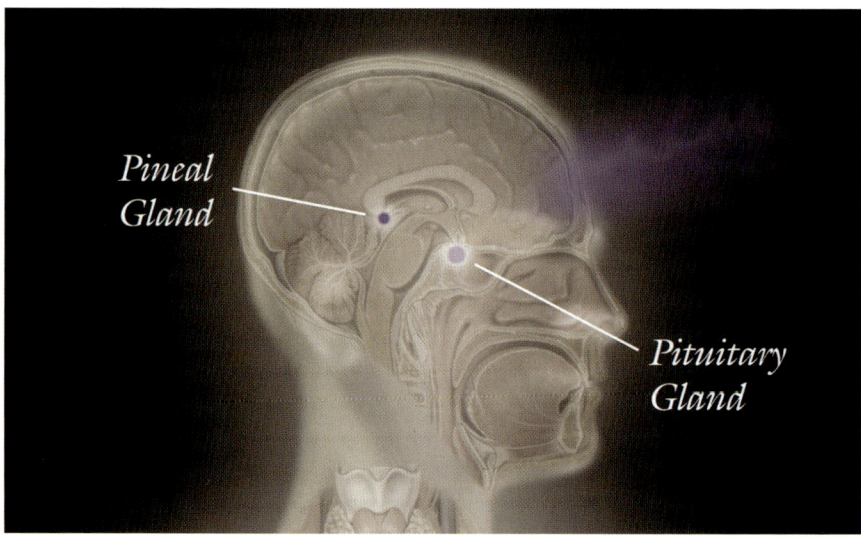

Copyright 2005 Alexis Cartwright, Keeper of the Crystals Pty Ltd.

Shift in Global Consciousness

The Earth's north/south axis has an angular inclination, so as the Earth rotates around its axis in an imperfect/uneven cone shape, the axis pointer or North Pole makes a very gradual *backward* movement through the 12 zodiacal signs. The backward movement through the *whole* Zodiac takes approximately 26,000 years and is called the *precession of the equinoxes*.

Its movement through *one* sign measures the length of time of one Zodiacal Age. As this polar axis leaves one sign and enters another, it creates a shift in global consciousness. *For example:* The Christ is associated with the sign of the fish and lived on the planet during the Age of Pisces whose symbol is two fish swimming in opposite directions. During the Age of Aries the ram, from 2000BC until the time of Christ, 'ram cults' developed in the Middle East and elsewhere. The Age of Taurus the bull, from 4000BC to 2000BC developed 'bull cults' such as the Egyptian Apis.

The phenomenon of the 'precession of the equinoxes' was an astronomical phenomenon discovered by the Egyptians. The present transition is moving from the *Age of Pisces* into the *Age of Aquarius* and is creating a global shift of frequency and consciousness is to create the fundamental changes necessary for us to integrate and live within the consciousness and reality of the fifth dimension.

The third eye chakra and corresponding pineal gland is being energetically impacted at this time because of the final transition process into this 'new' Age and is therefore supporting our *transference process* not only into the Age of Aquarius but also into the next dimension. The third eye, pineal and pituitary glands are energetically ruled by the planet Uranus, and by the constellation of Aquarius itself.

Everybody on the planet is going through a shift in consciousness. The third eye area and pineal gland, specifically, will go through consistent reactivations, until we can create the necessary changes in our body and consciousness. During this 'time of transition' the third eye chakra is slowly opening to filter through directly into the etheric body, the necessary universal energies to release old etheric and genetic or past life karmic patterning from the etheric body and DNA.

It is also weaving-in the necessary universal energies for the whole etheric body to begin to rejuvenate itself more independently so the physical body can heal and ascend. This is done by the third eye filtering through the necessary energies for the creation process of the lightbody.

Humanity, on a global level, is vibrationally shifting into the fifth dimension through this universal purification process, created by light filtering into the body and consciousness, via the pineal gland and third eye chakra. We are becoming *enlightened* through the healing and ascension process of the Earth and cosmic changes.

Pituitary Gland

The third eye chakra is energetically impacting the pituitary gland which is the master gland governing the whole endocrine system. As the **pineal** is purifying, repairing and revitalising the *etheric body* and consciousness and also *crystallising* more light into and within our body, the **pituitary** is simultaneously working to heal and revitalise all master glands and their corresponding organs.

The **pituitary** gland is activating the necessary *hormonal secretions* to heal and revitalise the *organs* within our anatomy, as well as heal and support the changes occurring within our *emotional* state of being. Therefore, the physical and spiritual dimensions of our body and consciousness are being radically impacted by the third eye, pineal and pituitary glands, at this point in time.

Through the opening of the third eye and as we shift into the New Age, a new and more universal level of consciousness is now 'awakening' within humanity. Through the opening of the third eye specific karmic memories and restrictions are being released from within so that as the etheric body and the DNA go through a universal purification process, genetic disease is slowly being wiped off the planet.

The 'minds eye' is releasing and shifting consciousness more rapidly
as we all go through a universal healing process to shift into higher
levels of consciousness. This is breaking down old belief systems
and unveiling and releasing layers of illusion. As we enter the next
dimension, during this time of the transition from 1999-2012, we
are all in the process of broadening our perception and enhancing
our psychic abilities

Procedures

Etheric surgery to clear an 'etheric web' in the third eye chakra.
This is an energetic buildup from imbalances occurring within the
etheric level of the chakra itself which creates an energetic barrier
within the chakra preventing universal light from filtering through
and into the brain, central nervous system and then throughout the
whole body to begin to alleviate specific lightbody symptoms such
as feeling heavy in the mind and brain area, disorientated, unable
to think clearly, loss of memory and/or overwhelming tiredness.

Visualisation

1. Look into the third eye area.

2. See/visualise/imagine an etheric web matrix which looks like
   a small wheel with a central hub.

3. See/visualise/imagine *some* of the matrix engorged with
   blackness.

4. Visualise (etherically) cutting out the blackness.

5. Sense and feel the chakra purifying itself with white light
   until the web-like formation of the chakra has crystallised
   and healed itself.

6. Visualise the colour purple in the third eye chakra so it can
   resonate at the optimum frequency and tone.

Essences

The **Cosmic Eye Essence** is a combination essence created for this specific procedure. It creates the following healing properties:

1.   Helps to clear 'webbing' distortion in the chakra.

2.   Works specifically with the third eye chakra, the pineal and pituitary glands as well as the brain itself.

3.   Supports the anchoring and manifestation process of the lightbody.

2.2.2 REVITALISING THE SEVEN MASTER GLANDS

The Lord's Prayer

The following meditation by Edgar Cayce is an excellent technique for revitalising the glandular system to create physical wellbeing and a spiritual enlightenment process. The original prayer that was initially channelled and written in the gospels now enables us to work directly with each specific gland.

Each appointed word within the prayer has a numerical vibration that resonates with each relevant gland and chakra, so they can heal themselves and therefore create a healing response throughout the whole body and consciousness. By giving proper focus to the meaning of the passage we can create a healing response within the glands and heart, to enable us to receive a vibrational healing impact from the universe.

Procedures: to revitalise the glandular system

1. The Lord's Prayer Meditation

1. Sit or lie down in a relaxed state.

2. Read or recite the first line of the Prayer:

Our FATHER which art in Heaven.

3. Quietly repeat to yourself, only the word in **capital letters**
   'FATHER', and with your eyes closed imagine the key word
   echoing within the (*pituitary*) gland centre.

   (VIOLET)

4. Remain still for at least 30 seconds.

5. Read or recite the next line:

   ### Hallowed be they NAME.

6. Quietly repeat to yourself, *only* the word in **capital letters**
   'NAME', and with your eyes closed, imagine the key word
   echoing within the (*pineal*) gland.

   (PURPLE)

Another dimension of healing is achieved through this meditation by visualising the colour of the chakra relating to the particular gland.

TONE 1A

DIAGRAM 6.5
The Lords Prayer Template: Colour/Gland and Planetary/ Sound Healing Meditation

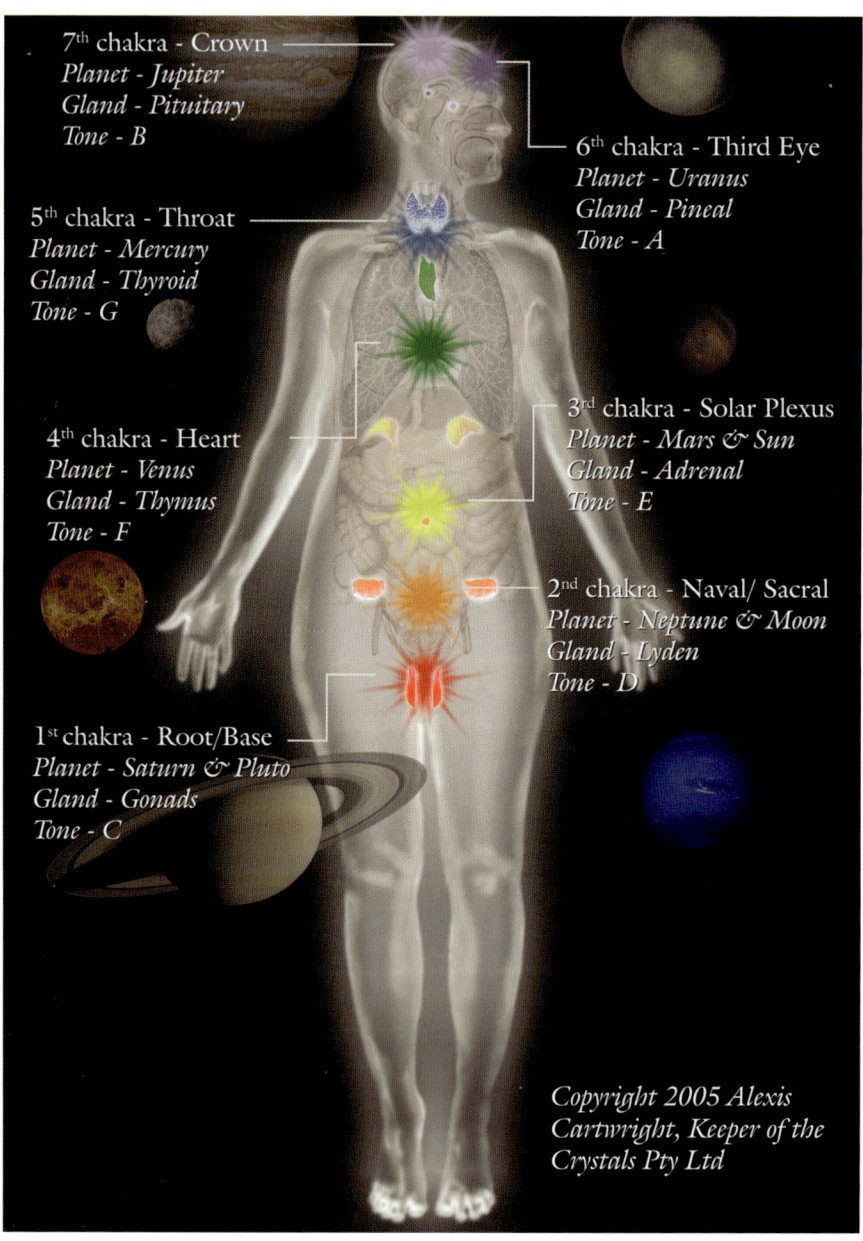

7th chakra - Crown
Planet - Jupiter
Gland - Pituitary
Tone - B

6th chakra - Third Eye
Planet - Uranus
Gland - Pineal
Tone - A

5th chakra - Throat
Planet - Mercury
Gland - Thyroid
Tone - G

4th chakra - Heart
Planet - Venus
Gland - Thymus
Tone - F

3rd chakra - Solar Plexus
Planet - Mars & Sun
Gland - Adrenal
Tone - E

2nd chakra - Naval/ Sacral
Planet - Neptune & Moon
Gland - Lyden
Tone - D

1st chakra - Root/Base
Planet - Saturn & Pluto
Gland - Gonads
Tone - C

Copyright 2005 Alexis Cartwright, Keeper of the Crystals Pty Ltd

THE LORD'S PRAYER

From Edgar Cayce

Our FATHER (pituitary) which art in Heaven,

Hallowed be thy NAME (pineal)

Thy KINGDOM come, thy WILL (thyroid) be done

In Earth, as it is in Heaven.

Give us this day, our daily BREAD (gonad)

and forgive us our DEBTS (adrenal)

as we forgive our debtors

and lead us not into TEMPTATION (lyden)

but deliver us from EVIL (thymus)

For thine is the KINGDOM (thyroid),

the POWER (pineal),

And the GLORY (pituitary),

for ever and ever – Amen

2. Amber drops to heal specific glands

Optional time saving procedure: if you do not have time to complete the above meditation, you can follow this simple procedure to heal specific glands.

Amber resonates a powerful electromagnetic charge when squeezed. It has a very powerful healing effect specifically when working with swollen or depleted glands.

1. Run your hands *up* the chakra system in the centre of the body.

2. When you intuitively feel to stop, imagine an etheric drop of amber going directly into the corresponding gland and then resonate the appropriate chakra colour throughout the whole chakra area.

3. Imagine the chakra spinning and re-energising that area of the body.

A small amber wand can also be used to perform this procedure. Just gently squeeze the amber over the depleted gland and corresponding chakra (for example: squeeze amber directly into the thyroid and then resonate blue throughout the whole throat chakra area). The vibrational healing properties of the amber and corresponding chakra colour will go directly into the master gland itself and begin to heal and revitalise it. This is a simple technique but a very powerful one for healing specific glands.

Essence: **Amber Essence** is available from the Lightbody Kit.

2.2.3 PERFECTING THE GLANDULAR AND CHAKRA SYSTEMS

By performing the Transference Procedures above we are perfecting the glandular and chakra systems and creating a 'state of enlightenment' on a day to day level to enable us to master the negative impact created by the Earth and cosmic changes at this time.

1. White Light

As the *chakras* continue to perfect themselves they begin to resonate at the tone and pitch corresponding to their planetary influence. They therefore come into a more balanced state with the Cosmos. The vibration of each colour and sound can then resonate through to the co-existing organs to energetically rejuvenate and revitalise them.

As each individual chakra and its corresponding colour and tone resonate into a state of perfection, the rainbow *colours* of the chakras begin to collate and resonate into one tone which creates an enlightened state of perfection by emanating through as one pure colour or 'ray' – **the White Ray.**

Through balancing and perfecting our chakra system, we are able to radiate and reflect the ray of white light to not only maintain a continual healing response within us at all times, but also to create a healing impact out into the world. At the precise time we master the chakra system, by holding and resonating the white light, we are *embodying* a state of true *'enlightenment'*.

2. Holding the Light

As each chakra resonates into a state of perfection a spontaneous Transference Healing impact is created on a multi-dimensional level.

Procedure: to begin to master the chakra system by holding and resonating white light.

1. Simply imagine white light resonating through and around you.

2. White light loved ones on a regular basis - a few times a day.

3.   White light after completing the previous glandular procedures, to stimulate an holistic healing and clearing process of the chakras and energy field of the body.

Essence: The **Radiant White Light Essence** is a combination essence for this specific procedure. This essence specifically balances the chakra system to enable us to begin to master radiating the white light.

2.2.4 BALANCING THE EMOTIONAL BODY

Every organ resonates emotions and thereby energetically impacts the body and consciousness. We can tap *directly* into the emotional level of the body through the *Metaphysical Diamond Procedure* in Transference Healing. This etheric diamond and its procedure filter through the cosmic colours and sounds necessary to begin to heal and repair each organ within the anatomy, via the chakra system.

To help maintain health and wellness during the transition, colour can also be directly integrated into the organs through visualisation and crystal essences.

I have included a simpler meditation/visualisation below to create a *colour healing process in the body*, through the chakras. This will begin to balance and maintain our energetic levels and emotional state of being. This procedure can alleviate painful symptoms from specific organs, release feelings of general tiredness and energetic or emotional depletion or distortion.

DIAGRAM 6.6

The Chakras and Corresponding Anatomy

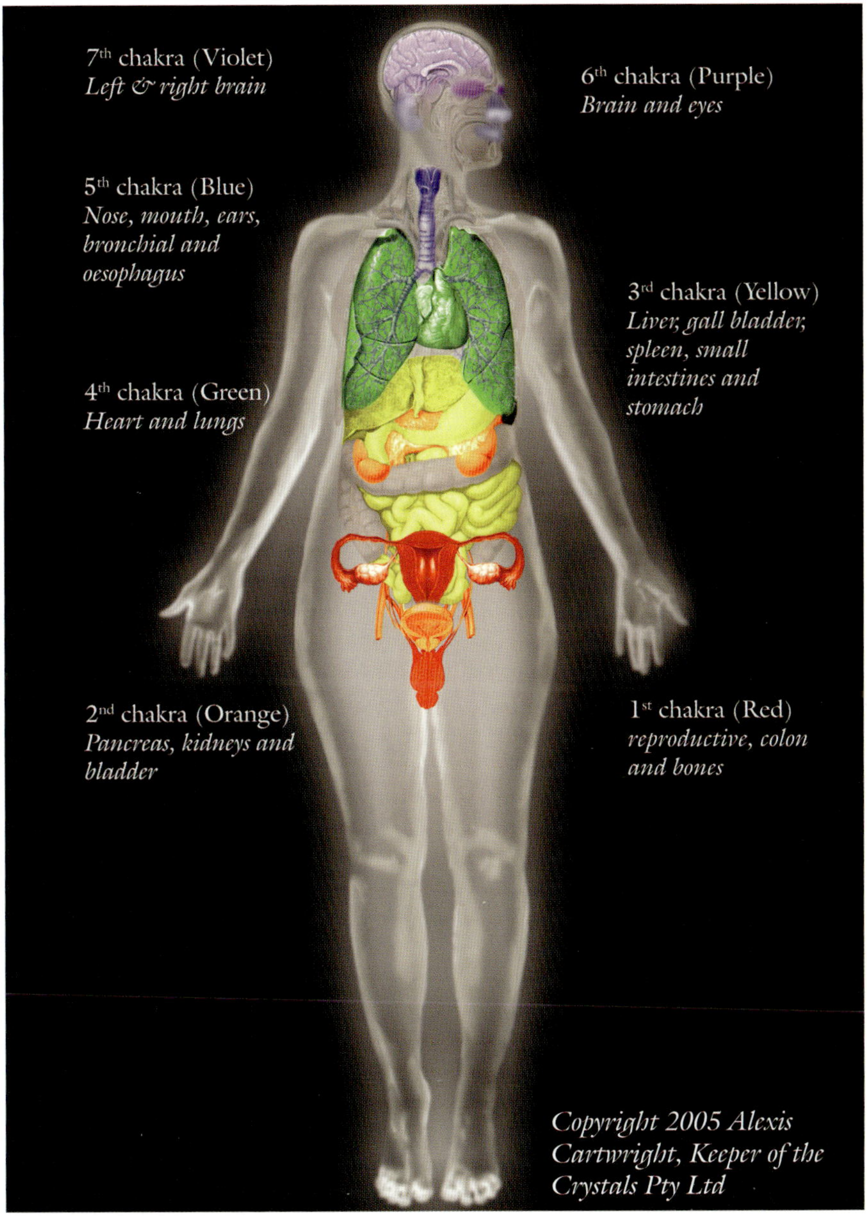

7th chakra (Violet)
Left & right brain

6th chakra (Purple)
Brain and eyes

5th chakra (Blue)
*Nose, mouth, ears,
bronchial and
oesophagus*

3rd chakra (Yellow)
*Liver, gall bladder,
spleen, small
intestines and
stomach*

4th chakra (Green)
Heart and lungs

2nd chakra (Orange)
*Pancreas, kidneys and
bladder*

1st chakra (Red)
*reproductive, colon
and bones*

*Copyright 2005 Alexis
Cartwright, Keeper of the
Crystals Pty Ltd*

1. Meditation/Visualisation

Procedure: to balance and maintain our energetic levels and emotions.

1. Sit in a meditative state.

2. Choose an organ, chakra and associated colour.

3. Close your eyes and visualise the area of the body or organ you have chosen to work on.

4. Set the intent to gently release any energy blockages in that area.

5. Then feel or visualise the dark shadows or energy blockages gently releasing themselves.

6. Alternatively to or with performing the procedure take seven drops of the **Rainbow Essence**.

7. To begin to heal the physical imbalances, direct the necessary colour from the appropriate chakra into the corresponding area or organ of the body that was struggling or creating a painful sensation.

8. Transmute all energetic and emotional distortion that is being released from the etheric patterning by visualising the colour purple resonating throughout the whole body and then white light to purify the body and consciousness.

9. The *Prayer of the New Millennium* that I have channelled through and is available in chapter 8 also clears the metaphysical diamond and supports the body and consciousness to ascend at this time.

Example 1

If balancing the stomach or a specific area of the abdomen, such as the intestines, visualise yellow resonating within and from the

solar plexus and then channel and feel this colour weave into
the intestines or stomach area and allow the organs to respond
accordingly. On an emotional and metaphysical level this will
create a state of empowerment, clear hypersensitivity and allow
manifestation through.

Example 2

Visualise purple resonating within and from the third eye and
then channel and feel this colour weave into the front lobe of the
brain and eyes and allow them to respond accordingly. On an
emotional and metaphysical level this will create more clarity, open
up clairvoyance, and enable one to shift into higher consciousness
more easily and anchor-in more of the lightbody.

2.2.5 PSYCHIC ATTACK OR ENERGY PLAYS

Indications of an energy play are old memories re-surfacing from
past relationships or ongoing issues with a particular person.
Karmic energy plays distort the glandular system creating feelings
of depletion, depression and even stagnation.

The following visualisation, procedure and essence are
catalysts for quickly clearing *karmic* situations, circumstances
and relationships in your life; help revitalise the master glands
and release old, restricted emotions; create rapid changes and
outcomes.

The key is to stay open to the changes - the more open you are, the
more powerful the healing and transference impact.

1.   Severing Karmic Pain and Sub-conscious Energy Plays

Procedure 1: to heal relationships by stopping energy plays and
resolving karma.

Place your finger on your naval and visualise pouring in an *etheric* drop of **Amber Essence** along with the colours gold and yellow.

Optional Procedure

1. Visualise yourself and the other person in separate pale blue bubbles attached together by a cord at the naval area.

2. Sense or see yourself cutting the cord and the other person drifting away.

3. Feel love emanating from your heart chakra as they drift away.

4. The further they drift, the more encouraged you are to feel unconditional love and the more settled you feel within your heart.

2.   Essence

Karmic Pain Release Combination Essence from the Lightbody Kit works specifically with the glandular system, the holding station of rigid thoughts and feelings, creating a purification and self- rejuvenation process so that new energies and emotions can be stimulated and created within.

1. Helps sever the energy plays and resolves the karma.

2. Revitalises the etheric and emotional body.

3. Helps more positive changes and outcomes to occur with corresponding or future relationships.

3.   The Feeling Vortex

The *feeling vortex* generates and vibrationally weaves energy throughout the whole etheric body. It is vital to work with the *feeling vortex* at this time. It has many dimensions within it and is very complex by nature. The area of the *feeling vortex* lies beneath and around the whole naval and solar plexus area.

If the feeling vortex is open:

1. It can create a depletion process by leaking energy from the etheric body. This creates a feeling of depletion and prevents a natural 'resourcing' process which is needed to rejuvenate the cells and anatomy of the body.

2. We are also susceptible to negative energetic impacts such as:

   - Distorted energies filtering through and into the body from the environment.

   - Distortion in the electromagnetic field of the body created by negative 'ultra violet rays' filtering through and into the body because of the intense *cosmic flare activity* occurring at this time.

3. Energy 'hook-ins' or plays also impact us more.

If the feeling vortex has been open *for a long time* and we have been constantly affected in ways mentioned above, then strange imbalances can begin to manifest more within the electromagnetic field of the body which can create more severe and even 'bizarre' lightbody symptoms, through to such deep levels of depletion that even cancer cells can begin to etherically manifest.

Closing down the feeling vortex will immediately begin to heal or even prevent these more severe symptoms from manifesting.

Procedure: to close the *feeling vortex.*

(Specifically brought through from the consciousness of the planet Chiron).

1. Place your hands one over the other just over your solar plexus - with the intent to shut down hypersensitivity and disassociate from pain and energy interference.

2. Imagine energy fibres extending out from the feeling vortex area like jellyfish tentacles.

3. Cut the fibres and send them to the light.

4. White light the feeling vortex.

5. Imagine the light rejuvenating and healing the solar plexus and *feeling vortex* area.

6. Count quickly from 1-100 as you imagine energy coming directly from Source into the feeling vortex area, thereby re-energising and rejuvenating the whole etheric/physical body. This will begin an intensive rejuvenation process throughout the whole anatomy.

7. Close down the feeling vortex by placing your thumbs and your index fingers together over the solar plexus area, and sliding them over each other until you have an etheric opening just the size of a 50 cent piece.

It is advisable to do this whole procedure a couple of times a day until you feel your energy levels have revived.

Essences: Dragon Power and Empowering Wisdom Essences support this procedure they are also available from the Lightbody Kit.

2.2.6 ALIEN INTERFERENCE: CLOSING THE 'DOORWAY' IN THE 'PATTERNING' TO PREVENT PAST OR FUTURE 'ALIEN INTERFERENCE'

There are many magnetic grid connection points in the Earth which create powerful electromagnetic charges. These connection points are like huge energy generators creating vortices from which *energetic portals* or *etheric Doorways* are created to connect us into other dimensions. The ancients understood the energy system of

the crystal Global Grid Matrix of the Earth and built sacred sites
where these **grid points** or *Doorways* are located on the planet.

Sometimes when we enter the area of a sacred space or site we
can experience an 'out of body' experience. Although this is a
positive thing some people feel the impact on a negative level and
experience what they perceive as an 'alien interference' process.
This usually occurs because there is a 'past life' aspect or weakness
within the etheric body or DNA needing to be healed so the Soul
can resolve issues from the past in this life, past lives and/or an
incarnation from other dimensions.

Triangular Star Diamond Doorway Point

If a negative experience occurs, we can clear the residue and cellular
memory by closing this *Triangular-Star Diamond Doorway Point*.

It is important to remember that all past traumas can be healed
by working with the *Triangular-Star Diamond Doorway Point*
(situated in the crown chakra area above the head). We can work
with this etheric Doorway to not only clear trauma from past
'galactic or Earth' lives but also from past *circumstances* in this
life. This Doorway in the patterning is etherically opening more
frequently now because of the energetic changes occurring to the
Global Grid Matrix so the Earth can readjust herself. It is creating
symptoms ranging from strange psychic experiences through to
general lightbody symptoms.

Example

When working on a client with recurring asthma, I saw her top
diamond *Triangular-Star Diamond Doorway* was open. As I closed
the Doorway and did a Transference Healing 'clearing of past
life patterning from the etheric body', I intuitively saw a painful
incident that had occurred in her late teenage years. As I talked to
her while closing the Doorway she confirmed this had happened.

Her father, who was an alcoholic had become violent one day and punched her in the face. This caused her to loose her front teeth and she was embarrassed about the replacement false teeth she now had. They were a constant reminder of this painful event.

As I closed her Doorway etherically, I told her that her sub-conscious would sometimes re-manifest the memory and traumatic emotions on a cellular level, at around the same time of day it had happened in the past. This triggered a feeling of anxiety and stress which then affected her lungs bringing through the symptoms of asthma. As we talked about it she began to see a pattern. She asked me if there was something else that could be done and I said 'No'. By closing the doorway point and doing a past life clearing of the etheric body via the doorway point, the trauma had been released from her sub-conscious mind and cellular body and the condition cleared.

It is important to access and heal past life aspects or even painful events from this life, so we can evolve at a more rapid rate through this time of transition. This is done in Transference Healing by working more extensively with the procedure of the *Triangular-Star Diamond Doorway Point*. It is not always necessary to understand the circumstances around past painful events, in this particular case I channelled through a reading while clearing this area in her body. However, just performing the procedure (working on this level energetically) will clear these kinds of symptoms.

Essences: The **Cosmic Shield of Connection and Protection** and **Chiron Essences** from the Lightbody Kit also work with doorway symptoms. They release trauma from this dimension of the patterning or diamond above the head which then clears painful sub-conscious memories of the past, from the DNA, cellular and etheric levels of the body.

2.2.7 PROTECTION AND CLEARING: CLEARING, WHITE LIGHTING & COLOUR BATHING

1. Protection from Scattered Energies

Procedures: to clear scattered energies creating scattered thought patterning; balance our energy field; detoxify and protect ourselves from negative ultra-violet rays creating distortion in our electromagnetic field:

1.   Visualise (or bathe) the colour cream over the whole body to detox the physical anatomy. Then visualise the colour of the 'radiant blue light' over the whole body which will purify the whole etheric body in parallel to the physical body.

2.   Keep clear quartz crystal on or around the body.

3.   Take **Cosmic Shield of Connection and Protection Essence** from the Lightbody Kit.

2. Protection from Negative Energies

Procedures: To clear *negative energies,* emotions, phobias and fears from the etheric body and subconscious mind:

1.   Visualise (or bathe) the body in the colour purple.

2.   Have amethyst with smoky quartz crystal on and around the body.

3.   Take the **Rainbow Essence** from the Lightbody Kit.

2.2.8 RELEASING ETHERIC IMBALANCES TO AWAKEN CHRIST CONSCIOUSNESS

The global awakening of Christ Consciousness on the planet began with the cosmic activation of the Grand Cross Alignment,

August 1999. This universal awakening is creating imbalances and symptomatic pain in the upper glandular and nervous system - from the heart through to the brain - as the dimensions of the body are trying to realign and heal to allow this new consciousness to awaken within.

Common lightbody symptoms or side-effects within the mind and body which are created by this awakening process range from, heart palpitations, throat and brain disease, headaches, lung disease and asthma, through to dé·jà vu. A great deal of underlying etheric stress is being released as this consciousness is being forced to awaken. We are not only experiencing difficulty in maintaining a healthy structural/cranial system, heart, lungs, throat and brain but also our sensory perception is changing and affecting the function of our eyes and nose and the inner ear which sustains a clear sense of perception, balance and co-ordination.

Essence: The **Crystal Cross Essence** from the Lightbody Kit helps maintain vitality and wellness through this area of the body and consciousness.

THE SELF-HELP PROCEDURES

These self-help procedures clear general lightbody symptoms now occurring on a global level. They alleviate the struggle and general feelings of fear, pain and possible despair at this time of transition. These procedures only take a few minutes to perform and allow us to self-master in our own healing process by making the necessary changes in our body and consciousness. **It is important to white light the body after performing each procedure.**

Each procedure refers to crystal or combination essences from the Transference Healing Lightbody Kit.

A separate smaller kit of combination essences specifically channelled to support the self-help procedures shared in this book is now available, it is called the 'Beyond Doorways Lightbody Kit'. Chapter 15 has more information on the kit, lightbody symptoms and these specific combination essences.

IMPORTANT: *Completion Ritual*

*Before you stop reading this chapter, run your finger from **right to left** across the sacred language below. This procedure will assist you to finalise the energies from this chapter.*

Your action, intent and the sacred vibration of this powerful language, will greatly assist you to fully integrate the information you have just read.

You can master the elements and learn to support your own healing and ascension process by attending a

'BEYOND DOORWAYS' WORKSHOP

These workshops are held regularly across the globe and are facilitated by certified Transference Healing® Teachers. The workshops aim to revise and solidify the lessons within this book, as well as, explaining first-hand the procedures in this book.

Level 1 – Workshop (1 day)

Includes: Templates and 15 Doorways Lightbody Essences.

Enables you to better understand and work with the fundamental level teachings and healing procedures contained within this book. *The key focus is on empowering you to participate in your own healing and ascension process at this time*. You will understand from a higher perspective how and why the Earth and humanity are ascending into a new dimension. Why you are a part of this shift and what you can do to minimise the negative impact of it on your life, while maximising your personal growth and enlightenment.

Level 2 – Workshop (1 day)

Includes: Crystal gridding kit with corresponding templates.

The focus of this workshop is to increase your understanding of the Mystery School concepts and teachings of Transference Healing, the workshop provides new information and is *not* revision work. You will undertake crystal scull, gridding and templating activities and explore the technology of matter and light.

Join a Workshop Now!

Go to the transference website to view the workshops being held by Alexis Cartwright herself OR to locate a certified teacher who is offering the workshops in your locality.

www.TRANSFERENCEHEALING.com

IMPORTANT: Commencement Ritual

*Before reading chapter 7, run your finger from **left to right** across the sacred language below.*

Your action, intent and the sacred vibration of this powerful language, will ensure that you are fully open to receiving and integrating the information within.

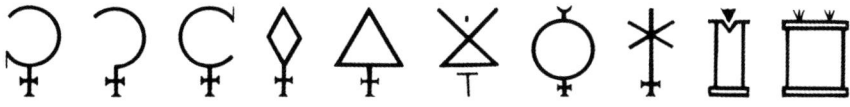

The above symbols are alchemical symbols depicting specific asteroids that were named after certain Goddesses. They include the asteroids Ceres - after the Greek Goddess of harvest, Pallas - after Pallas Athena the Greek Goddess of wisdom, Juno - after the Roman Goddess who rules marriages and is married to Jupiter and finally Vesta - after the Roman Goddess of the Earth.

These symbols energetically connect you to certain powers that filter down from the Cosmos, thereby anchoring certain principles and properties of the Goddess.

CHANNELLED TEACHINGS OF THE CHRIST

CHAPTER OVERVIEW

In this chapter you will learn:

* That Transference Healing procedures and Mystery School teachings have been anchored through at this time of the new millennium to help humanity obtain the Divine power and teachings of the Christ, supporting us through the rebirth of our planet.

* That the new book being written by Alexis is called 'Revelations' and be given a detailed overview of its profound contents.

* How we have been denied knowledge of the Christ's true belief system, spiritual principles, practices and teachings. We have lost the true essence, source, contents and magical properties that where once practiced and taught in ancient times.

* How the essence of the Feminine Principle has been misrepresented and disregarded, forsaking the beauty and compassion of the Goddess and leading to a 'solar powered' unbalanced society.

* How once humanity reconnects and becomes conscious of the powers of the Feminine Principle within, they will regain the internal resources to obtain the powers of the Holy Spirit such as:
  - **Awakening the Kundalini**; which opens the chakra system enabling us to obtain higher levels of consciousness and filters energies throughout our systems to energetically and alchemically support the healing process of our etheric/physical body.
  - **Awakening the psyche**; enabling us to open up dimensions of the brain and consciousness which enable us to see and obtain or channel Divine inspiration and sacred information.

* The true reason why Jesus established *Christianity* on the planet, was to create a sacred space where **all** people, not just those of a particular culture or religion, had the opportunity to learn to obtain the powers and principles of the Christ.

The Christ teachings are an ancient and more **celestial** or **cosmic** belief system or consciousness, which instilled the ability to heal through 'light'. The Church system was created by Jesus to provide a service to humanity. It was a system to create an *initiate of the Christ* who learnt the principles of Nature to then master the healing powers of Nature and then be of service to humanity by passing this knowledge onto others.

* As the true essence of the Christ teachings are universally re-established within the heart of humanity and onto the planet, they will establish a new universal belief system that will come to be identified as Mystic or Millennium Christianity.

* Jesus, the man, anchored the template to become the energetic and physical way (tool) through which the Earth and humanity would be able to take the next vital step in evolution and enter into a new world and reality energetically connected to the parallel 'kingdoms' and worlds which co-exist within higher levels of frequency, matter and consciousness within the Cosmos. He changed our concept of time, space and matter.

* During Jesus' final incarnation, he began the process of perfecting the ego and mastering the *Feminine Principle* so that he could complete a state of Mastership by balancing and embodying the *androgynous* nature of both the Feminine and Masculine Principles of the God/Goddess. He was then able to filter in the universal and alchemical powers and elements of Nature - the Earth and cosmic energies - to be create the profound healing and alchemical resources within, enabling him to change his body's composition into higher frequencies and properties. Jesus, therefore resurrected his *androgynous* lightbody, mineralising it with such electromagnetic force that he anchored in his Christbody - while in a state of *physical* incarnation. This completed his ascension process on Earth.

* The 'Grand Cross' astrological template of 1999 cosmically and energetically imprinted the template of Christ's return on a universal level.

◆

THE BOOK OF REVELATIONS AND TRANSFERENCE HEALING

The Transference Healing procedures and Mystery School teachings have been anchored through at this time of the new Millennium to help humanity obtain the Divine power and teachings of the Christ (encoded within the 'Book of Revelations'). They will support humanity to take a quantum leap of faith to *'physically master'* during this overwhelming time of rebirth on our planet.

Transference Healing is the physical tool and energy system channelled to support, teach and empower us to *embody* these energies and the teachings of the Christ (to be revealed in greater detail in my new book 'Revelations'). It will interpret and reveal the hidden message from the 'Book of Revelations' on *how* the Earth and Cosmos are energetically changing and how these changes are supporting our healing and ascension process.

'Revelations' will provide:

1. An in-depth understanding of the etheric/physical anatomy and body.

2. Specific information on the energy changes, their effects on the physical body and the *outcome* for the planet and humanity after this time of transition, on Earth.

3. Insight on astrological, cosmic, elemental and galactic phenomena creating energetic and physical changes within the body, consciousness, Earth and Cosmos.

4. Information on **the true essence of alchemy** and how to create the alchemical changes within, to create the new anatomy of **the fifth dimensional body** - biblically know as the **Adam Kadmon** body.

5. New details on the technology of **the new lightbody system.**

6. Geometric and geographic information on specific **crystal and light grid lines, ley lines or dragon lines** within the Earth and Cosmos and:

    i.   How they are to support the creation process of the electromagnetic field and lightbody system that is to come into full manifestation.

    ii. Where the grid points exist, interconnect and open up stellar Doorways into parallel Galactic and Ethereal Kingdoms or worlds.

    iii. Where they create corridors into specific dimensions which are the parallel worlds we will come to co-exist within, in the far future.

    iv. How the grid points resonate and emanate the healing and ascension powers of the Holy Grail.

7. Information on how the frequency changes occurring within these crystal grid lines are changing **the frequency of water** on the planet:

    i.   How the internal technology involved in the shifting of the frequency of water will change the vibrational level of the anatomy and also the atomic and molecular structure of the cells within the body.

    ii. Locations will be given where 'holy water' will once again manifest through healing wells.

8. Information on **the new DNA:**

    i.   How **crystallised** energies will resonate through from crystal grid lines and cosmic energies from stellar gateway systems to filter and weave into the DNA for the re-weaving and perfection process of a 22-strand DNA system.

    ii. How these crystal and cosmic frequencies are also resonating through to re-weave and rejuvenate distortion in the **etheric body.**

    iii. Specific information will also be given on how the healing and restoration of the DNA and etheric body will create the alchemical powers and internal resources to heal 'Chiron or core wounding' so the new anatomy and lightbody system can begin to the co-create itself with more ease.

    iv. Insight will be given on the source and reasons why there is distortion in the etheric/physical body and DNA and also the origins and reasons why genetic diseases and viruses exist today.

9.   Information on **the technology of crystals**, how they amplify healing, ascension and prognostic ability.

10.   Channelled information on **the true essence of Christianity:**

    i. Why Jesus established the Christ teachings on the planet.

    ii. The lineage and origins from which these teaching came.

    iii. The true relationship between **Mary Magdalene and Jesus.**

    iv. The spiritual practices that occurred between them and the reasons why.

    v. The incarnations Christ has had on the planet and the true reason for his resurrection process.

11.   Information on the **Merkabah body** and **Christbody** system.

12.   Information on the **origin of the Kabala**:

    i. The hidden meaning of certain teachings of the **Kabala.**

    ii. The reason for the political and spiritual unrest between the East and the West.

13. Information on the **ancient civilisations** of Lemuria, Atlantis, Egypt, Greece, India the Mayan, and of the Arthurian times:

   i. Their spiritual practices, ritual ceremonies, belief systems, crystal and mythical knowledge and healing procedures to sustain aspects of the principles and true teachings of the Celestial Christ.

   ii. How remnants of these lost teachings are still sustained today within certain religions, philosophical societies, cults and cultural belief systems.

14. Sacred and new information on the location, lineage holders and lost teachings of the **'Great Central Moon'**:

   i. The lineage holders and mysteries were handed down through a specific line of initiates who worshipped the powers and knowledge of the long forgotten **Goddess.** This was the sacred knowledge Eve internally received through the awakening of her kundalini and chakra system - which created her enlightenment and ascension process.

   ii. The 'priestess order' or initiates sustained and passed down these teachings on the planet and protected them to ensure they stayed pure. They were sustained and only handed down to women who were selected as the 'Keeper of the Crystal' (from which the concept of the 'Holy Grail' came into manifestation).

   iii. Insight into the nature and lives of certain lineage holders of the Goddess that existed on Earth such as Isis, Mother Mary, Mary Magdalene and Morgan La Fay, will be shared in this book Also new information will be channelled and brought through from these Divine Beings, so that certain powers and teachings of the Goddess, can be revealed once again to humanity.

15. Topics channelled from specific Ascended Masters and Archangelic beings such as Thoth, Isis, Archangel Michael, Lady Nada, Buddha, and so on share information regarding:

    i. **The technology of sacred knowledge and powers** created by geometry, crystals, alchemy, the kundalini, astrology, cosmology, metaphysics, sound, colour and the rays etc.

    ii. **The Divine forces of Nature and the Goddess,** the essence from which we were created which will allow us to understand the concept of creation, genesis and the Adam and Eve story through to the meaning and know how of our evolutionary process and the dimensions in which we will come to exist within.

    iii. Information on the parallel dimensions the **Celestial Christ** exists on and within.

    iv. The location of grid points creating corridors into specific dimensions that are the parallel worlds we will come to co-exist within, in the far future.

A NEW BELIEF SYSTEM

The spiritual teachings and New Age perspective to be revealed in my new book 'Revelations', hold more of *the Feminine Principle and esoteric teachings and powers of Nature and the Goddess*- which the church identifies as the essence of the Holy Spirit. Jesus was able to understand and master the *alchemical* and *magical* healing powers of Nature by integrating these ancient teachings and embodying the powers and principles of the Goddess which he studied and practiced within the Mystery Schools of India and Egypt.

These magical teachings and Divine powers, channelled and practiced by the Christ, have been lost through time because of the manipulation of the information by some of the founding members of the Church who disregarded the essence, magical properties and powers of the Goddess.

The church itself has disregarded or even misrepresented these original teachings of the essence of the Feminine Principle and forsaken the beauty and compassion of the Goddess. It has become a 'solar powered', *man made,* institutionalised belief system based on preaching rather than experience.

The pure teachings and principles of Nature, the Christ revealed while on Earth, were inscribed into the gospels by his apostles and believers in ancient times. However, they have been manipulated ever since, beginning with the founding members of the Church. Through this process the Church itself *contained* and *sustained* certain powers and knowledge to control global consciousness and also control and manipulate the economy of the planet for their own gain. Money and knowledge is power.

Therefore we have been denied knowledge of the Christ's true belief system, spiritual principles, practices and teachings. We have lost the true essence, source, contents, and magical properties that were once practiced and taught in ancient times. The Bible is now preached and taught in a literal sense and the true nature of its words, healing powers and teachings are withheld from human consciousness. Once humanity reconnects and becomes conscious of the powers of the Feminine Principle within, they will regain the internal resources to obtain the powers of the Holy Spirit such as:

1. AWAKENING THE KUNDALINI

The Kundalini opens the chakra system enabling us to obtain higher levels of consciousness and filters energies from the chakra system throughout the pranic system of the body to energetically and alchemically support the healing process of the etheric/physical body. Therefore, the Kundalini enables us to ascend into higher level of consciousness, re-connecting us to our Higher Self to obtain the powers and ability to begin to '*heal thyself*.'

This will give hope back to the people and empower their personal and *direct* healing and ascension process through and by the Christ.

2. AWAKENING THE PSYCHE

This enables us to open up dimensions of the brain and consciousness which enable us to see and obtain or channel Divine inspiration and sacred information. We will then be able to look *within* to Source for spiritual connection and thereby obtain the intellectual resources and knowledge to understand the meaning behind the veil. We will begin to establish and understand the meaning of life and Nature and thereby master more within our own personal and spiritual growth process. We will link directly into the Christ in consciousness to obtain universal information and also obtain direct connection to the Christ. This will once again empower our personal growth process and remove the need for the institution of the Church. We will be *living* our own belief system through our direct connection to the Christ.

THE TRUE ESSENCE OF CHRISTIANITY

The true reason why Jesus established *Christianity* on the planet, was to create a sacred space where **all** people, not just those of a particular culture or religion, had the opportunity to learn to obtain the powers and principles of the Christ. The Christ teachings are an ancient and more **celestial** or **cosmic** belief system or consciousness which instilled the ability to heal through 'light'.

The Church system was created by Jesus to provide a service to humanity. It was a system to create an *initiate of the Christ* who learnt the principles of Nature to then master the healing powers of Nature. Through obtaining the inner technology and teachings of the Christ, they could then be of service to humanity by relaying them onto others. Those attending a particular service could therefore experience the magical properties of a 'Divine and sacred enlightenment and healing process' created by the initiate or Christ channeller. Even the name Jesus (Greek Iesous) means 'great of magic'.

The followers of Jesus who were the first initiates of the order, such as the apostles, were also educated to empower others to develop themselves to channel the healing, enlightenment, spiritual powers and principles of the Christ - to then 'awaken' and ascend into a more evolved state of consciousness and being.

The Earth and cosmic principles, information and teachings of the Christ are now taught in the Transference Healing procedures I have channelled and anchored onto the planet. Also the more advanced teachings of the Christ, will be given to graduates who choose to *master* the Christ teachings and powers, by attending the 7th Mystery School commencing in 2006. *(See page 301 for more information on the 7th Mystery School)*

> **As some of the true essence, hidden codes and teachings of the Christ are channelled and revealed through my new book 'Revelations,' and by other Christ channellers, grid masters and historians on Earth, the sacred powers and teachings of the Christ will be universally re-established within the heart of humanity and onto the planet. These teachings will establish a new universal belief system that will come to be identified as Mystic or Millennium Christianity.**

MYSTIC OR MILLENNIUM CHRISTIANITY

The time and birth of Jesus was recognised by the ancient magicians and esoteric masters, as that prophesised for the Divine birth of a master who would establish the true essence of faith, 'Christianity' and salvation for the planet and all humanity. Astrology foretold the incarnation of the 'template' of a *Divine cosmic being* who would physically restore and unite the principles and properties of the God/Goddess within and on the planet. Through his own physical and spiritual ascension process on Earth, through mastering the elements of Nature- he would complete his ascension and thereby template his wisdom and teachings so the rest of humanity could understand and eventually heal and ascend also.

Jesus, the man, anchored the template to become the energetic and physical way (tool) through which the Earth and humanity would be able to take the next vital step in evolution and enter into a new world and reality energetically connected to the parallel 'kingdoms' and worlds which co-exist within higher levels of frequency, matter and consciousness within the Cosmos. He changed our concept of time, space and matter by teaching us how to break down and transfer through the illusion of separation, duality and the elements of matter which restrict us from re-connecting and integrating back into the Divine Essence and nature of spirit - in physical body and consciousness.

Jesus was to become '*the way*' to obtain Salvation because he templated and created the teachings and tools through which humanity could and would ascend.

THE CONCEPT OF TIME

Even though the *exact* date and year of Jesus' birth are unknown, the event itself created a turning point in human consciousness, history, and the nature or concept of time.

1. The birth of Jesus was seen as a Divine birth, prophesised as the 'Coming of Christ'. Events prior to this time were viewed as a *preparation* for a 'universal restoration and awakening' of humanity.

2. Many different calendars existed throughout history until 46 BC when the Julian Calendar of Rome first attempted to create a standard record of time. The popes of Christian Europe later adopted the Julian Calendar from the Roman Empire. However, in 525, the monk Dionysius Exiguus was asked to prepare a standardised Christian calendar for the Western Church and counted years from a year he *assumed Christ was born*. The Western Church 'split' our record of time into events occurring before the birth of Christ - now expressed by the abbreviation of BC and dates of events occurring after the birth of Christ - expressed by the abbreviation AD, *Anno Domini* or year of our Lord (The later reform of the Julian calendar in 1582 came to be known as the Gregorian calendar after Pope Gregory XIII.).

3. Christianity also changed our general concept of time from circular to linear by removing the Law of Reincarnation from Christian doctrine. They preached the human Soul existed for only one lifetime or incarnation to master the principal teachings of Christianity in order to be saved and go to Heaven for eternity.

REINCARNATION

The ancients believed in *circular* time based on the Universal Laws of Karma and Reincarnation and karma created the *circumstances* to learn and evolve through. Most of the 'New Age' spiritual community today, also believe the Soul evolves through many incarnations or multiple cycles of death and rebirth, to learn the principal laws of the Universe and reach a state of Mastership.

Reincarnation states the spirit comes to the Earth plane many times in order to experience physical life under a variety of circumstances and conditions. Even though we incarnate into different bodies while taking on different personalities, surrounded by different people while occupying Earth at different times and within different cultures - our spiritual evolution continues, unbroken and uninterrupted. The spirit evolves toward oneness with the God/Goddess through physical evolution.

FULFILLING A PROPHECY

During Jesus' final incarnation, he began the process of perfecting the ego and mastering the *Feminine Principle* - the once forbidden powers of the *Goddess*. He also began to master the female aspects of the 'psyche' such as the Divine 'gifts and talents' of 'intuition and channelling'.

Jesus no longer only worshipped the *Solar Power* of the Cosmos like most practicing initiates of ascension, but began to also honour and worship the ancient teachings of the *Lunar Power* of the Earth,

Moon and Cosmos. By doing so he began to filter into his body and consciousness, the Divine properties and attributes of the Feminine Principle so he could complete **a state of Mastership** by balancing and embodying the *androgynous* nature of both the Feminine and Masculine Principles of the God/Goddess. He could then begin to filter in the universal and alchemical powers and elements of Nature - the Earth and cosmic energies - to be able to create the profound healing and alchemical resources within, enabling him to change his body's composition into higher frequencies and properties.

> **Jesus, therefore resurrected his *androgynous* lightbody, mineralising it with such electromagnetic force that he anchored in his Christbody - while in a state of *physical* incarnation.**

This completed his ascension process on Earth. The man Jesus, therefore fulfilled the prophecy of a Saviour, who was to incarnate and become the long-awaited 'Christ' on Earth. Through balancing the forces of duality and by refining the ego, body and consciousness, Jesus came to anchor, resonate and also *embody* all dimensions of the light/Christbody which sustains the genetics of the *galactic and angelic aspects of the Self on Earth*. Through *embodying* the totality of his divinity and Higher Self, he broke through the restriction of time and space. He therefore resurrected his Cosmic Self, body and consciousness, while in a *physical* incarnation, and imprinted this template into our dimension and universe.

At that precise time, while in a state of total 'enlightenment', he also recognised that he was to return to Earth as *cosmic energy,* at the turn of the millennium. He would complete his destiny as the Saviour by templating a universal healing and ascension process so the Earth and all of humanity could evolve.

The 'Grand Cross' astrological template of 1999 cosmically and energetically imprinted the template of Christ's return on a universal level. In divine synchronicity, the ancient prophecy was fulfilled that the planet and humanity would evolve through the internal technology and resources of the Celestial Christ.

REINCARNATION AND RESURRECTION

Humanity on a global level came to see the man Jesus was the *'Chosen One'*. At the time of his crucifixion he *embodied* his lightbody/Christbody thereby resurrecting into the higher dimensional frequency of the incarnated Christ. He had fulfilled the spiritual prophesies by creating *a universal salvation/ascension process* on Earth.

Jesus fulfilled his destiny as the *Saviour of* Mankind through this resurrection process (not by saving humanity from their sins). He demonstrated that the process of human evolution was a process of ascension and resurrection not disease and reincarnation. Humanity no longer needed to be eternally *crucified on* the *third dimensional' cross* of matter' bound by the 'law of cause and effect or karma.'

The true reason why reincarnation was not found within the teachings of Jesus was that he taught the concept of *resurrection,* not reincarnation. He introduced a belief in *immortality* as he knew genetic disease would eventually be decoded from the DNA as we anchored in the lightbody and therefore the process of reincarnation would eventually cease to exist.

This is a clearer perspective on re-incarnation and resurrection and foretells that reincarnation will exist only until we can begin to anchor in and resurrect the lightbody to release ourselves from a process of 'death and rebirth' through the laws of 'gravity and duality' - and begin to embody divinity, longevity and eventually immortality.

THE 'SECOND COMING'

The astrological 'Grand Cross,' 1999, announced Christ's cosmic resurrection in the Heavens and 'Second Coming' to Earth. Through the creation and cosmic activation of this 'Grand Cross', the Earth began many changes to support the healing process of the human body within this third dimension, by filtering in the universal Earth and cosmic healing energies and properties necessary to decode genetic disease from the DNA.

This universal 'Grand Cross' template weaves through the necessary inter-dimensional energies to also create a new DNA system within humanity to support the resurrection of the new anatomy or fifth dimensional body as well as the new lightbody system. This process will therefore create more wellness and longevity. Through the astrological 'Grand Cross Activation' all of humanity will come to create a natural healing and resurrection process and overcome the need for reincarnation as we have known it.

CHRIST TEACHINGS

Christ is the name or title of an office held by Jesus. He was chosen to *embody* and master the Divine powers of Nature and the God/Goddess here on Earth to teach the world how to self-master their own healing and ascension process into higher consciousness and physical reality, *through a Divine template.*

Jesus taught about the healing nature of the Earth and Cosmos and about *other dimensions* that are an aspect of the totality of our DNA. He referred to these dimensions as the 'Kingdoms of Heaven'. He also taught about a more evolved lightbody that would electromagnetically integrate within *higher dimensions* of the etheric body.

PARALLEL DIMENSIONS AND REALITIES

The *true* concept of linear time reflects the concept of *physical immortality* - the belief that there is no physical death as we no longer have to continue to suffer through the death and rebirth process of physical reincarnation (circular time).

Below I have given a brief description of the *four planes of transformation* and the four bodies, which determine the linear and circular cycles of our existence. These bodies sustain the technology, energies, elements and properties necessary to support our innate ability to *transfer* into parallel worlds and realities. These are the parallel worlds within other dimensions where we also co-exist between our *more physical* incarnations on Earth. In this way our spirit, life force and consciousness can experience other forces of Nature and therefore come to understand the workings of creation.

Through shifting frequency, life force and consciousness we take on different expressions of Nature and the elements through which a body forms. This body sustains itself within each different reality for only a period of time at each level of existence, so we can understand different aspects of ourselves.

THE FOUR BODIES

It is important to recognise that we live within different periods of time and space, within different levels of consciousness, at different levels of frequency so we can sustain a physical and spiritual existence. I have briefly explained the four bodies, which enable us to do this. It is a very complex process, which needs to be explained at this time in order to understand what it means to 'anchor in' the lightbody so we can enter into the fifth dimension.

It is a vital part of the teachings of the 'Christ' and even though I have just touched on the subject in this chapter, a more conclusive explanation will be given in 'Revelations.'

1. MORTALITY – THIRD DIMENSIONAL PHYSICAL BODY

DIAGRAM 7.1
Third Dimensional Physical Body Symbol

Copyright 2005 Alexis Cartwright, Keeper of the Crystals Pty Ltd.

The third dimensional physical body is the aspect of the Self, which sustains itself on the 'cross of matter' *through reincarnation* so we can learn to purify and master the limitations within ourselves. The body's physical mass and compounds are sustained within the third dimensional hologram of the body, which sustains us within the third dimensional hologram of our reality and visible dimension.

This third dimensional level of the etheric/physical body and consciousness contains the *lower nature* and corresponding *genetic* weaknesses that re-manifest disease through the eternal birth and death process of reincarnation and mortality. *This body is also identified as the mortal 'Earth' body and sustains us within the concept of circular time.*

2. IMMORTALITY – SIXTH DIMENSIONAL LIGHTBODY

DIAGRAM 7.2
Sixth Dimensional Lightbody Symbol

Copyright 2005 Alexis Cartwright, Keeper of the Crystals Pty Ltd.

The lightbody resonates energetically within higher frequencies beyond the layers of the third dimensional physical mass of the body. It is more electromagnetic and crystalline in nature and its elements or compounds are sustained more within the sixth dimensional hologram of the body. The *Higher Self* and lightbody maintains our connection with the immortal aspect of the Self, and is connected more to the invisible worlds within our reality.

This dimension of our body *indefinitely* sustains our life force and consciousness in higher dimensions of more *ethereal mass,* as we co-exist within different levels of consciousness and realities at different times. We have not yet mastered this sixth dimensional body and level of consciousness. *This body is also identified as the immortal 'cosmic' body* and sustains us within the concept of linear time.

3. ADAM KADMON - FIFTH DIMENSIONAL 'NEW ANATOMY' BODY

D IAGRAM 7.3
Fifth Dimensional New Anatomy Body Symbol

Copyright 2005 Alexis Cartwright, Keeper of the Crystals Pty Ltd.

The 'New Anatomy' body is not only made up of the four elements, earth, air, fire water like the third dimensional body, but has also mastered an alchemical infusion of these elements, to a certain degree. As these elements are infused with more electromagnetic frequencies they also sustain more ether making it more electromagnetic and *ethereal* in is elemental composition. It is a body, which enables us to transfer from a more condensed form of mass and consciousness to obtain a more *enlightened* and *ethereal* form of mass and consciousness.

The Adam Kadmon is the template through which we can transfer and exist within physical substance and form and also integrate more electromagnetic light to co-exist within more ether and light. It is a vehicle through which we can *unite* the aspects of physical mass with light and therefore sustain a *physical lightbody* while living in a more physical reality like Earth. It is the body, which enables us to live in higher consciousness while in a state of duality or 'Earth-like' *physical* incarnation. It sustains the holographic template through which it is possible to ascend from the third dimension into the sixth dimension while living within the fifth dimension - and therefore co-exist in both. *This body is also identified as the' ethereal body' and exist more within a semi-state of alpha consciousness where we don't really feel any concept or consequence of time.*

4. CHRISTBODY - SEVENTH DIMENSIONAL CELESTIAL BODY

DIAGRAM 7.4
Seventh Dimensional Celestial Body Symbol

Copyright 2005 Alexis Cartwright, Keeper of the Crystals Pty Ltd.

Each human being is living within the substances of the above three bodies to different degrees. Over the next 1,000 years all will learn to master and integrate all aspects of them into a more perfect state of proportion and composition, to obtain the ability to heal and mineralise the etheric/physical and ethereal or lightbody into a Christbody. When an individual perfects this process they will begin to live within the seventh dimension while the rest of humanity still exists within the fifth. *This body is also identified as the celestial body where light is mineralised and crystallised.* One lives in a state of higher consciousness and there is no concept or relation to time because time does not exist at this level of consciousness and being.

CHRIST TEACHINGS ON ALCHEMY

Time, as we have known it up to the time of the 'Grand Cross' in 1999, will no longer exist. Everything is now *speeding up* because we are in the process of entering into the fifth dimension and will begin to live within a whole new level of consciousness and being. Everyone will learn to integrate more of the properties of the higher dimensional bodies as we enter into and begin to live more within the fifth dimension. At this level of consciousness we can begin to *master* the elements and therefore embody more of the *powers of alchemy.* This will then enable us to evolve with the planet, during its rapid but gentle evolutionary changes over the next 1,000 years.

During this period of time the Earth and humanity will evolve from the fifth dimension and also be able to co-exist more within the sixth and seventh dimensions. Remember that our concept of time will be continually altering and changing throughout this process as the boundaries of space and time that have sustained our body and consciousness within a third dimensional hologram and its elemental compositions and properties, are beginning to break down and disperse.

We are truly being reborn into the light. We can begin to live within higher levels of frequencies and consciousness, and therefore struggle less with our *physical transference process,* as we co-exist more within the ever-increasing, inter-changeable realities. This will be a similar level of consciousness to the quasi-dimensional existence of the Lemurians who had the ability and consciousness to live within different altered states within several levels of time and space.

Over the next 1,000 years everybody will therefore complete a cycle of 'third dimensional re-incarnation', as they slowly *resurrect* and *ascend* through and into the Christbody and Consciousness. The Christbody sustains the elements of the new anatomy and lightbody system so we can become more conscious of the parallel levels of existence experienced when co-existing *within the four planes of transformation.*

RETURNING TO A TIME LIKE LEMURIA AND ATLANTIS

Over the next 1,000 years we will be returning to a time similar to when Atlantis existed sometime between 1,000,000-10,000 BC. Our technology and resources as well as consciousness and lifestyle will change radically as the Earth and global consciousness make a progressive shift in their evolutionary process. We are therefore re-establishing aspects of ourselves from when we were evolving and 'existing within matter', at different times of Lemuria and Atlantis.

When we can integrate, manipulate and co-create the right proportion of elements, properties and minerals within our body, we can then co-exist more easily within the *four planes of transformation.* We will able to sustain a more perfected level of existence by *transferring our* body and consciousness at will so we can maintain control of our body, life force and consciousness.

When we can *master* creating *alchemical transference* shifts in the elemental compositions in the mass of the physical body while sustaining consciousness, we are beginning to live more within a concept of linear time and a more seventh dimensional reality. We can then sustain more of our chosen level of existence and reality at any given time.

This process will take aeons of time to master - from 3013. Remember that time will not be as relative at that point and global consciousness will be at a much higher level. Humanity will be learning to understand and create the *powers of alchemy* itself. At this level of Mastership we have begun to hold the elusive 'Holy Grail'.

THE TRUE TEACHINGS OF CHRISTIANITY

Jesus, through his own *salvation/ascension process,* established *the true teachings of Christianity.* He taught how to obtain the innate powers of self-healing, mastery and ascension *while in a state of incarnation*. *'Salvation'* therefore releases us from the suffering of ongoing mortality, the death/rebirth process of continual reincarnation created by the imperfection the DNA and consequently the etheric and physical body.

Jesus mastered these magical and Divine powers of Nature for healing, ascension, manifestation and 'Mastership into a state of illumination and light'. However, the churches manipulated this ancient, magical and Divine principle and teaching by distorting the true, esoteric, alchemical knowledge, ritual powers and teachings of the Christ.

THE 'SECOND COMING' AND THE CHRIST LIGHT

Christians, who have considered themselves the 'Chosen Ones', have been preparing themselves for the *'Second Coming'* for the past 2000 years. The astrological 'Grand Cross Alignment', August 1999 energetically activated and vibrationally registered the time of the *'Second Coming'* and *mass ascension* onto Earth and into the etheric/physical bodies of all humanity. It began the elimination of reincarnation by activating the embodiment of the lightbody /ascension process.

The Church defines 'Christians' as those who are christened by and attend the church. However, the true essence of the term 'Christianity' refers to those who have 'awakened' by anchoring in the foundations of their lightbody through which they can obtain the internal resources and know-how to ascend through and by the Light of Christ.

> *Anchoring the lightbody is an aspect of the resurrection process, which can only manifest through embodying different elements and frequencies of light.*

CHRISTENED MASTERS

Christ and his teachings have been preparing humanity to shift into the next dimension for 2000 years - from the time of his birth until the Millennium. Now is the time of the spiritual 'awakening' when every *body* will *begin* a Divine and vital ascension process.

The Celestial Christ is now revealing the true teachings of alchemy and Nature to the first wave of *Lightworkers* or initial channellers who will awaken during this crucial time of transition and transference, from 1999 – 2012.

They will become the crusaders of the Christ. They will be the initial *masters* who will personally anchor more of the new anatomy and lightbody system and therefore shift into a higher state of frequency and consciousness before the rest of humanity. By doing so they will anchor 'Christ light' not only into their body and consciousness but also onto the planet. They will ascend at a more rapid rate and therefore support the rest of humanity to also heal and ascend through the Earth changes.

The Christened Masters will not only channel through the necessary energies, procedures and information to support humanity and the planet during this vital time of transition from 1999 to 2012, but will also provide the *foundations* so all who incarnate to complete a cycle of third dimensional incarnation and resurrection, will also be able to eventually awaken and ascend.

REVIEW

The period after 2012 will not be as difficult as the transition of 1999-2012. By the end of the transition, a lot of the physical, political and spiritual unrest will have found some lasting resolution and the world and global consciousness will have progressed to a higher level.

By 2012 specific people on the planet will have created the essential foundations to support a new, more spiritual level of existence on Earth and the ongoing shifts within global consciousness, which will gently and progressively come about over the next 1,000 years.

The Christ will be able to complete a process of global salvation and resurrection, as 'energy' is the source through which all will evolve, heal and ascend. The power will be taken away from the man-made institutions and given to the initiates serving humanity. The true essence of Christianity is not to be established through the Church but by the alchemical forces of Nature. Those who have been *universally* initiated to become the *masters* within humanity will support the 'Celestial Christ's' global ascension process. Jesus referred to these key channellers and healers as the 'Christened Ones.'

The 'Christened Ones' will continue to filter through new information and support during this time. They are the 'Christ channellers' of the future who will heal sickness and resolve fears. The healers themselves will channel through the necessary healing technology and energies of the Christ to continually provide the resources to clear the manifestation of ongoing lightbody symptoms. 'Grid channellers' will also heal the planet.

The Power in Heaven will be transferred to Earth through the anchoring of more light within the body and consciousness, and all will eventually *master* in their healing and ascension process. Through the electromagnetic changes now occurring within the etheric heart of humanity, the lightbody can begin to manifest and begin *a self-mastery process.*

The masters will slowly replace those in power and position in the Church and economic system as it naturally begins to break down. The hierarchical systems of the many Christian religions on the planet will no longer hold a space for humanity in the old way.

However, everyone will *eventually* become naturally 'christened' through the *Grand Cross Alignment* and the corresponding *Earth and cosmic changes*, which are creating the resurrection of humanity.

The ascension process into a higher state of existence in the next dimension and beyond has begun. The Christ will bring in a *new way* for humanity to ascend via the unification of all Christian teachings, the Christ channellers, healers and grid workers, and the *Earth and cosmic changes* initiated within our Universe at the time of the astrological *Grand Cross Activation, 1999*.

> **"Blessed is he that readeth and they that hear the words of this prophecy, and keep those things which are written therein; for the time is at hand."**
>
> *Revelation of John the Divine 1:3*

IMPORTANT: *Completion Ritual*

*Before you stop reading this chapter, run your finger from **right to left** across the sacred language below. This procedure will assist you to finalise the energies from this chapter.*

Your action, intent and the sacred vibration of this powerful language, will greatly assist you to fully integrate the information you have just read.

THE 7ᵀᴴ GOLDEN AGE MYSTERY SCHOOL

Sacred Mystery School Teachings for the Ascending Masters

Commencing in 2006

Alexis Cartwright has been initiated by the Celestial Christ to create the 7ᵗʰ Golden Age Mystery School on Earth. This is the 7ᵗʰ Mystery School to be established on EARTH, and she has channelled its teachings through the *Prism of Lyra*.

This school is a doorway through which you can take your next step into the celestial learning and teachings of the Thoth Mystery School. These teachings, which have been re-channelled in purified form, enable the Mystery School Initiates to live within the higher dimensions on Earth before the rest of evolving humanity.

Training will take place over a period of three years. It will be taught during a 2-4 week live-in retreat, held in different locations around the world.

To enrol in the Mystery School you must have first completed all levels of the Transference Healing Training.

All school teachings are channelled sacred teachings of the Celestial Christ, overseen by Melchizedek.

To learn about the course outlines, review costs and book a place visit the Transference Healing website.

www.TRANSFERENCEHEALING.com

IMPORTANT: *Commencement Ritual*

*Before reading chapter 8, run your finger from **left to right** across the sacred language below.*

Your action, intent and the sacred vibration of this powerful language, will ensure that you are fully open to receiving and integrating the information within.

These are the three symbols of the Green Ray, used in Transference Healing (Swastika, Om and Cross) for the healing and opening of the heart chakra.

When worked with, they create a healing and enlightenment process. The *Swastika* 'faces clockwise' and is an ancient Sanskrit symbol for the heart, the endless wheel from which stems all life. The *Om* is an ancient Hindu symbol, it creates and generates the power of being in a state of perfection and oneness with the God/Goddess and finally, the *Balanced Cross*, gathers and unites universal energies into a state of perfect balance within. This creates wellness and holistic oneness with the universe.

The combination of these symbols, when initiated within the heart chakra, will unlock the purest energies from the heart and allow it to spiral out into your aura field creating the vibration of love and abundance. They support you in obtaining the ability to demonstrate your divinity.

THE PRAYER OF THE NEW MILLENIUM

CHAPTER OVERVIEW

This chapter reminds us that:

♦ During the current transition everyone is being energetically impacted on a personal level. The heart chakra is re-templating, healing and opening. We are feeling pushed to understand our deepest emotions, while any illusion held within on any level is rapidly breaking down.

♦ The changes we are experiencing within our body, reality and on a global scale, can make us feel overwhelmed. At these times remember that there is always a blessing to come from the darkest and most fearful of times in our lives. It is also very comforting to know that we all have within us the innate resources to obtain inner strength, wellness and knowing.

♦ The self-healing procedures in this book are empowering. They give us practical tools to clear blockages, imbalances and lightbody symptoms as well as enabling us to clear the emotional body and open the heart chakra to activate new levels of enlightenment.

♦ Opening the heart chakra is the key to creating 'Divine healing and enlightenment' and it also supports anchoring the lightbody, which is vital for transformation and ascension.

♦ We are also given a channelled inspirational and spiritual prayer for healing and opening the heart. The 'Prayer of the New Millennium' has come through to support humanity to heal and ascend at this time.

♦

MESSAGE TO THE PEOPLE

During this time of transition from 1999 – 2012, everyone is being energetically impacted on a personal level to open the deeper chambers of the heart chakra. The heart chakra is re-templating, healing and opening more because of the energetic changes occurring on our planet at this time. Therefore humanity is feeling pushed to get in touch with and understand the depth of their emotions. Illusion held within the heart, ego and mind is rapidly breaking down at this time.

At times some are feeling overwhelmed because of the changes that they are feeling or experiencing in their own body and reality, but also because of the changes that are also occurring within the planet on a global level. However, there is always a light to be obtained within the darkest and most fearful times in our lives and it is comforting to know that we all sustain the innate resources within, to obtain inner strength, wellness and knowing.

The self- healing procedures in this book give us practical tools that enable us to clear energy blockages or imbalances so that we can elevate lightbody symptoms and at the same time clear and heal the emotional body to create a clearer sense of *perception* and *understanding*. We are thereby opening and healing the heart chakra on a deeper level to activate new levels of *enlightenment* within the body and consciousness.

THE INNER CHAMBERS OF THE HEART

Activating the inner chambers of the heart chakra is the key to creating a 'Divine healing and enlightenment' response and also supports the anchoring of the lightbody, which is the vital key for creating a 'self-transformation and ascension process'.

This can all be supported through the technology and resources created by the *electromagnetic field* of the inner chambers of the physical heart and also its chakra. (This is explained further in chapter 13). The more we clear our emotions, the deeper we reach into the inner self and begin to heal *core* wounding from within the heart. On a parallel level, the more we open the inner chambers of the heart chakra, the more our self-healing powers; enlightenment and ascension process are supported. As we master the above, we also awaken a new level of consciousness *within the heart chakra* - **Christ Consciousness**.

THE PRAYER OF THE NEW MILLENNIUM

The following inspirational and spiritual prayer was guided to be channelled through, to support humanity at this time. It is a prayer of healing, opening the heart and thereby clearing the emotions and purifying the vibrational levels of the body.

I was intuitively told at the time that the prayer came through, that the New Testament 'Lord's Prayer' was anchored through to help humanity heal, open the heart chakra, and *connect* to the Higher

Self. The 'Prayer of the New Millennium' has come through to also support humanity, in a *new way.*

It is here to support humanity *to heal and ascend* at this time. It opens our heart chakra to enable us to *anchor and embody* our Higher Self and our new lightbody system. It also supports us to master our own healing and ascension process during this time of global change.

The new prayer works on a parallel level to the Lord's Prayer and was channelled through for the New Millennium. It encourages and energetically supports us to release deep inner fears, live in truth and feel more unconditional love from a heart-based perspective, to enable faith to manifest through more into our consciousness.

CLEARING AND PURIFICATION

The prayer encourages and enables us to look into our heart, feel our heart based emotions and follow through with what our heart tells us is 'true'. It supports and encourages us to take the necessary steps to create personal change, self-healing, transformation and the next step in our personal/spiritual growth process.

Magical powers and properties lie within each word and sound, clearing the *emotional body* and also any imbalances sustained within the energetic and electromagnetic fields of the etheric/ physical body. It is so important to respond more positively to the Earth and cosmic changes at this time - this prayer enables us to 'clear in the moment.'

It supports us to master on a daily level by enabling us to clear feelings of confusion so we can make clear decisions, overcome personal struggle and release painful feelings which manifest as lightbody symptoms. It also supports and encourages us to let go of old patterning around the' need to control' thereby creating surrender, faith and trust in the Universe and a deep sense of purification on all levels within the body and consciousness.

As we say the Prayer it will trigger an energetic healing response from the heart chakra to open and activate a healing process within the inner-heart. This will then create an energetic healing response throughout the cellular levels of the body, enabling the body and consciousness to ascend into a higher state of being.

> **If we follow our heart with pure intent, the Universe will respond accordingly.**

The 'Prayer of the New Millennium' is available for purchase as an A4 poster. Go to page 389 for more details.

THE PRAYER OF THE NEW MILLENNIUM

OUR FATHER/MOTHER IN HEAVEN AND EARTH

Give me the power of feeling. Give me the strength to counteract attack with love. My force is pure. Allow me to release old emotions. Give me joy. Release pressure. Give me strength. Release all restrictions to create positive action and outcome. Release uncertainty. Create courage.

Harmonise and allow transformation of Divine Will, so that my gifts and talents will come through. Revitalise and re-energise me. Release the fear of pain for others. Release my feelings of isolation and loneliness. Create compassion and sensitivity. Help me respond to life with a feeling of faith and trust.

Release all judgement to allow rejuvenation. Allow opportunities to flourish and flow. Allow fear of direction to go. Release a shattered feeling. Allow me to find inner peace. My inner voice will know and challenges will create new endeavours. Energy will come and tiredness will go.

I will understand all tests of spirituality allow transformation and become whole. I will remain grounded through the changes. Fear will be released and I will be filled with energy as I bring in Divine Blue and release all pain. I have psychic talents and no suppression. I feel freedom of feeling. I feel no pain or isolation, only oneness and unconditional love for all.

Let my creative energies flow. I bring through Divine Will. I will become the Philosopher, Do-er, Healer, the Magician and the Master of Self. I respond to my higher and future self.
I now transcend.
I see and become clear.
I am The Light

Kodoish, Kodoish, Kodoish Adonai
Tsebayoth/Sabayoth

IMPORTANT: Completion Ritual

*Before you stop reading this chapter, run your finger from **right to left** across the sacred language below. This procedure will assist you to finalise the energies from this chapter.*

Your action, intent and the sacred vibration of this powerful language, will greatly assist you to fully integrate the information you have just read.

IMPORTANT: Commencement Ritual

*Before reading chapter 9, run your finger from **left to right** across the sacred language below.*

Your action, intent and the sacred vibration of this powerful language, will ensure that you are fully open to receiving and integrating the information within.

| CHIRON | NESSUS | CHARIKLO | PHOLUS | ASBOLUS | DAMOCLES |

There are at least 40 Centaurian bodies that we know exist at this time within our solar system. Above are the symbols of the centaurs that are named and used by astrologers today, they include: Chiron, Nessus, Pylenor, Chariklo, Pholus, Asbolus and Damocles. By connecting to these symbols you are integrating the energetic qualities that these celestial bodies create and resonate as they transit the different planets and astrological house of your natal chart and orbit within our solar system.

Symbol for Pholus (c) 1994 Zane B Stein

CHIRON: THE PLANET AND MYTHOLOGY

By Astrologer Lucy Lyne

ABOUT THE AUTHOR OF THIS CHAPTER - LUCY LYNE

Lucy is a highly respected professional Astrologer, Spiritual Counsellor, Healer and Teacher. She is the Principal of the "Chiron College of Astrology and Healing" based in Brisbane, Australia.

Lucy was originally trained as a nurse. Her spiritual journey started to unfold in 1984 when she began studying Astrology. Her learning did not cease upon completion of her studies. In fact her path of growth since then has led her to learn about the many healing properties of crystals along with the Tarot, Reiki, Crystal Toning, Vibrational Healing including Transference Healing and vibrational essences. Throughout her journey Lucy has continued to expand and improve her knowledge and understanding of Astrology. Her particular passion is centred upon the placement of the planet Chiron in her clients' charts and the effects of the Soul wounding this carries; this is a well-refined and profound aspect of her astrology readings. Lucy is now considered a leading expert on the subject of Chiron and its effects on the individual.

Lucy met Alexis Cartwright in 1995. As a result of their mutual respect and shared interest in Chiron, Alexis invited Lucy to write a chapter in her first book "Doorways" entitled "Chiron: The Planet and Mythology". As a result of positive feedback in relation to this chapter in the first book, Alexis has asked Lucy to provide an even more detailed chapter for this her second book.

Lucy has a strong connection with Transference Healing. In 2000 she was strongly guided to learn Transference Healing with Alexis. She completed her training and became one of her first ever graduates. Transference Healing integrated in one modality all the aspects of healing that Lucy was so passionate about. Lucy is now accredited as both a Practitioner and Teacher of Transference Healing, she is also a member of the Transference Healing Team presenting and running workshops at the International Transference Healing Conferences.

Lucy can be contacted at astro@transferencehealing.com

CHAPTER OVERVIEW

In this chapter you will discover that:

- Chiron is a 'Centaur' that was discovered in 1977. It is known as the 'Wounded Healer' and its role is to teach us to face our emotional wounds and heal ourselves.

- Chiron is associated with healing (particularly vibrational), higher consciousness, sexual discrimination, philosophy and teaching (particularly relating to separation, reincarnation, karma and metaphysics), as well as, ecology and healing the planet.

- Since Chiron's discovery there has been a resurgence of alternative therapies for healing and a significant shift in our attitude towards death and the environment.

- There is a gift in every wound. The path to true healing and the gift the wound contains lies through the wound not around it.

- As Chiron *moves around our astrological chart*, connecting with our planets, it strips down our defences so that true healing can occur. Chiron is the emotional can-opener of the universe, opening deep wounds and getting to the core of the issue so that true healing can take place. It teaches us to accept personal responsibility for our own lives and connect to our higher mind.

- The healing journey back to love involves a re-balancing of our perceptions about a wound and learning to love everything about ourselves, including our wounds. It is a journey of growth and evolution towards wholeness and love back to our Divine origin to be LOVE and to be connected to God within ourselves.

- The placement of Chiron in our *natal astrology chart* by sign, house and its aspects of connection to other planets is extremely significant and indicates our *inner-wounds and blockages*. The *'sign'* in which Chiron is located in our chart indicates where the wounding has occurred, the *'house'* tells of the area it will manifest into our life and where healing needs to take place for us to be on our Souls journey and the *'aspects'* further define issues associated with the wounding.

- Chiron has a 50-year cycle and will transit a natal chart four significant times in this cycle. The first trigger occurs between four and 23 years of age and is a time of realising our separateness from spirit. The second is a critical time when circumstances can push us in a different direction in life and we can glimpse our true path. The third is a painful time of self-discovery when blockages to our emotions become evident and wounds come to the surface for healing. The fourth occurs at age 50 when Chiron returns to the sign and place it was at your birth. It is a time to questions 'what am I going to do with the rest of my life".

- Chiron will either be healing and give insights or be felt as additional wounding resulting in further defending and blocking. The degree of readiness to confront out issues will determine the actual healing that takes place.

- The wound is only our perception and can become our greatest gift once we have used the key that Chiron offers to unlock the emotions and allow true healing to occur.

◆

CHIRON 'THE WOUNDED HEALER'

hiron was discovered in 1977 by a Californian astronomer called Charles Kowal. Since its discovery there has been much debate as to what Chiron actually is - a planet, an asteroid or a planetoid - but it has now been officially named as a new type of Heavenly body called a 'Centaur'.

DIAGRAM 8.1
The Centaur Chiron

Copyright 2005 Alexis Cartwright, Keeper of the Crystals Pty Ltd

Several centaurs have since been discovered. They belong to the Kyper Belt outside of our solar system. Because of their elliptical orbit they enter the orbit of our outer planets. Chiron's orbit is between Saturn (the conservative, conformist planet) and Uranus (the radical, revolutionary planet). Chiron is seen as a 'bridge' between the inner and more distant outer planets of our solar system.

Chiron is known as the **'Wounded Healer'**, whose role is to teach us to face our *emotional wounds* and heal ourselves. The knowledge of how to heal can then be passed on to others, to aid in their healing.

The symbol for Chiron is a **key,** a key to unlock the door to the psyche. Once our wounds are healed the door can be locked behind us. We are then able to move forward in our life, healed and with a greater understanding and compassion for others. To truly understand another's pain, we need to have experienced wounding and pain ourselves.

> **Through our own healing, true compassion for another person's suffering can develop.**

CHIROΠ IS SAID TO RULE OR BE ASSOCIATED WITH:

- Healing - particularly vibrational healing using the hands and crystals.

- Higher consciousness - the ability to alter and heal the physical body through the Mind and Spirit.

- Sexual discrimination - the ability to use willpower to rise above the basic animal instincts to a higher level of oneness and love.

- Philosophy and teaching about death, karma and rebirth - the ability to develop a more positive attitude about loss and separation and to face our inevitable death, without fear.

- Ecology and healing our planet.

Since Chiron was discovered in 1977 there has been a remarkable resurgence in the use of alternative therapies for healing. Our attitude to death and the environment has also dramatically altered.

- 'Chiron' means hand and **'healing with the hands'**. Techniques such as Reiki, Transference Healing, Chiropractic, Chironics and 'Laying on of Hands' have become more widely accepted since Chiron's discovery.

- **Vibrational essences and the use of crystals** are more widely acknowledged for their healing potential.

- The use of the **'mind'** in overcoming illness through visualisation, positive affirmation and meditation has also become more accepted.

- AIDS first surfaced in 1977 in Africa and has since extended throughout the world so that indiscriminate sexual activity is a major concern and **sexual discrimination** has become more important to us all.

- Also in 1977 Dr. Elizabeth Kubler-Ross established her counselling clinic for the terminally ill. **Death** is now a subject that is more openly discussed and less feared. In fact people who had never heard of karma and past lives are becoming very interested in these subjects.

- **Ecological and environmental issues.** Healing the Earth and accepting responsibility for pollution on a personal and global level are becoming a priority for individuals as well as governments.

> **There is an ancient North American prophecy that says: "When the healing planet is discovered in the sky then the sacred warrior teachings will return to Earth".**

It is now time to listen and act on the information that Chiron brings, to help us heal our wounds on a personal level and those of the Earth on a global level. It is time to reconnect to the God within and Christ Consciousness.

THE MYTHOLOGY OF CHIRON

When planets or other Heavenly bodies have been discovered and named by astronomers, it is very interesting how the mythology surrounding the choice of name fits the vibrational energy that is associated with that Heavenly body. The myth of Chiron is one such amazing example.

In Greek mythology, Chiron was the offspring of Saturn, God of Agriculture and Philyra the Nymph. He was born as a **Centaur** (half-man, half-horse) symbolising the dichotomy between the lower animal nature and the higher human nature. His appearance so disgusted his mother she rejected him at birth and abandoned him. This was the first and deepest **wound** Chiron experienced. Chiron never knew who his real father was, this created **another** deep **wounding.** He was fostered and raised by Apollo, the god of the Sun, music, prophecy and healing.

Chiron was accidentally wounded in his leg. The wound was incurable and having the immortality of the gods he was doomed to suffer forever. This wound became a constant reminder to him of the suffering that he and others endured. Chiron spent his life searching for a cure and learning about the various healing arts. During his constant search for a cure for his own wound, he became a very knowledgeable healer, full of wisdom and compassion, with the ability to help others.

Chiron had tremendous intuitive wisdom and spoke the truth with honesty and love, while assisting in teaching others to also develop their higher minds. He passed his knowledge of the healing arts onto others so they could heal themselves and become self-sufficient and whole. However, through all of this he remained unable to heal himself - he carried the burden of his incurable wound, hence his name the 'wounded healer'.

Eventually, Chiron met Prometheus, who was being punished for stealing fire from the gods and giving it to humanity as a gift. He asked Zeus to allow him to trade his immortality and suffering by changing places with Prometheus. Zeus agreed and Chiron gave up his immortality and faced his own death thus being released from his suffering.

Chiron's journey after death took him beyond the perceived limitations of life to find the answer to his wounding. By facing death and the fear surrounding it he learned that death was not the end but a new beginning, a change or transference of energy. Chiron was finally honoured by the gods and reincarnated into a Heavenly body between Saturn and Uranus. His 'wounding' had been released.

This is the ultimate journey of growth and healing for all of us, a spiritual journey which allows us to reconnect to God, to connect to the light, to connect to the *LOVE* within ourselves.

THE WOUND

> **Chiron says, "There is a gift in every wound. The path of true healing and the gift the wound contains lies *through the wound not around it*".**

A **wounding** by a person, situation or circumstance and the emotions associated with it can be avoided, or so we think, by controlling situations in our life. We develop structures, defences and behaviours that we think protect us from further wounding, but in fact we tend to lock love out of our life and often create dis-ease as a result.

Chiron, *astrologically in our natal chart and by transit,* has enlightened messages for each of us about healing, the higher mind, sexuality and death. Chiron's keywords are '**wounding, healing and reconstruction**'.

- Chiron, as it moves around our astrological chart, connecting with our planets, strips down our defences so that **true healing** can occur.

- Chiron is the emotional can-opener of the universe, opening deep wounds and getting to the core of the issue so that true healing can take place.

- Chiron teaches us to accept personal responsibility for our own lives and connect to our higher mind.

- Chiron is the teacher and philosopher teaching about separation, sexual discrimination, death, near death experiences, karma past lives and the metaphysical.

THE HEALING JOURNEY BACK TO LOVE

This journey involves the process of re-balancing our perceptions and learning to love everything about ourselves, including our wounds. It is one of growth and evolution towards wholeness and love back to our Divine origin to be *LOVE* and to be connected to God within ourselves.

What we call a 'wound' in our lives is only our perception of the situation where we feel others have caused us emotional pain. In reality this is a judgment on our part, a judgment perceiving the situation as a wrong doing or imbalance of energy. Often part of this judgment is based on previous experiences and the pain we still carry from an earlier wounding.

When making a judgment about an event, circumstance or person, the lower mind, connecting with the *lower three chakras* say 'more suffering than happiness, more wrong than right and more heartache than joy'. By holding onto the 'wound' and the associated painful emotions we turn away from the love and light within, the God within, thus blocking our growth and evolution. This can then create dis-ease and ill health in our physical body.

The *higher mind*, connecting with the *upper chakras*, holds the other side of the perception, but this is hidden within us like a secret waiting to be revealed. Chiron is the key to unlock this hidden, repressed perception of what really took place at the time of the wounding and reveals the gift the wounding contains. It can bring light to the secret and begin the healing of the 'wound'. It offers us the opportunity to see all that we truly are with loving compassion and to grow and evolve by connecting to the God within.

When we can release all judgments, grudges and emotional pain and move beyond holding onto past trauma and wanting revenge, then and only then is true healing able to take place. We are able to reconnect our head to our heart and allow love and light to enter our being. We are able to experience true peace with life and the universe, to be one with God.

ASTROLOGY CHARTS

We can obtain information as to the nature of our wounds by having our natal astrology chart read by a professional astrologer. This gives us a greater understanding of how we can work through the Wound to achieve healing and the gift contained within the wound. The most important thing Chiron indicates in our astrological chart is our opportunity to Heal, to **'LET GO AND LET GOD'**.

In our **natal astrology chart** the placement of Chiron by sign, house and its aspects or connection to other planets is extremely significant as it indicates our inner wounds and blockages.

- **The sign** that Chiron is in indicates **where** wounding has occurred.

- **The house** that Chiron is in tells the **area** it will manifest in our life and where healing needs to take place for us to be on our Soul's journey.

- **The aspects** or the **effect** Chiron has on other planets in our chart further defines issues associated with the wounding and indicate what areas need to be reconnected for healing.

> **When Chiron, in our natal chart, is strongly connected by challenging aspects to our personal planets, the heart chakra is often severely blocked.**

Chiron's placement (by sign, house and aspect) shows *where* we are cut off physically, emotionally mentally or spiritually due to painful or traumatic experiences and indicates our particular and unique path of service. The degree to which we are on our true path depends on how we have healed our wounds and raised our level of consciousness.

Remember the '*wound*' is only our perception. It can become our greatest gift once we have used the key that Chiron offers to unlock the emotions and allow true healing to occur, thereby awakening our connection to God and the Christ Consciousness.

TRANSITS

In our *natal chart* the planets have a fixed position determined by the date, time and place of our birth. However, all planets continually move through the various signs of the zodiac. Transits occur when these moving planets connect to the natal planets. When the natal planets are stimulated or triggered, the lessons they contain can then be learned, the potentials can be developed and growth occurs. Chiron takes approximately 50 years to make a complete transit or cycle of the natal chart to return to its exact placement at the time of our birth.

Chiron's orbit is between Saturn (28-year cycle) and Uranus (84-year cycle) and it is seen as *'The Rainbow Bridge'* between the inner, personal planets and the outer, impersonal planets. As we take responsibility for our own healing and change our perceptions of past wounds, we cross the bridge to reunite with the love within and become the exceptional individual we were meant to be.

Saturn by transit says 'stop blaming others and outside circumstances for your wounds, take responsibility for the choices you have made in your life'.

Chiron by transit offers us the key to heal and resolve issues regarding the perceptions of our wounds, to LOVE everything about ourselves; to love our life and connect to the God within.

Uranus by transit says 'use detachment and be unique, stand up for what you truly believe in. Be the unique and special individual you truly are'.

TRANSITS BY CHIRON

Chiron itself is one of these moving planets and therefore will connect with each of the planets in the natal chart during its 50 year cycle. Transits by Chiron indicate significant times in our life when *emotional* wounds can occur and also times when *past* wounds will come to the surface out of the subconscious, hidden or repressed area of the mind, to be dealt with. At times, if or when our perception of the past pain and wounding alters and we can see the gift contained in the 'wound', true healing can take place.

Chiron, as it moves around the chart in transit, brings light to the unresolved and un-healed issues of various aspects of our life. It gives us the opportunity to heal the area indicated by the planet and house involved.

MAJOR TRANSITS TO CHIRON

There are four significant times that Chiron will trigger itself in its 50 year cycle. The *house area* of the natal chart that Chiron is transiting at these times is very significant. An astrology reading can pin point these times and areas, show the healing potential and how to obtain the *'gift within the wound'*.

The **first** trigger is a time of realising we are Earth bound and separated from spirit; that we are physical beings. This has a vastly different effect depending on how old we are when it occurs. The time is not the same for everyone and can occur any time between the ages of four and 23.

The **second** is a critical time when circumstances can push us in a different direction, a time when our life's purpose can become evident, when we can get a glimpse of our true path in life.

The **third** is a painful time of self-discovery when blockages to our emotions become evident and wounds come to the surface for healing.

The **fourth** trigger occurs at age 50 when Chiron returns to the sign and place where it was when we were born. It is a time to question 'What am I going to do with the rest of my life?', 'What are my past achievements and what of the future?'

The *initial* Chiron wounding is like a thorn piercing us. We remove the thorn and believe that healing can now occur but a small piece of the thorn is left embedded. The wound may appear to heal, only to fester again at a later time. It is not until the wound is painfully lanced and the last fragment of the thorn or original wounding is removed once and for all, that true healing can take place.

This analogy depicts how a Chiron transit works in astrology, digging deep into the emotional pain of the wound so it can be healed from the base/core issue. As a result, the trauma or wound does not continue to infect future situations and cloud our judgment or perception about events in our life.

THE INTERPRETATION OF CHIRON BY ASTROLOGICAL SIGN

Chiron is the teacher and philosopher, teaching about sexual discrimination, separation, death, karma and the metaphysical. Chiron is the healer showing us the spiritual wounding we have come to heal and in return the gift we have to offer.

The **astrological sign** that Chiron is in at the time of our birth indicates what the wounding is that we carry with us and also our gift.

The **sign** our Chiron is in can be looked up in the chart provided below. It is usually different to your Sun or natal sign. This is only a quick reference however, and a full astrological reading of your birth chart will give you a more complete picture of the wounding, showing the astrological house area or *where* Chiron falls and the connection or aspects it makes to other personal planets.

THE INTERPRETATION OF CHIRON BY ASTROLOGICAL SIGN - A GUIDE TO YOUR CHIRON SIGN

These dates are for GMT London and are a quick guide only, for a full and accurate interpretation of your Chiron, a natal astrology chart is recommended.

DATE OF BIRTH	CHIRON SIGN
13/01/1905 to 19/03/1910	Aquarius
20/03/1910 to 28/08/1910	Pisces
29/08/1910 to 14/01/1911	Aquarius
15/01/1911 to 30/03/1918	Pisces
31/03/1918 to 22/10/1918	Aries
23/10/1918 to 28/01/1919	Pisces
29/01/1919 to 24/05/1926	Aries
25/05/1926 to 19/10/1926	Taurus
20/10/1926 to 24/03/1927	Aries
25/03/1927 to 06/06/1933	Taurus
07/06/1933 to 21/12/1933	Gemini
22/12/1933 to 22/03/1934	Taurus
23/03/1934 to 27/08/1937	Gemini
28/08/1937 to 22/11/1937	Cancer
23/11/1937 to 27/05/1938	Gemini
28/05/1938 to 29/09/1940	Cancer

DATE OF BIRTH	CHIRON SIGN
30/09/1940 to 26/12/1940	Leo
27/12/1940 to 16/06/1941	Cancer
17/06/1941 to 26/07/1943	Leo
27/07/1943 to 17/11/1944	Virgo
18/11/1944 to 23/03/1945	Libra
24/03/1945 to 22/07/1945	Virgo
23/07/1945 to 09/11/1946	Libra
10/11/1946 to 28/11/1948	Scorpio
29/11/1948 to 08/02/1951	Sagittarius
09/02/1951 to 17/06/1951	Capricorn
18/06/1951 to 08/11/1951	Sagittarius
09/11/1951 to 27/01/1955	Capricorn
28/01/1955 to 26/03/1960	Aquarius
27/03/1960 to 18/08/1960	Pisces
19/08/1960 to 20/01/1961	Aquarius
21/01/1961 to 31/03/1968	Pisces
04/04/1968 to 18/10/1968	Aries
19/10/1968 to 29/01/1969	Pisces
30/01/1969 to 27/05/1976	Aries
28/05/1976 to 13/10/1976	Taurus
14/10/1976 to 28/03/1977	Aries
29/03/1977 to 21/06/1983	Taurus
22/06/1983 to 28/11/1983	Gemini
29/11/1983 to 10/04/1984	Taurus
11/04/1984 to 20/06/1988	Gemini
21/06/1998 to 21/07/1991	Cancer

DATE OF BIRTH	CHIRON SIGN
22/07/1991 to 03/09/1993	Leo
04/09/1993 to 09/09/1995	Virgo
10/09/1995 to 29/12/1996	Libra
30/12/1996 to 04/04/1997	Scorpio
05/04/1997 to 02/09/1997	Libra
09/09/1997 to 07/01/1999	Scorpio
08/01/1999 to 01/06/1999	Sagittarius
02/06/1999 to 21/09/1999	Scorpio
22/09/1999 to 11/12/2001	Sagittarius
12/12/2001 to 21/02/2005	Capricorn
22/02/2005 to 01/08/2005	Aquarius
02/08/2005 to 05/12/2005	Capricorn
06/12/2005 to 19/04/2010	Aquarius
20/04/2010 to 20/07/2010	Pisces
21/07/2010 to 08/02/2011	Aquarius
09/02/2011 to 16/04/2018	Pisces
17/04/2018 to 25/09/2018	Aries
26/09/2018 to 17/02/2019	Pisces
18/02/2019 to 2020	Aries

ARIES

This **wound** is a deep fear of rejection. The 'I am' is wounded in childhood due to feeling unloved and unworthy. We tend to have great difficulty in asking others for help.

Healing takes place when the fear of rejection is faced and the door to self-love is unlocked when we are able to say 'I am worthy'.

The Gift becomes obvious: Self-worth and the ability to truly trust and help others through the flow of the healing energy of love.

TAURUS

This **wound** is a feeling of insecurity and lack of resources or abundance. Accruing material possessions and having strict values are seen as a way to gain security.

Healing takes place when our personal values can be defined outside of material possessions and security comes from connecting to the God within.

The gift is realised: Trusting and valuing self, with a knowing that all our needs will be met. A true knowing that life is abundant.

GEMINI

This **wound** is a disbelief in personal ideas and concepts and a feeling that we are not being heard or listened to. There is wounding in the area of communication, intelligence, and the thinking process.

Healing takes place when we trust and articulate our own ideas with conviction and also *verbally* express our feelings.

The gift becomes visible: The awareness of the power of **both** thought and word. A thirst for knowledge and sharing with others that comes from the heart.

CANCER

This **wound** is one of separation. We feel unloved or abandoned by our family. Combined with an immense compassion for humanity we have a great need to be needed by others.

Healing takes place once the emotional bonds and attitudes to family are reconciled within our heart.

The gift becomes obvious: The ability to help heal the family of mankind and assist others by giving them love without rescuing.

LEO

This **wound** is to the inner child and the ego. The ability to be spontaneous is damaged drama and ego issues abound in our life.

Healing takes place when we connect to our inner child and release the need for drama in our life

The gift becomes evident: Creativity and self-expression replace drama. Spontaneity and fun can abound in our life.

VIRGO

This **wound** is around the issue of control, either perfectionism or total lack of control, particularly in the area of health.

Healing takes place when we release the need to control and realise that how and what we think does affect our life

The gift can be used: The ability to see our work as healing therapy and be of service to others, passing on information and knowledge for others to use as they see fit.

LIBRA

This **wound** involves traumatic relationships in the early years. There is a craving for love and adoration despite the defences and walls we have been built up throughout our life. Crisis can occur in relationships.

Healing takes place when significant relationships are seen as mirrors for self-healing instead of the cause of our difficulties.

The gift is reflected: Understanding that we are whole and have the ability to be a mirror for others to help them heal relationship issues.

SCORPIO

This **wound** is very deep and it could indicate birth trauma, illness, loss of a parent and even death encountered at a very early age. Often abuse is an issue or struggles involving power, sex or money.

Healing takes place when we accept change and transformation as a part of life and use personal power in a positive way to benefit all.

The gift is very precious: Attaining a new attitude to sexuality, power, death and rebirth thus giving peace to our Soul.

SAGITTARIUS

This **wound** involves battles over religion, faith or spirituality. There is a feeling of being deceived, misled or conspired against by religion or God. Our parents may have disagreed over religion or we could become the victim of a false guru.

Healing takes place when we open our heart and connect to our Higher Self and the God within to find our own truth.

The gift becomes obvious: Joy in following our true path and using our great inner wisdom to benefit others.

CAPRICORN

This **wound** involves authority figures and a feeling of lack of acknowledgement or appreciation. It often relates to a wound involving the father or unreasonably high parental expectations. Our achievement may be thwarted.

Healing takes place when we recognise and acknowledge our own true value, thus accepting personal responsibility for our life

The gift can be used: Self-mastery and leadership skills become evident along with the ability to help others see their own true potential.

AQUARIUS

This **wound** is a fear of group contact and believing that our individuality will be swallowed up. There is a feeling of being different or even a burning need to be unique yet a yearning to fit in. Betrayal by the group can occur.

Healing takes place when we accept and love the individuality, differences and diversity of self and others.

The gift is obtained: The ability to detach yet not disconnect from those around us. To be able to freely share our unique gifts, creativity and visions.

PISCES

This **wound** is knowing the disconnection from God and feeling that the Universe has betrayed us. There is a feeling of having come for a higher purpose but not knowing how to achieve this. The intuition is highly developed and there is a tendency to be self sacrificing.

Healing takes place through a process of learning from many guides and teachers, without following one in particular, then accepting our inner wisdom or Divine guidance and reconnecting to 'God Consciousness'.

The Gift is to realise: The Universe can be full of 'love' and our gift can be used to benefit humanity by embracing the divinity of all life, becoming the teacher and mystic and assisting others to connect to the God within.

SUMMARY

Chiron as the emotional can-opener of the Universe helps us to open our deep hidden wounds so that true healing can take place. It unlocks the doors to the past to help us understand and heal old wounds. We can then get on with life without reacting emotionally from past traumas. It is the teacher and philosopher, teaching about separation, death, sexual discrimination, karma and the metaphysical.

Chiron can stop us in our tracks, teaching us to connect to our heart and listen to the 'silent voice' within. Chiron will either be healing and give insights or be felt as additional wounding resulting in further defending and blocking. The degree of readiness to confront our issues will determine the actual healing that takes place.

Chiron transits will open old wounds and encourage us to find the path to healing our wounds, to re-balancing and healing deeply from our core. They can be major turning points of emotional crisis that influence our life path and direction.

As Chiron transits our natal chart it will trigger each of our planets during its 50 year cycle, activating the **core wounding** issues of our lives. This offers a chance to radically alter old and painful patterns, to release the perceptions and make quantum leaps in healing the self.

> **A Chiron transit opens the heart chakra to connect the head with the heart.**

IMPORTANT: *Completion Ritual*

*Before you stop reading this chapter, run your finger from **right to left** across the sacred language below. This procedure will assist you to finalise the energies from this chapter.*

Your action, intent and the sacred vibration of this powerful language, will greatly assist you to fully integrate the information you have just read.

CHIRON   NESSUS   CHARIKLO   PHOLUS   ASBOLUS   DAMOCLES

IMPORTANT: Commencement Ritual

*Before reading chapter 10, run your finger from **left to right** across the sacred language below.*

Your action, intent and the sacred vibration of this powerful language, will ensure that you are fully open to receiving and integrating the information within.

Ogham served as an alphabet for one of the ancient Celtic languages. Its origin is uncertain - it may have been adapted from a sign language. Current understanding is that the names of the main twenty letters are also the names of 20 trees sacred to the Druids. A 15th century treatise on Ogham, The Book of Ballymote, confirms that Ogham was a secret ritualistic language.

Above is an "ogham line" showing all 25 "letters" of the Ogham Alphabet.

When integrating the properties of this ancient language you are connecting to the inner nature of the trees and also the inner realms of the Earth, thereby enhancing your ability to channel through the magical healing properties of the Trees and the Earth. By working with these symbols you are also supporting the awakening process of your third eye and a deeper level of your *psychic* abilities thereby enhancing your ability to master the prophetic powers of the Goddess.

RAVEN POWER, THE BLACK MADONNA AND BLACK RAY OF THE GODDESS

CHAPTER OVERVIEW

- *Raven Power* in Transference Healing symbolises the powers held by the ancient magicians and priestesses, who worked at mastering the powers of the *Black Madonna* (a lineage of *Goddess teachings* that support those accessing the powers hidden within the *Black Ray* and all elements sustained within *Nature* itself).

- The Black Ray has been misunderstood and mistakenly feared.

- *Ravens* symbolise those who choose to interpret, understand and master the mysteries - the mystical knowledge and transference powers of Nature, geometry and light specifically the Black Ray, to obtain the ultimate power of all ' Alchemy'. These people are servants of Divine purpose and impart a powerful, creative and directive force into the world.

- You can begin to master channelling the properties of the Black Ray through developing your personal and spiritual growth process. Opening the deeper chambers of the heart, purifying the ego, intent and the third eye, can do this.

- The raven is also the guardian of ceremonial magic, healing and transformation and is the symbol of the Black Ray.

- The Black Ray is the colour of a vibration that filters through from beyond the *Void*; providing the necessary geometric frequencies to create a healing response that enables matter to reform and shape. It is the opposite polarity to the White Ray. When the two rays are worked together, they create the Divine healing properties and power of the 'infinity' symbol (which is a symbol of purification and unification).

- *Harmony Alignment Point 16* is located in the third eye area. When it is energetically activated and healed dimensions of the lightbody begin to anchor. We then resonate encoded energies into the Universe communicating that we have reached a certain level of 'enlightenment'. As a result Sirian codes and keys then filter through into our DNA and etheric body creating a frequency shift within the body and third eye. This enables us to hold our light and become spiritually empowered. We become a Lightworker on Earth, able to hold our light through the darkest of times and the most difficult of initiations. We can intuitively see the reason behind the circumstances creating learning curves in our everyday life. We also obtain the natural ability to access the White and Black Rays through our consciousness, we can access the unknown and create powerful alchemical healing and transformation processes for others and ourselves. We being to obtain the power of the Black Madonna, becoming a magician and master of self.

◆

aven Power in Transference Healing, symbolises the powers held by the ancient magicians and priestesses. The magician/priestess worked at mastering the powers of the Black Madonna: which is a linage of Goddess teachings that supports one in accessing the magical, healing and transformative powers hidden within the Black Ray and all elements sustained within Nature itself.

Ravens symbolise those who choose to interpret and decipher the mysteries. They work towards understanding the mystical knowledge and transference powers of Nature, geometry and light specifically the **Black Ray**, to obtain the ultimate power of all: Alchemy.

Those who dedicate themselves to this level of Mastership, (raven power magic), work towards understanding the true essence of the Black Madonna teachings. They are enhancing their spiritual and psychic abilities so that they can come to understand the *mysteries* held within Nature and the Universe. They therefore become 'channellers' and by doing so obtain access to the magical healing powers of *Nature,* while living by the spiritual principles sustained by the *Universal Laws* that govern our universe.

They are the 'Redeemed'. As servants of Divine purpose they imparted a powerful, creative and directive force into the world. They are the truth seekers and usually go into realms of consciousness where others fear to tread. They recognise that there is a supreme science sustaining the knowledge and power of the *Goddess* within Nature itself and that these magical properties of the Goddess can be accessed at any time.

DIAGRAM 10.1
The Raven Card from the Transference: Animal Magic Deck

Raven

In the past, a veil of symbols and myths were employed to conceal the essential teachings of the Black Madonna. This 'veil' concealing the arcane (knowledge) existed to protect **wisdom.** However, the power and knowledge of the *mysteries* have universally infiltrated into the modern world via artists, scholars, astrologers, cosmologists and teachers of esoteric knowledge: the tarot, Kabala, sacred geometry etc. Those who work with these tools and mediums are working at channelling the powers and wisdom of the *Goddess* by understanding the inner technology and wisdom of the Black Madonna teachings.

RAVEN POWER

You can begin to master channelling the properties of the Black Ray through developing your personal and spiritual growth process. This can be done by opening the deeper chambers of the heart, purifying the ego, intent and third eye. Through this ray you will begin to filter through the *magical* properties that supersede and create all life within our Earth, Universe and dimension. Mastering the elements of the Black Ray when 'running' energy will therefore enable you to create a more profound or *magical* healing response or impact that is *divinely* orchestrated and can not be controlled or rationalised by the ego or consciousness mind.

The raven is the guardian of ceremonial magic, healing and transformation and is the symbol of the Black Ray. This ray has been channelled and anchored, as a fundamental property and vibration of Transference Healing. Transference Healing, not only works with the seven main rays (red through to violet) and also the White, Pink, Silver and Gold Rays, but most importantly the Black Ray; the ray that always seems to be overlooked because of general ignorance and fear.

This is what is so unique about the Transference Energy and its teachings, it gives us the opportunity to 'tap into' channel and work towards mastering the ability to access the sacred information and powers of the Black Ray, thereby reconnecting us once again to the hidden power and teachings of the Black Madonna.

PROPERTIES OF THE BLACK RAY

The Black Ray is the colour of a vibration that filters through from beyond the Void; thereby providing the necessary geometric frequencies to create a healing response that enables matter to reform and shape. It is the opposite polarity to the White Ray and when these two rays are accessed and worked together, they create the Divine healing properties and power of the **infinity** symbol. This is a symbol of purification and unification.

The infinity symbol reflects how the Black Ray weaves through the properties needed from the Void and while doing so transfers them into the pure healing properties that constitute the White Ray. As the Black Ray transforms matter into higher levels of frequency or light, a more evolved state of consciousness and being can come into manifestation. A magical transference shift begins to occur within matter, because the Black Ray filters through the necessary magical healing energies and properties previously hidden in the normally unobtainable dimensions within Nature. Therefore it is the Black Ray that gives Transference Healing its unique and *magical* quality.

The Black Ray channels the healing powers of Nature itself to create a healing and *transference* response and process that can only be created by Nature and the Goddess, and not by humans. When one masters (the raven power technique) in Transference Healing, it enables them to personally access

more effectively the powers of the **Black Ray. This ray provides the necessary resources to create a Divine and** *magical* **healing response, by dispelling and transmuting disease or illness instantaneously. Therefore one begins to master holding and sustaining the power of The Light at all times.**

INITIATIONS INTO RAVEN POWER

By meditating on the raven we:

+ Enhance the powers of mysticism.

+ Make a universal initiation to serve and heal humanity.

+ work to heal all aspects of ourselves.

+ Step into the Void to learn, discover and witness where all knowledge begins.

+ Listen to our inner voice and the Goddess within, at the same time.

+ Take responsibility for ourselves and our own process of Salvation.

+ Choose to live unconditionally and to receive knowledge and power to help others rather than 'ourselves'.

UNIVERSAL KNOWLEDGE

The Universe and the forces and properties of Nature itself provide, contain and store all resources and knowledge necessary for our healing and growth process. I believe all universal energies; knowledge and information are available universally through higher consciousness and can be accessed through the mediums and tools mentioned above, (tarot, astrology etc). All the knowledge I have accessed, to obtain inner knowing and peace of mind has come through and from N*ature* and the *universe*. The Black Ray enables us to access and channel sacred universal energies and knowledge, which then create a self-empowering and healing process for others and ourselves.

RAVEN POWER PROCEDURE

HARMONY ALIGNMENT POINT 16

There is an energetic point existing around the third eye area within the etheric body, called Harmony Alignment Point 16. When it is energetically activated and healed, certain dimensions of the lightbody begin to anchor through.

We then resonate encoded, geometric energies out into the Universe conveying the 'message' that we have reached a certain degree of frequency in our body and consciousness; in other words we have reached a certain level of consciousness or 'enlightenment'.

Sirian codes and keys then begin to filter through into the DNA and etheric body to create a frequency shift within the body and third eye. It is like switching on a light bulb, enabling us to 'hold our light' to such an extent we become spiritually empowered. Through 'holding our light' we become an instrument for the light, channeller of The Light and a 'Lightworker' on Earth.

We are able to *hold our light* through the darkest times or in the most difficult times of initiation and also intuitively *see* the reason *behind* the circumstances creating learning curves in our day-today life. We are able to begin to channel energies whose unique frequency would normally be too hard to hold, as they would create physical stress and send the mind into overload. We are then able to begin to *master* 'free will' which enables us to then live by 'Divine Will'.

ACCESS POINTS

When we reach this level of vibration, frequency and consciousness, we begin to obtain the natural ability to access and channel not only the White Ray through our consciousness, but also the forgotten and mistakenly feared Black Ray. We have earned our 'right of passage' into the unknown. We are able to enter into the realms of the **Elemental** Kingdom, channel and decipher new and universal information giving answers to existing mysteries and universal concerns as well as access and create a powerful *alchemical* healing and transformation process within others and ourselves. **We begin to obtain the power of the Black Madonna, the *magician* and *master of self.***

INITIATION TECHNIQUES

There are two techniques in Transference Healing which create an initiation and healing process enabling us to master Raven Power or the energies of the Black Ray. They are 'Harmony Alignment Point 16' and the 'Holding Power of Light Technique'. I have also made the **Raven Power Essence** to help us work on this level.

PROCEDURE

♦ Enter a mild meditative state.

♦ With a power finger and through intent, visualise and sense the colour of White light and the tone of high C going directly into the third eye area of the body where Harmony Alignment Point 16 lies.

- Hold this colour and frequency or vibration for about 30 seconds.

- This procedure should only be performed a couple of times a week as it can create initiations into a *rapid* state of *purification* to obtain new levels of empowerment and enlightenment - putting some into spiritual and physical overload.

Raven Power Essence initiates the awakening of the psyche so we can begin to understand the process of universal spiritual initiations and receive the internal resources to master them.

- It enables us to 'hold our light' through the darkest times of initiation and rebirth.

- It preventatively takes care of lightbody symptoms so we can master and become a more empowered instrument of light.

- It enhances our ability to see into the unknown, overcome fear of the unknown and access The Light when needed, within any circumstance we find ourselves in.

Raven Power Essence also helps us master the attributes of light so we can master the ability to access universal knowledge, energy and resources. It helps us see the *source of negativity or pain*, whether from an earthbound energy or a negative energy block and helps us transmute negativity, through intent, into the light.

Even though this essence integrates the Harmony Alignment Point 16 Technique, by taking the essence everyday we are performing this technique everyday. It can therefore bring up issues to look at and can sometimes make us feel a little overwhelmed through the process of releasing negativity.

Therefore, adults need to use their discernment when taking this essence. It should be taken in small doses and not very often. The recommended dose is seven drops per day until the bottle is finished, which takes around 2-3 weeks. However, if you want to stop during this time please follow your intuition. You can continue the dosage at a later time.

Please note: This essence should not be given to children.

Note:
If you resonate with the Raven Power procedure and essence you can integrate and master its magical qualities by reading the channelled divination card of the Raven, available in the Transference Healing Animal Magic Deck *(refer to page 355 for more details)*.

IMPORTANT: *Completion Ritual*

*Before you stop reading this chapter, run your finger from **right to left** across the sacred language below. This procedure will assist you to finalise the energies from this chapter.*

Your action, intent and the sacred vibration of this powerful language, will greatly assist you to fully integrate the information you have just read.

THE TRANSFERENCE HEALING®
ANIMAL MAGIC DECK

A new insight into the magical qualities of animals and how they are supporting us at this time!

This exciting new card deck is a world first and features 55 magical divination cards with individual, powerful and transformational images representing the unique qualities and kingdoms of each:

+ Earth Animal.
+ Mythical Animal - including Pegasus, Unicorn, Griffin and Gargoyle.
+ Elemental Being - including Dryads, Sylth, Crystal Fairy and Selendyne.

Supporting the cards is a beautifully presented book offering readers detailed information channelled by Alexis Cartwright. You will learn of the healing and empowering qualities of each animal, as well as a corresponding message offering both insight and wisdom.

Now you can access the Animal Magic used by the *Native American Indians, Shaman Healers and Celtic cultures* to not only understand the forces at play in your daily life, but also to gain a deeper sense of personal awareness and an expanded consciousness.

The insight you gain when using these cards will support you on an energetic level to master the changing elements occurring as we shift to the fifth dimension.

If you strongly resonate with a particular card, you can also purchase it as an A4 poster, allowing you to integrate its energy into your home or office environment.

Place your order at www.TRANSFERENCEHEALING.com

IMPORTANT: *Commencement Ritual*

*Before reading chapter 11, run your finger over this symbol,
imagining you are placing it into your heart chakra.*

*Your action, intent and the sacred vibration of this powerful
language, will ensure that you are fully open to receiving and
integrating the information within.*

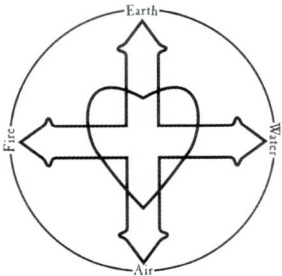

This symbol completes the initiation of the Dragon Power.

Christ Consciousness activates the empowerment of Divine Will, helping
you with your own power. The infinite intelligence of God brings through
the wisdom and power of Divine Will. This enables access to cosmic and
spiritual energies of higher frequencies for healing and ascension.

Running your fingers over this symbol can help you increase your energy
if you are very depleted or if you need extra energy to deal with a difficult
situation. It can also help counteract dis-ease or negativity and negative
energy plays.

CHAPTER
11

DRAGON
POWER

CHAPTER OVERVIEW

In this chapter you will discover that:

* Dragon Power is a technique that enables us to *hold our light* in any situation. It energetically heals and spiritually/emotionally supports *sensitive,* intuitive or psychic people who are being depleted by leaking energy to others. It revitalises our *power centre* if channelling is energetically draining us or we are being depleted by the Earth and cosmic changes. It protects against *direct* psychic attack and also counteracts negative feelings or thought projection against us.

* If we are being energetically depleted, then electromagnetic light becomes deficient in our body. This affects our cellular body and glandular system. If we become depleted on a deeper level, our etheric body becomes weak and we do not have the reserves of energy needed to counteract symptoms and diseases. Consequently, there are not enough resources from the *etheric body* to revitalise our electromagnetic body, which creates even more distortion through the cellular and glandular system. Various symptoms then begin to manifest more rapidly such as viruses, genetic weakness and in some extreme cases even cancer.

* Cancer physically manifests because we cannot therapeutically sustain enough *electromagnetic light* within the body to allow the cells to rapidly change by absorbing the necessary hormonal secretions for the cellular body to *rejuvenate* more effectively. The Dragon Power technique can be utilised to assist sufferers to counteract and transmute pain and disease from their etheric/physical body and consciousness, while also creating a rapid cellular rejuvenation process.

- *Self-worth* is the last hurdle to overcome before coming into a state of oneness by mastering all limitations within the self. Suppressed or painful memories of times of *abuse* and *persecution* stored within our DNA have caused us to become dis-empowered to such an extent that we have lost some of our instinctive and intuitive abilities and weakened the energetic resources within our etheric body.

- As we learn to raise our own **Dragon Power** and master our own inner forces, we can begin to master the *ego* and *intent*. Through this process our innate abilities and spiritual 'gifts and talents' will begin to manifest, enabling us to heal ourselves by releasing hidden and built up pain from the *heart chakra*, sub-conscious mind and deeper energetic levels of the etheric/physical body. We begin to transmute negativity for physical, mental and emotional purification, our inner-self then strengthens. On a global level a purer world will be created.

- At this time of transition we are being forced to understand our spiritual power source. We are going through a state of initiation so we can begin to self-heal dormant weaknesses that have restricted our sense of self-empowerment. The key is to own the Power of the Dragon within.

- This procedure is only to be used to empower you to defend yourself against negativity not to empower you to attack others – whatever the circumstances. Used wrongly an energy implosion will be created within the perpetrator.

◆

DIVINE EMPOWERMENT

Dragon Power is a technique which channelled through to support me when I was developing my psychic and spiritual gifts and abilities. It enables us to *hold our light* in any situation; energetically heals or spiritually and emotionally supports *sensitive*, intuitive or psychic people who are being generally depleted by leaking energy to others; and revitalises our *power centre* if channelling is energetically draining us or we are being depleted because of the Earth and cosmic changes.

Dragon Power is a technique for protection against *direct* psychic attack and also counteracts negative feelings or thought projection against us. When we start to master our *power centre* and show unique and Divine attributes, we can sometimes confront people around us who, out of general ignorance and fear, have conflicting feelings of judgment towards us.

DIAGRAM 11.1
Dragon Card from the Transference Healing Animal Magic Deck

Dragon

THE ANCIENTS

When this technique and its principles and teaching came through, I was told that Masters from ancient times learnt to master this technique and their *power centre* at times of initiation for ascension. If an initiate were put in a situation of personal attack, procedures to activate Dragon Power would awaken naturally from within, to enable them to protect themselves.

These ancient spiritual masters existed within many cultures and religions at different times – as Druidic priests in Europe, Buddhist monks in Tibet and Samurai warriors in Japan. They were all intuitively guided, through their own spiritual Mastership process, to develop this level of 'self-empowerment'. However, as each culture interpreted this spiritual self-development and empowerment technique in their own unique way, the procedures varied. Although these procedures were channelled to create a state of *spiritual* empowerment on an *energetic* level, remnants have been handed down, developed and utilised within many physical forms of martial arts such as Tai Chi, Judo and specifically Tae Kwan Do.

SYMPTOMS

If we are being energetically depleted, then electromagnetic light, which is similar to and identified as the compound or mineral known as magnesium becomes deficient in our body. This then affects our cellular body and glandular system. If we have become depleted on a deeper level, our etheric body becomes weak and we do not have the reserves of energy needed to counteract symptoms and diseases. Consequently, there are not enough internal energetic resources from the *etheric body* to revitalise our electromagnetic body, which then creates even more distortion through the cellular and glandular system. Various symptoms then begin to manifest at a more rapid rate, such as viruses, genetic weakness and in some extreme cases even cancer.

Cancer is a metaphysical eating away of the Soul's innate power and ability to sustain the light through the 'darkest times'. Cancer physically manifests because we cannot therapeutically sustain enough *electromagnetic light* within the body to allow the cells to rapidly change by absorbing the necessary hormonal secretions for the cellular body to *rejuvenate* more effectively. I have sometimes used this **Dragon Power** technique to draw up the Dragon Power within a person to '*resource*' their etheric field and cellular body' so they can begin to counteract and transmute pain and disease from their etheric/physical body and consciousness and while doing so create a rapid cellular rejuvenation process. This enables the *core* or root of the weakness or disease to not only be released but also decoded out of the body, to sustain more long-term wellness.

SELF-EMPOWERMENT

Over time and through different incarnations, painful experiences have occurred and impacted the body and consciousness. They have weakened our internal resistance and resources, thereby affecting our inner feelings of self-worth. **Self-worth** is the last hurdle to overcome before coming into a state of oneness by mastering all limitations within the self. Suppressed or painful memories of times of *abuse* and *persecution* stored within our DNA have caused us to become dis-empowered to such an extent that we have lost some of our instinctive and intuitive abilities. This has also weakened energetic resources within the etheric body; from our ability to sustain a longer life span through to 'trusting in Source' so we can obtain the healing necessary to master our personal growth and spiritual abilities at difficult times of spiritual initiation.

As we learn to raise our own **Dragon Power** and master our own inner forces, we can begin to master the *ego* and *intent*. Through this process our innate abilities and spiritual 'gifts and talents' will begin to manifest, enabling us to heal ourselves by releasing hidden and built up pain from the *heart chakra,* sub-conscious mind and deeper energetic levels of the etheric/physical body. In this way, we will begin to transmute negativity into the light, for physical, mental and emotional purification. As our emotional void is filled, our inner-self will strengthen and build. On a global level, a purer world will be created as general feelings of judgment and negativity are released.

SELF-HEALING

Now, at this time of transition of (1999–2012), we are once again being forced to understand our *spiritual power source* so we can purify our emotions, consciousness, intent and ego. We are being energetically activated through the third eye area to open up our instinctive and intuitive nature; revitalise our life force to begin to heal genetic weaknesses from within; develop our psychic abilities and protect ourselves against all forms of energetic bombardment from the Earth and cosmic changes. During this time of transition, negativity on a global level is being released. Humanity is going through a state of initiation so we can begin to self-heal dormant weaknesses that have restricted our sense of self-empowerment.

The key is to *own the Power of the Dragon within*. Dragon Power gives us the energetic resources, on all levels, to begin to heal ourselves so we can deal with difficult times and situations by counteracting all kinds of negativity. It helps us counteract and master fear, personal limitation and negativity and through this process, learn to hold our light on a day-to-day level. 'Holding our light' means we are anchoring and sustaining the light thereby creating an *electromagnetic field* or *shield* to protect us at all times. Dragon Power therefore provides a *protective shield* to defend us against energy attacks from others and the environment at large.

> ### Remember:
> **this procedure is only to be used to empower you** *to defend yourself against negativity* **not to empower you to attack others - whatever the circumstances. Black magic and sorcery use Dragon Power in a negative way. If this procedure is used in this way, it will create an energy implosion within the perpetrator.**

RAISING THE DRAGON

If we need extra energy to deal with a particular situation, or to obtain strength to counteract disease within ourselves, we can raise our own Dragon.

It must be raised carefully for only a minute or so and then put back again. You will be working with your solar plexus, heart and third eye chakras and the four elements of earth, air, fire and water (located at the four points of a cross over your heart).

DIAGRAM 11.2
Dragon Power Symbol

Copyright 2005 Alexis Cartwright, Keeper of the Crystals Pty Ltd

PROCEDURE

1. **Embed the Sign of the Cross** over your heart chakra *vibrationally:*

    ♥ **Imagine** a circle over the heart chakra in the centre of your chest *(see diagram 11.2)*.

    ♥ **Polarise the *four elements*** by using the middle finger of either hand to touch the circle over your heart chakra in the following sequence:

    Top: **Earth;** Bottom: **Air;** Left: **Fire;** Right: **Water.**

Through the intent of your heart, (from your heart) *ask* the Power of the Dragon to 'Counteract attack through Divine Will' and then:

2.   **Raise the Dragon:**

1. *Raise* both arms to shoulder level - horizontally from the sides of your body, with palms facing downwards.

2. *Visualise* scooping universal energy as you immediately begin to *lower them* to your sides and around to the front of your body.

3. *Stop* your hands at the front of your body, below your base chakra – place the fingers of one hand on top of the fingers of the other hand with palms facing upwards. Keep both hands in this position.

4. *Visualise* you are drawing universal energy up through your body to your heart as you *raise* both hands vertically up the front of your body.

5. *Place* your hands on your heart chakra - *hold* the energy for a couple of minutes in the heart with the *intent* of owning the Power of the Dragon – ask to '**Bring the Dragon Power into consciousness**'.

6. *Lower* your hands slowly down the side of your body at the conclusion of this procedure.

After performing this procedure approximately twice a week for about a month you will begin to manifest the force of Divine Will from within you to counteract painful issues or symptoms and any negative energy plays that might be occurring against you at the time. This empowerment process will remain for the purpose at hand.

As the initiation is mastered, you will create a new level of empowerment for yourself in your day-to-day life. From that point on you will have the instinctual ability to raise your power to master any situation on a similar level.

To *perfect* **Dragon Power** to master this ancient lineage of empowerment, you can perform this procedure about three times a week until you feel you have mastered it enough to counteract any feeling of attack that might come through - for whatever reason. You can then repeat it whenever you need to.

Dragon Power Essence: helps you master this procedure and its corresponding principles. You can also ask for the dragon to be your guide while taking the essence.

Take seven drops of the essence each morning and night, over the three weeks or until the essence is finished.

Please note: this essence should only be given to children in small doses – about two drops in the morning and night and no longer than 2-3 weeks.

Note:
If you resonate with the Dragon Power procedure and essence you can integrate and master its magical qualities by reading the channelled divination card of the Dragon, available in the Transference Healing Animal Magic Deck *(refer to page 355 for more details)*.

IMPORTANT: *Completion Ritual*

Before you stop reading this chapter, run your finger over this symbol, imagining you are placing it into your heart chakra. This procedure will assist you to finalise the energies from this chapter.

Your action, intent and the sacred vibration of this powerful language, will greatly assist you to fully integrate the information you have just read.

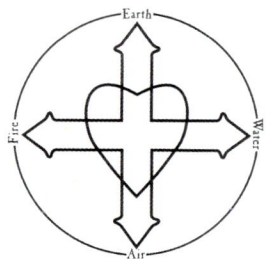

NOW AVAILABLE
AN AUDIO PRESENTATION
FEATURING ALEXIS CARTWRIGHT

Hear Alexis speak about:

- Her personal journey.

- The Earth changes towards 2012.

- The ascension beings supporting the ascension process.

- Transference Healing®.

PLUS - Experience and benefit from a powerful mass healing and meditation.

This Bardon Conference CD was recorded live in 2000 after Alexis was advised by the Celestial Christ to record her presentation/healing at that conference.

The Celestial Christ and other Ascension Beings resonate through the recording, supporting Alexis and the mass Transference Healing and ascension process. As such, the recording continues to resonate a Divine healing and ascension process with every playing.

"It is electrifying and mesmerising. Alexis will captivate your attention. The powerful energies supporting the presentation are tangible! You will be dramatically altered - you will be impacted and your life will be permanently changed!"

Duration: approximately 40 minutes

Place your order at www.TRANSFERENCEHEALING.com

IMPORTANT: Commencement Ritual

*Before reading chapter 12, run your finger from **left to right** across the sacred language below.*

Your action, intent and the sacred vibration of this powerful language, will ensure that you are fully open to receiving and integrating the information within.

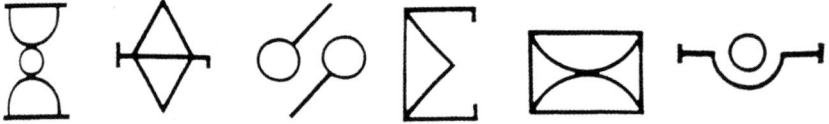

The above symbols, according to ancient astrologers represent the divination and duration of time. They are the symbols representing an hour, day, night, week, month and year.

These symbols therefore create the powers of gestation throughout the duration of time. When you integrate these symbols you are able to let go of control and live in synchronicity with the forces of your destiny, nature and the universe.

CHAPTER
12

CHILDREN OF
THE LIGHT

CHAPTER OVERVIEW

In this chapter you will discover:

♦ Before coming onto the Earth your Soul reviews its evolutionary progress and determines what lessons are necessary for its future growth. While you are in the womb your Soul exists in an altered state within an astral dimension that is connected to your developing physical body. At this time you reflect on your chosen incoming 'essence', the life and connections your will make and the karmic forces behind them. You integrate this process into your new physical body and are then born into the world. This enables you to embody the revelations made while in your altered state. Mastering the karmic forces at play in your life creates a new sense of identity and being.

♦ Your 'force of destiny' is geometrically embedded into the etheric templates of the chakra system, glandular system and DNA while you are in the womb. As the Soul reflects on its destiny it creates a spectrum of emotions which are vibrationally embedded into every cell of every organ of the body by the hormonal and chemical secretions from the heart, brain and nerves – embedding consciousness and the Souls unique identity into the body.

♦ Unique emotional aspects of the Soul show up as energetic imbalances in the etheric patterning of the body through the Metaphysical Diamond. Transference Healing assists in clearing any imbalances impacting the body. You can also clear these through understanding your emotions and the true nature of your mind.

♦ Karmic forces manifest in life through relationships with family members, friends and associates who trigger ongoing reconciliation, resolution and completion. Personal growth and enlightenment occurs by healing both *negative emotions* experienced in relationships and *negative circumstances* which manifest in our personal life through our own karmic forces of destiny.

- The energetic changes post 1999 has allowed incoming Souls to enter at a higher frequency level then before. Children born since the 1990's have been born into a fifth dimensional frequency and have different perspectives and feelings as a result. These patterning changes within new incomings Souls will become more and more obvious towards 2012.

- Being born with a fifth dimensional template is forcing these children to master their gifts, talents and lightbody integration at a much faster rate. Their spiritual values, specific Soul gifts and levels of consciousness are also evolving at a much faster rate. Their personalities are more unique and spiritual than ours were at the same age.

- Some children identified as 'Indigo' or 'Crystal' Children have shown even more extreme or unusual personality traits and are generally seen as having more unusual symptoms or behavioural patterns than those around them. These children can seem 'ungrounded' or even 'disconnected' from the world. They are more hypersensitive and psychic in nature, more telepathic and have more 'Doorway' experiences. They often have very creative 'gifts and talents'. They are working with the masters on Earth, to become the foundation builders of the new systems of the seventh Golden Age, beginning to manifest at this time.

◆

HUMAN GESTATION

efore reincarnating onto the Earth, incoming Souls review the progress of their evolutionary journey and determine the lessons necessary for future growth. During human gestation the consciousness of incoming Souls exist within an altered sense of time and reality on an astral dimension connected to the developing human, physical body.

They reflect on the *chosen* essence of their incoming incarnation - the connections they will make and the karmic forces behind the circumstances their life will create for them on Earth. After integrating this process with the physical body, the Souls are born into a world which will enable them to *embody* the revelations made while in this altered state of consciousness. Through mastering the karmic forces at play in their lives they can create this new sense of identity and being.

FORCES OF DESTINY

Their 'force of destiny' is geometrically embedded into the etheric templates of the chakra system, glandular system and DNA as the body evolves within a mother's protective womb. As the consciousness of the Soul reflects on its life to come, it creates a resonance of emotions which are vibrationally embedded into every cell of every *organ* within the body by the hormonal and chemical secretions from the heart, brain and nerves. In this way, consciousness is embedded into the body and the Soul's unique identity or signature is also templated within the body and consciousness.

These unique emotional aspects of the Soul show up energetic distortions within the etheric patterning of the body through what I call the 'Metaphysical Diamond'. This Metaphysical Diamond energetically interplays through the body and you see it as colour resonating from the different areas of the body. By intuitively 'tuning' into this dimension of the body and working with colour and sound through Transference Healing, you can clear any emotional/energetic imbalances that impact the body when dealing with different life circumstances.

EMOTIONAL HEALING

You can also work at clearing the metaphysical dimensions of the body through understanding your emotions more, as well as the true nature of your inner mind. Louise Hay explained in great detail the metaphysical reasons behind disease in 'You Can Heal Your Life'. She says that clearing different emotions can heal different symptoms and dimensions of the body and Soul eg. our liver is diseased because it is holding our anger and therefore *clearing* anger heals the liver; or *clearing* grief heals the lungs. How we run or express our emotions therefore determines how effectively we sustain long-term health and wellness in our body and consciousness.

THE AURA

Our inner nature or emotions reflect out into the electromagnetic or auric field of the body as colour and everyone around us responds to the flow of these energetic responses. If we feel lighter and more positive emotions such as love and joy then the electromagnetic colours that resonate into our aura, emanate a more positive flow. The more our Soul clears imbalances and heals the emotions within the body and consciousness, the more we master in life. We can then achieve more personal fulfilment in our relationships, have less stress and more ease in our body so therefore maintaining more of a state of wellness and also create more opportunities for our personal growth and income because we are able to let go and allow synchronicity and new opportunities to manifest.

MASTERING THE INNER SELF

Karmic forces manifest in life through relationships with family members, friends and associates who trigger ongoing reconciliation, resolution and completion. Emotional buttons force the consciousness of the Soul to look at and heal old behaviour 'patterns' and personality traits. Personal growth and enlightenment occurs by healing both *negative emotions* experienced in relationships and *negative circumstances* which manifest in our personal life through our own karmic forces of destiny. The Soul reflects and unfolds its true, inner nature to itself and the world through the day to day experiences and circumstances created by karma.

When the Soul clears and heals *old patterning* by purifying the emotions and mastering the inner self, all karmic relationships and day to day issues are also mastered more effectively and we begin to have a more fulfilling and fruitful existence. As we master circumstances in our daily life through the consistency of our own healing process and personal growth and development, we acquire the ability to become a master.

NEW AGE CHILDREN

NEW TEMPLATE

The energetic changes on the planet at this time of transition from 1999-2012, are not only healing the heart of humanity on a mass level but are also embedding a new template within the etheric body, life-force and consciousness of incoming Souls. This is allowing them to exist on a higher frequency level than was generally possible before 1999. The energetic changes are creating the energetic resources for Souls to be born into and exist within a different reality or hologram of existence on Earth.

FIFTH DIMENSIONAL FREQUENCY

Children born since the 1990's have been born into a fifth dimensional frequency and have a different perspective within their thoughts and feelings than those born before. The 'patterning' changes occurring within new, incoming Souls will become more obvious as we go through this time of transition (1999-2012) - for example, the new Souls who are being born during this time are showing even more *unique* qualities and attributes.

GIFTS AND TALENTS

Being born with this new fifth dimensional template is forcing them to master their gifts, talents and lightbody integration at a much faster rate. Their spiritual values, specific Soul gifts and levels of consciousness are also evolving at a much faster rate. Therefore, their personalities are more unique and spiritual than ours were at the same age.

DNA COSMIC CODING

Through the Earth's transition, all of the new incoming Souls are being forced at an early age to learn to deal with more on an inner level and are given less time to live out karmic patterning and old, out-dated, archetypal personality traits. They have embodied more of their Higher Selves because they are more balanced within their psyche and have a more *cosmic coding system within their DNA*. This coding connects their consciousness into parallel realms and realities which filter through insight on behaviour patterning that is of a more *spiritual nature* (ethereal or even sometimes galactic) than what has been established or identified as *normal* 'personality traits' on Earth.

INDIGO CHILDREN

Some have shown even more extreme or unusual personality traits and are generally seen as having more unusual symptoms or behavioural patterns than those around them. These children can seem 'ungrounded' or even more 'disconnected' from the world as it re-establishes itself around them. They are now identified as, or termed 'Indigo' or 'Crystal' Children. They are working with the masters on Earth, to become the foundation builders of the new systems of the seventh Golden Age, beginning to manifest at this time.

BEHAVIOUR PROBLEMS

Some show behaviour problems or defiant personality traits which simply reflect a different level of perception and ideals than what is being taught to them. This so-called *negative, defiant or oppositional behaviour patterning* usually comes through because of a feeling of personal restriction, spiritual suppression or energetic suffocation. Some of these 'behaviour patterns' correspond with physical symptoms ranging from eating disorders and allergies to glandular deficiencies, low immunity and middle ear and pineal gland imbalances. The children experience and draw unusual circumstances into their lives and cry from general lightbody pains in the body, which can't be explained.

NEW PERCEPTUAL POWERS

In the past, usually very 'gifted' or 'disturbed' children showed odd or abnormal behaviour patterns. However, all children are now expressing some odd behavioural 'patterning' ranging from their own personal views of the world, the way they express their emotions and their personal interests through to 'general symptoms' they might be bringing into their physical bodies. Many children are prescribed behaviour medication simply because they are utilising different sensory perceptual powers and living within a different level of consciousness than what is generally considered normal. Some show a sense of sadness or bewilderment because they feel different to their immediate world environment.

PSYCHIC SENSES

Children of today sense and see things beyond what the general mind can rationalise and understand. They are more hypersensitive and psychic in nature. They are more telepathic, have more frequent 'Doorway' experiences, so speak of things or occurrences happening from and within other dimensions and from previous times. They also see more clearly into other realms, feel energy more intensely and show unique and spiritual 'gifts and talents' at an early age.

CREATIVITY

Children who are classified with 'learning difficulties' often have very creative 'gifts and talents', ranging from psychic to artistic abilities which create abstract thoughts beneficial for writing, drawing, painting, music and performing. They have extreme energy fluctuations, co-ordination problems and 'learning difficulties', usually because they have a more creative way of thinking and show interest in fields of study that are usually not available at the primary level or within the academic curricula of most of today's schools.

CHILDREN OF THE TRANSITION

Children born during this time of transition, from 1999-2012, feel, know and sense more than they understand – seemingly being torn between two worlds - the third dimensional Old World and the fifth dimensional New World. Sometimes their Soul's consciousness and *etheric* body resonates faster within their physical bodies so they are magnetically lighter. Their consciousness is then continually altering and their bodies continually shifting on a vibrational and cellular level.

NEW DNA

These children are forming another DNA helix like the adults undergoing self-mastery. Those born after 1999 already have the third helix in their DNA system and are mutating their 12-strand DNA more rapidly than most adults who are still living within the old matrix. Consequently, they are suffering with more lightbody symptoms than most adults. However, because they are born with the new fifth dimensional holographic matrix within their etheric body they have the internal resources, spiritual and energetic connections and internal know-how to heal themselves more rapidly if worked on energetically or if living in a more spiritual or templated (gridded with energy) environment.

TRANSITIONAL PAIN

More and more unknown symptoms are going to appear and disappear. This is *transitional* pain. The pain only seems to last a couple of weeks and can recur from time to time. Simply interacting with the children using the suggestions mentioned below, will help them *master* these recurring *transitional* symptoms and enable them to develop and grow very quickly and easily.

HELPING THE NEW CHILDREN ALIGN WITH THEIR SOUL'S PURPOSE

As we shift our consciousness we can understand and encourage the children to express what they truly feel, see and know, so they can evolve in consciousness at a more rapid pace and express their own unique personality, attributes and internal wisdom without fear. Through this process they will help shift global consciousness.

'CHILDREN OF THE LIGHT'

The children of today are the
'Children of the Light'.
Guide them to emanate their Soul's reflection.
In return they will help us transcend into other
realities so we can shift our consciousness by making
the necessary changes in our perception, values and
life - through this time of transition.

SUGGESTIONS TO HELP THE NEW CHILDREN

1. Let them see the angels, elementals and galactic/ lightbeings.

2. Encourage them to ask their angels and guides for assistance and help to relieve their pain, confusion and fear.

3. Let them talk of past or parallel lives they are feeling, living or seeing.

4. Have their astrology and numerology readings done so you can understand their strengths and weaknesses and be divinely guided to work with them on the necessary levels.

5. Help them develop and express their uniqueness and individuality into the world.

DIAGRAM 12.1
Inner Child Soul Portrait

A spiritual, Soul portrait of a client and friend, Alexandra Payne - aged 9. Channelled and painted by Celeste, a spiritual artist living in Sedona, Arizona, USA.

6. Encourage their personal interests and help develop their 'gifts and talents' so they can fulfil their destiny and purpose in this incarnation.

7. Encourage them to utilise their 'gifts and talents' to express their inner knowing with more ease. This will release built up stress, frustration, feelings of limitation and issues of self-worth.

8. Don't ignore their outbursts of pain.

9. Talk to them about energy and teach them to run simple procedures to support their own healing process.

10. Don't limit their mind's perception.

11. Listen to them and what they truly feel.

12. Communicate with them on topics that interest them by **listening** and then discussing on the levels they need to.

13. Teach them to meditate.

14. Allow and encourage them to play with the crystals that they are attracted to.

15. Give them lightbody essences *(see chapter 15)*.

    The Inner Child Combination Essence *for fifteen year olds and over:*

    Enables them to let go of, and also begin to heal, painful memories and wounding from childhood. It also supports pure child like-feelings such as joy, love and faith to come back into manifestation and consciousness.

    The Child of Light Combination Essence *for fourteen year olds and under:*

    Enables 'transitional children' - those born during this *time of transition* - to obtain a templating and vibrational healing response which helps counteract viruses and lightbody symptoms they could already be feeling physically or becoming more susceptible to.

Recommended Dosage: Take seven drops of a single essence, twice a day.

> **Be kind to the children.**
> **Allow them to share their light with you.**

IMPORTANT: Completion Ritual

*Before you stop reading this chapter, run your finger from **right to left** across the sacred language below. This procedure will assist you to finalise the energies from this chapter.*

Your action, intent and the sacred vibration of this powerful language, will greatly assist you to fully integrate the information you have just read.

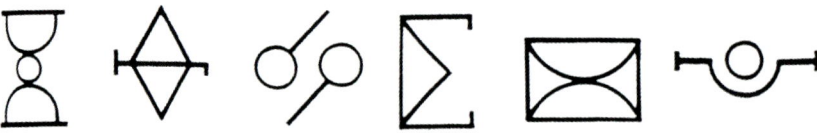

THE PRAYER OF THE NEW MILLENIUM

As featured in chapter 8 of this book.

Is now available as a beautiful and powerful quality A4 colour poster so you can integrate this profound frequency into your home or workplace.

"The perfect gift for yourself or a loved one."

Alexis Cartwright channelled this profound prayer in 2000. The prayer came through the Celestial Christ to support humanity to heal and ascend at this time in a new way.

The Prayer opens the heart chakra enabling the reader to anchor and embody their Higher Self and their new lightbody system.

It also supports the reader to master their own healing and ascension process during this time of global change, encouraging them to take the necessary steps to create personal change, self-healing, transformation and the next step in their personal/spiritual growth process.

Place your order at www.TRANSFERENCEHEALING.com

IMPORTANT: *Commencement Ritual*

*Before reading chapter 13, run your finger from **left to right** across the sacred language below.*

Your action, intent and the sacred vibration of this powerful language, will ensure that you are fully open to receiving and integrating the information within.

7ะርUጠ ㄎﾉ7ヒ7ㄎ

ㄎርꓶ7Uะ±7 ㄎﾉะ77

U7ヒꓵ±ะU77 ㄎጠะㄎርะ7

Written above are the words "EARTH", "COSMIC", "CRYSTALS", "CODES", "TEMPLATES", and "CHAKRAS" using letters from the Angelic language called 'The Enochian Alphabet', which is a Language of Light that reflects the wisdom of Enoch.

These symbols will filter or weave through the necessary *Earth* and *crystal technology* to support your reconnection process to the Divine and co-existing Kingdoms of the Lyran, Arcturian, Pleiadian, Orion and Sirian dimensions. This gridding process will enable you to filter through the necessary *Earth* and *cosmic crystal codes* that will support your *chakra system* and *DNA* to *re-template* and thereby enable you to physically anchor through more of your **celestial lightbody** system.

THE EARTH AND ITS DOORWAYS INTO CO-EXISTING ANGELIC, ELEMENTAL AND GALACTIC DIMENSIONS

FROM THE AUTHOR

As you read through chapters 13 and 14 it is not important to consciously comprehend the details as you will receive an energetic coding or 'gridding' process of the information through your DNA.

As the codes filter into your DNA, they create a healing response so you might feel strange sensations through the middle ear, third eye area and the base of the back of the brain. I therefore advise you to 'ground' yourself after reading these chapters, or even parts of them, by going into a short meditation:

Visualise a small star a few inches beneath each foot; then, from the base of each foot, extend a silver line to join down into the point of a V at the earth star chakra, six inches beneath the feet.

Together, the chapters introduce the galactic and spiritual parallel dimensions, co-existing within and around us which are part of the totality of our DNA. These are the dimensions supporting us through this time of evolutionary transition so we can ascend into the fifth dimension.

Chapter 13 concentrates on the spiritual technology which allows us to access these dimensions. The crystals and templates, the Earth and the different energy systems of the heart, chakras and subtle and physical bodies of the human anatomy, that support the co-creation process of the lightbody and the technology to master connecting through and into these dimensions.

There are three parts to chapter 13.

1. Part One is technical. It has new viewpoints on the creation process of the Earth and humanity and provides information on the spiritual technology and tools to create a more inter-dimensional reality and the ability to lightbody travel.

2. Part Two is written from a heart-based (spiritual and emotional) perspective. It describes the three chambers of the heart chakra and how they impact our consciousness.

3. Part Three is a review or summary of the key points of the chapter.

Chapter 14 provides information on the different grid points and gateways in space and specific information about these parallel dimensions and worlds.

> *Please understand the difficulty of trying to accurately convey metaphysical concepts and processes using current 'scientific' terminology or language as they don't necessarily fit conventional scientific models.*

Alexis

CHAPTER OVERVIEW

In this profound chapter, you will discover:

Part 1 – Creation of the Earth

- The Earth formed from ethereal gases that underwent a process of alchemical change transforming into cosmic crystals, some of which evolved into Earth crystals, which were the first forms of life within our dimension.

- Crystals sustain etheric templates, which hold the internal technology that created the dimensions of the human electromagnetic field, etheric and physical bodies.

- Crystals create a vibrational purification and transference process that amplifies the healing and co-creative process.

- There are parallel dimensions co-existing within different frequency levels of the Earth and Cosmos. These are spiritual worlds or kingdoms ranging from the Elemental Kingdom to Galactic Kingdoms. These dimensions filter through into our DNA, etheric body and lightbody codes and frequencies that allow us to enter them.

- Elemental lightbeings and extra-terrestrial lightbeings co-exist with us on Earth, however they exist within different realms sustained within different frequency levels of the Earth and Cosmos respectively.

- Crystals sustain the internal technology and codes to create the *Merkabah body*, which is the etheric vehicle in which the lightbody travels through space into parallel dimensions.

- The Pleiadians utilised the technology of the crystals to create the template from which the Human Race evolved. The first genetic structure and nature "template" of the human physical body and consciousness is known as ADAM and was Pleiadian. The Soul that incarnated as this 'first-born' son of the God/Goddess latter reincarnated as Jesus. His DNA sustained the first complete etheric coding system to be able to access and become conscious of the Higher Self, Divine Spirit and Tree of Life.

- We co-exist from and within the third (physical body), fourth (etheric/lightbody) and fifth (cosmic/lightbody) dimensional 'bodies' it is this trinity that allows us to evolve into higher levels of consciousness.

- The etheric body *co-creates* the dimensions of the physical anatomy within the third dimensional physical body. The *etheric/lightbody* sustains the human body and *consciousness* within the fourth dimension, this continuously filters through allowing for the continual evolutionary process of the physical form. We see this body as our inner-child, emotional and creative aspects of our heart and Soul, reflecting our personality and inner nature into the world. The *cosmic/lightbody* sustains itself within the fifth dimension filtering through what is needed to create our androgynous Higher Self and the technological aspects of the mind or brain that allow us to reflect out our perceptions, thoughts and intellectual attributes to the world. This dimension allows us to continuously heal our lightbody, as well as, heal and evolve our physical anatomy.

Part 2 – The Heart Centre of Parallel Realities and Universes

- The physical core of the Earth sustains the central gravity point of the physical human body.

- As many parallel galaxies and universes co-exist with Earth, the crystallised core of Earth is also the central grid point for universal healing and ascension.

- The Earths' crystal core emanates a specific 'OM' vibration in the frequency of F# (having changed from F in 1999), between 2012-2013 it will transfer to the tone of G. This shift is creating pressure within the physical and emotional 'heart of humanity' creating a rapid purification and evolution of global consciousness from the current third dimensional reality to a fifth dimensional heart-based perspective.

- The Earths core is a cosmic Doorway into realities within and on the Earth for healing and ascension, for this reason lightbodies gravitate here to receive and create the necessary elements to heal, grow and ascend. What is so unique about Earth is that she enables these lightbodies to anchor in the vibration and formation of the heart chakra and the physical and emotional heart.

- Nothing ever dies. Frequencies of energy can never be created or destroyed; they can only be transferred from one state of being into another through a divinely orchestrated evolutionary process, so that consciousness can experience many holographic realities to understand the meaning of life.

- Our fundamental chakra system is divided into two lower and higher levels. The lower chakra system (base, naval, solar plexus and heart chakras) sustains and maintains the Lower Self (physical form and substance), while the higher chakra system (heart, throat, third eye and crown chakras) sustains and maintains the Higher Self (spiritual consciousness and the lightbody system). The heart chakra divides and integrates the lower and higher levels/selves.

- The heart chakra absorbs its gridding and electromagnetic impulses directly from the *crystallised core of the Earth, which* it then filters through directly into the physical heart.

- There are three energetic chambers of the heart chakra. As we emotionally and intellectually reach higher levels of consciousness via the chakra system, a deeper chamber of the heart can open. It is only through the heart chakra that we can absorb universal energies and knowledge.

- The first chamber of the heart chakra resonates through the Green Ray and stimulates the emotion of love. It creates a general healing process in the physical body and a subtle refinement process in the etheric and emotional body. At this time 99% of us are working towards mastering this chamber.

- The second chamber of the heart chakra resonates through the Pink Ray and stimulates the emotion of unconditional love. Those 1% of humanity becoming masters are working towards opening, functioning from and mastering this chamber. As we open this chakra our consciousness evolves and we begin to create the 'cosmic lightbody' and 'Merkabah' system.. We are then able to access, through higher consciousness, what is needed to understand the purpose, meaning and direction of our life. We are also able to evolve and ascend into higher levels of consciousness by anchoring through artistic, psychic and spiritual gifts and talents and create a more profound healing response and process for others and ourselves by channelling universal insight and energies.

- The third chamber of the heart chakra resonates through the radiant **Blue Ray** and stimulates the emotion of *compassion*. It only opens with assistance from the four upper chakras - **stellar gateway, soul star, causal and earth star chakras** - which exist beyond the seven main chakras. To be working with this chamber one would need to be living in a higher and more multidimensional level of consciousness of an ascending master. The very few working towards opening this chamber at this time have come to Earth specifically to ascend into a state of Mastership and embody the necessary energies to become an ascending master at this time, becoming a vital support system for the Celestial Christ on Earth.

• The old concept 'to be spiritual is to suffer' is no longer a reality within our new world.

• The word YHWH creates the perfection process of the three chambers of the *heart chakra* so that all dimensions of the *heart chakra* can integrate and work in *harmony* with the other six chakras. It also initiates the healing and ascension powers symbolised and encoded within the 'Book of Revelations'.

Part 3 – Review

• This section of the chapter not only reviews the proceeding information but provides additional information on the Source and the principles/properties of creation itself. Topics discussed include: Genesis, The Master Christ Template Set, the laws of genetic engineering, the Crystal Prism of Lyra, crystal alchemy and grid points into inter-dimensional Kingdoms, the seven levels of the chakra system, universal healing of the Earth and Nature through the 'heart", expanding into Christ Consciousness and heart mastery.

◆

- PART 1 -
THE CREATION OF
THE EARTH

GENESIS

The physical planet Earth formed from ethereal gases - *frequencies of ether* - which filtered into our area of 'space' from other dimensions, beyond and through 'the Void.' These ethereal gases underwent a process of alchemical infusions which formed them into cosmic crystals (sustaining geometric *etheric* templates.) Some of these cosmic crystals evolved into *physical* Earth crystals.

> **Earth crystals were therefore the first physical life forms to exist within our dimension.**

DIFFERENT DIMENSIONS OF MATTER

Each crystal is made up of many different frequency levels of 'light' from within the Cosmos - ranging from the *stars, ultra-violet light* and *rays* through to the different frequencies of minerals within the Earth. This infusion of geometric, 'electromagnetic frequencies and gasses' is solidified on a higher vibrational level before being birthed and formed through an intensive 'thermal' process within the inner layers of the physical Earth. I see crystals as frozen particles of light.

'Earth' crystals are therefore also 'cosmic' in origin and nature and sustain etheric templates. These etheric templates hold the internal technology for the ethereal gasses to crystallise and create the elemental properties and compounds which ultimately create all dimensions or aspects of physical 'matter,' within our planet, body and universe. This internal technology not only created the dimensions of the *electromagnetic field* and the *etheric body,* but also created the different dimensions of the *human physical body* and *anatomy.* So, as the Earth is supporting the formation process of the crystals, the crystals in return are energetically supporting the co-creation process on Earth.

> **Crystals not only amplify the necessary energetic and electromagnetic frequencies for the healing and co-creative process of the *etheric/physical body* but also for the healing and co-creative process of the *lightbody.***

The energetic and organic makeup of Earth crystals is of a finer, purer frequency than humans. They therapeutically impact our physical body and consciousness by emanating a purer vibration of energy which stimulates a magical, alchemical integration and infusion process of chemicals, elements, gasses, sound and colour frequencies. This process then co-creates a *purer* alchemical healing process within the etheric/physical body so it can ultimately become more ethereal in nature.

Crystals, therefore, create a vibrational purification and transference process within the elements of Nature from and through, both the Earth and Cosmos.

> # The planet Earth herself is a 'crystal' hologram consisting of 'matter' sustained within many energetic levels.

DIAGRAM 13.1
Becker-Hagens Earth Star

The geometry of the Earth Star presented by R. Buckminster Fuller was originally published by Russian researchers. It is a '**Rhombic Triacontahedron**'. It is the etheric hologram of the crystallised dimension of the Earth consisting of four basic triangles *within which are 30 diamonds within a 120 polyhedron and sphere*.

CO-EXISTING PARALLEL DIMENSIONS TO EARTH

There are parallel dimensions co-existing within different frequency levels of the **Earth** and **Cosmos.** They are spiritual worlds or kingdoms - ranging from the Elemental or Fairy Kingdom sustained through and within the formation of *Earth crystals* through to the Galactic Kingdoms which exist within the Cosmos through different formations of the *cosmic crystals.*

Elemental lightbeings or 'fairies' co-exist with us but within different realms sustained within different frequency levels *within the Earth*.

Terrestrial lightbeings from the 'Galactic' Kingdoms also co-exist with us here on Earth but within different realms sustained within different frequency levels *within the Cosmos or space*.

These dimensions not only co-exist with us but filter through into our DNA, etheric body and lightbody - through consciousness and light - the necessary **codes** and **frequencies** enabling us to enter into these parallel dimensions or worlds which are part of the totality of our gene pool and DNA.

At this point in time, most of humanity does not acknowledge or explore these dimensions within and around us. However, all of humanity will come to understand more about them now that our lightbodies are being activated to manifest through, during this time of transition from 1999-2012. After the transition into the fifth dimension, humanity will not only understand more about the dimensions of these realities and worlds but will begin to access them.

THE MERKABAH BODY

The lightbody and co-existing Merkabah technology give us the resources to lightbody travel into parallel dimensions and co-existing worlds.

Earth and cosmic crystals not only create and sustain the formation and manifestation process of the etheric/physical and lightbodies, but also sustain and resonate the internal technology and geometric codes to create the Merkabah body. The crystals resonate the geometric codes from the *stellar gateways* into our DNA which in turn filters them into the lightbody's electromagnetic field - to create the Merkabah body.

The Merkabah is the etheric vehicle in which the lightbody travels through space and into parallel dimensions and co-existing worlds within the Earth and Cosmos.

MULTIDIMENSIONAL EXISTENCE

The etheric, crystallised structures or templates which manifest as Earth and cosmic crystals create all forms of 'matter'. They sustain the internal technology (geometry) to crystallise frequencies of 'ether' into particles of *light* and *matter* to create all life forms within and beyond our dimension - the multidimensional kingdoms or worlds existing within parallel universes to Earth. These life forms which co-exist with us are part of our multidimensional gene pool and spiritual lineage.

CRYSTALS

1. Crystals 'Transferred' the Pleiadian Race into our Dimension.

As mentioned in chapter 2, the Pleiadians lived *within* and became the first civilisation to physically exist *on* Earth. By evolving different dimensions of their etheric/lightbody they were able to transfer from their previous *galactic dimensions* (outside of Earth in the constellation of Taurus) through and into the *Elemental Kingdoms of Earth*. When entering this kingdom they began the process of reforming and crystallising human lightbodies. This process took millions of years in our concept of time. Their consciousness entered the Earth's outer planes, or levels of existence, with the assistance of the *Earth and cosmic crystals.*

2. Crystals 'sustained' the Pleiadians' life force in and on Earth.

At the time Nature was creating the elements and environment of the Earth, which became lush with all the resources necessary for biological life, the Pleiadians still existed as translucent lightbodies in the ethereal planes and etherically absorbed the elements and pranic healing properties of Nature.

When the Earth and cosmic crystals were creating Earth, the Pleiadians lived within the Elemental or Fairy Kingdoms *within* the Earth crystals. The internal technology and electromagnetic frequencies of the Earth crystals sustained and created their humanoid etheric/lightbodies, chakras and pranic energy system. The Pleiadians were then able to access and etherically absorb the necessary elements and resources from Nature and planet Earth to materialise and eventually evolve the *physical body*. Over millions of years they slowly manifested and materialised into the third dimensional world to become the first physical humanoid forms to exist on Earth.

Lemuria was the name of the civilisation on Earth, at that time. The Pleiadians became the first lightbeings to co-exist *within* and *on* the Earth. They created the first template from which the Human Race evolved both physically and spiritually. Therefore the genetic structure and nature of the 'first Adam' was Pleiadian.

ADAM

The Soul who later became Jesus, incarnated as Adam, the 'first-born' son of the God/Goddess who was and did obtain, the 'consciousness of light' on Earth. He was the first Soul to etherically template *specific* frequencies into the etheric body and DNA, to create the first 'perfected' blueprint or mould of the human physical body and consciousness.

His DNA sustained the first complete *etheric coding system* to be able to access and become conscious of the *Higher Self, Divine Spirit and Tree of Life*. It enabled him to access higher or more human and Divine levels of consciousness than had been accessed on Earth until that time. Before and around the time of Adam other life forms of a more a primitive nature, physical form and consciousness also existed. They have mutated their DNA to evolve into the different species of animals (around 800 species) that exist on Earth today.

EARTH'S ROLE AS THE HEALING PLANET

Planet Earth naturally evolved to create/birth and *sustain* the physical human body through which consciousness could evolve.

It was the internal technology and properties of the Earth and cosmic crystals that created the Earth and the Global Grid Matrix whose *centre point* is the crystallised *core* of the Earth. I have seen how this crystallised core *sustains* the central 'gravity point' of the physical human body within the third to fifth dimensions, for universal healing and ascension.

THE GLOBAL GRID MATRIX AND 'TRINITY' LEVELS OF THE HUMAN PHYSICAL BODY AND CONSCIOUSNESS

> **We could not evolve into higher levels of consciousness and being without sustaining and co-existing from and within *all* of the dimensional 'bodies' mentioned below.**

THE THIRD DIMENSIONAL PHYSICAL BODY

The Global Grid Matrix is responsible for creating and sustaining the necessary dimensions of the *etheric* body which then co-creates the dimensions of the *physical anatomy* within the *third dimension*. The etheric body does this by filtering in all of the necessary minerals and elements from the *physical* Earth and Cosmos, to co-create the outer layers known and seen as the (physical) human body.

THE FOURTH DIMENSIONAL ETHERIC/LIGHTBODY

The etheric/lightbody sustains the human body and consciousness, on a parallel level to the third dimension, within the *fourth dimension*. This dimension of the body continually filters in and weaves through all the necessary elements such as 'ether' and *the frequencies or vibrational properties of Nature*, so the **etheric**/physical body can co-create the elemental secretions for the continual evolutionary process of the physical form. The *inner* layers of our etheric/lightbody co-create qualities of consciousness that we see as our inner child-like qualities and the emotional and creative aspects of the heart and Soul which reflect our personality and inner nature out into the world.

THE FIFTH DIMENSIONAL COSMIC/LIGHTBODY

The cosmic/lightbody sustains itself on a parallel level within the *fifth dimension*. It filters in necessary *elements* such *as electromagnetic frequencies and stellar gateway* codes from the Cosmos. They create the dimensions of our lightbody we know as the androgynous Higher Self and also the technological aspects of the mind or brain which enable us to reflect our perceptions, thoughts and intellectual attributes out into the world. This dimension of the body continually weaves through the necessary electromagnetic frequencies so the **etheric/lightbody** can continue to heal itself and evolve and in turn continue the ongoing healing and evolutionary process of the **physical anatomy.**

> **The etheric/physical body can only sustain a life force and continue to ascend if there is also an evolving lightbody system.**

The Global Grid Matrix not only enables the human body to co-exist within all energetic and physical elements and dimensions mentioned above, but also *alchemically* transfers the compositions within the elements so more light and ether can be co-created and sustained within our physical body and consciousness. It is this inner technology which will ultimately enable us to ascend into the parallel dimensions and worlds that co-exist with us, such as the realms of the Pleiades, Sirius and Orion.

As we ascend through and by the elements we can also start to *consciously* co-exist within these parallel dimensions while evolving on Earth. This is because the energetic properties that constitute the organic make-up of the dimensional levels of the etheric/lightbody, which sustains our energetic Nature in this world, is similar to their lightbodies. However, as they are more evolved than we are, they exist on higher levels of frequency, matter and consciousness. *(The dimensions are explained further in chapter 14)*.

- PART 2 -
THE HEART CENTRE OF PARALLEL REALITIES AND UNIVERSES

THE CRYSTAL CORE OF THE EARTH

The internal *physical* structure of Earth's core mostly consists of iron, with smaller amounts of nickel and other metals. It has a solid inner core and a liquid outer core; the mantle is made of different types of rocks and magma; the crust (c 0.1% of the diameter) is made up of solid rocks.

Earth's physical centre core, as explained above, is a *crystallised core* that creates an electromagnetic field and *pull*, so therefore has the role of a *gravity point* (or centre point) that supports us in sustaining multidimensional levels within our etheric/body and consciousness - while in physical incarnation on the planet.

MIDWAY STATION WITHIN THE UNIVERSE

As mentioned previously, I have seen how the crystallised core of our planet sustains the central gravity point of *the physical human body* so it can sustain its life force within the third to fifth dimensions. However, since many parallel galaxies and universes co-exist with Earth, on a multidimensional level within lower and higher frequency levels of space, the crystallised core of planet Earth is also the *central grid point for **universal** healing and ascension* - it is a midway station *within the universe.*

EARTH'S FREQUENCY

This **crystal core** emanates *a specific* 'OM' *tone* and *vibration* in the frequency of F#. However, it is on such a pure and high vibrational level we can't hear it with normal sensory perception. In 1999, through psychic perception, I felt and heard the frequency of the Earth's core change. The initial tone of F changed to F# where it will remain until 2012. Between 2012-2013 it will then gently transfer again, into the tone of G.

Since this crystal core also sustains the electromagnetic frequencies which in turn sustain the **physical** foundations of the heart, this shift is creating abnormally high levels of energetic pressure within the physical and emotional 'heart of humanity'.

Everybody is being energetically pushed to shift the frequency of the heart on a physical and metaphysical level so the 'heart of humanity' can purify and evolve, at a more rapid rate. This is how global consciousness is now evolving so rapidly between 1999-2012 from a third dimensional reality and heart-based (emotional and spiritual) perspective to a fifth dimensional reality and heart-based perspective. We are evolving more rapidly on an emotional and spiritual level to enter into a higher and more evolved state of consciousness.

THE 'HEART'S CORE' TRANSMISSION

At the time of Earth's creation, the vibration of the crystal core resonated and transmitted out to many parallel struggling dimensions and their existing worlds, entities and beings, the message that 'Earth provides a *crystal Doorway* through which healing and ascension can occur'. It is now also transmitting a new 'holographic sound frequency' to the parallel worlds and realities that the 'heart of humanity' is *now* making a dimensional shift into a new level of consciousness. *Now* is the most pivotal point in time to enter this dimension and world as it holds the greatest possibility/probability for obtaining a higher level of evolution. The energies are now available on Earth, to obtain more ether and light through a new 'transference process of the body and consciousness.'

STEPS OF CONSCIOUSNESS

The global consciousness of planet Earth impacts all other parallel worlds that are aspects of our genetic DNA. In this way we are all inter-connected and 'one.' During a physical death process we go through many steps of consciousness. It is a time of transition to enable us to shift consciousness while we ascend through our lightbody into a parallel dimension or reality inter-dimensional lightbeings interact within and between these worlds as part of their evolutionary process.

The lightbody enables us to sustain our essence or life force between incarnations. In time we all will come to re-connect with loved ones either on a more evolved planet Earth, or within different dimensions at different times in our evolutionary process. We are all spiritually inter-active, so will continue to co-exist with each other in different relationships as we grow.

Nothing ever dies. Frequencies of energy can never be created or destroyed; they can only be transferred from one state of being into another through a divinely orchestrated evolutionary process, so that consciousness can experience many holographic realities *to understand the meaning of life.*

EARTH'S COSMIC DOORWAY

The Earth's core and planet Earth herself are the 'Doorway' into the 'Kingdoms of Heaven'.

The energetic **'core'** of planet Earth is a **cosmic Doorway** into realities within and on the Earth for healing and ascension.

Lightbodies gravitate here to receive and create the necessary properties and elements to heal the consciousness of the Soul and to ascend through the different dimensions and experiences of life on Earth. Eventually they ascend through Earth and the Gateway of Orion to enter into other physical realms or parallel worlds of higher vibration and consciousness for a more evolved life force, experience and existence - such as the higher galactic and ethereal dimensions and worlds of the Pleiades, Orion and Sirius.

HEART MASTERY
THE VITAL EVOLUTIONARY KEY

What is so unique about Earth is that she enables incoming Souls/lightbodies to anchor in the vibration and formation of *the heart chakra and the physical and emotional heart*.

The *crystal core*, *template* and *electromagnetic field* created by the molten rock and crystallised formation of the **core** of the Earth, sustain the electromagnetic field for the creation process of the *physical heart*.

EVOLUTIONARY KEY

Forming a human heart is a vital evolutionary step as the physical and energetic heart creates:

+ The dimensions of the *emotional body*.

+ Certain 'geometric' electromagnetic frequencies so the lightbody can manifest and evolve.

+ The frequency changes in consciousness to resonate into a higher vibrational level and into a more evolved etheric/physical or ethereal state of being.

Souls/lightbeings choose to incarnate, heal and grow through planet Earth and this dimension because 'consciousness' obtains more wisdom, depth and comprehension from the internal technology of the heart. As the heart energetically heals within, we emotionally purify and evolve and become more connected to the God/Goddess.

A UNIVERSAL VIEWPOINT OF THE SEVEN MAIN CHAKRAS

Our primary or fundamental chakra system is basically divided into two levels - the lower and higher levels. The heart chakra divides and integrates the Lower Self (base, naval and solar plexus chakras) from and with the Higher Self (throat, third eye and crown chakras).

THE LOWER CHAKRA SYSTEM: BASE, SACRAL/NAVAL, SOLAR PLEXUS AND HEART CHAKRAS

This system sustains and maintains *physical form and substance*. It is vital for the evolutionary process of the etheric/physical body. The three main lower chakras are designed to sustain and maintain our physical body, function and wellness by integrating through the four elements (earth, air, fire and water) from the Earth and Cosmos. They absorb the four elements to manifest a physical body or template which can maintain our Soul's sense of *physical identity* at all times, in all worlds sustained within the third to fifth dimensions.

The Lower Self and lower chakra system integrates our consciousness into the lower worlds and realities which constitute the experiences, realms and realities we can master when living in a more physical third dimensional world like planet Earth, or even into higher dimensional *physical* worlds within the fifth dimension. It is also an energy system designed to help us integrate the human and Divine aspects, emotions and energies for the *heart/fourth chakra* to continue to open and evolve. (There are actually three energetic levels to the *heart chakra* which will be explained later in this chapter).

THE HIGHER CHAKRA SYSTEM:
HEART, THROAT, THIRD EYE AND CROWN CHAKRAS

This system sustains and maintains *spiritual 'consciousness'* and the *lightbody system*. It sustains the electromagnetic fields within the etheric/physical body and monitors the integration process of the Lower Self or the lower chakra system so the Higher Self and lightbody system can weave through and into manifestation.

These chakras absorb the more *refined* ethereal substances of the four elements. They therefore enable the manifestation of the lightbody so we can sustain our essence or life force between incarnations and within higher realms of consciousness within worlds co-existing within the fifth to seventh dimensions. The Higher Self (heart, throat, third eye and crown chakras) enables us to open up the creative and spiritual side of our nature.

The Higher Self and higher chakra system monitor and weave through into the physical body, the internal technology and knowledge to maintain automatic function, life force and consciousness.

TEMPLATING

The chakras are energetic vortices that resonate clockwise and/or anti-clockwise to absorb the elements and ether for the etheric/ physical body to continually revitalise and nourish itself. The chakras also grid-in and absorb the necessary geometric templates and energies from the Earth and Cosmos so we can evolve, grow spiritually and refine the emotions to begin to function within *higher levels of consciousness*. They grid/weave and encode through specific etheric geometries directly from the *crystals* and the *Global Grid Matrix* to enable us to evolve, self-master and become more enlightened in body and consciousness.

> The technology or templating system of
> the chakras can also absorb the necessary
> energies and elements to create the
> *new anatomy* of the *Adam Kadmon* and
> eventually bring the whole lightbody system
> into manifestation so we can master our
> ascension process.

THE 'TRINITY' OF THE HEART CHAKRA

The heart chakra absorbs its gridding and electromagnetic impulses directly from the *crystallised core of the Earth* which it then filters through directly into the physical heart.

The geometric coding system of the *heart chakra* determines the health of the physical heart and its adjoining organs such as the thymus gland (immune system) and lungs. The energetic coding/ gridding system of the *heart chakra* also determines which of the three chambers - the levels, rays and templates - of the heart and consciousness the body is working from. (These three energetic chambers are explained further in following paragraphs).

The other six chakras absorb their gridding and electromagnetic impulses directly from the gridding system of the Global Grid Matrix which is sustained by *the crystals of the Earth and Cosmos.*

They respond to each other and also independently interact with the *heart chakra*. Therefore, since the *heart chakra* operates through and with each of the other chakras, the health, consciousness and ascension process is determined by the degree to which the *heart chakra* is resonating from, with and to, each of the chakras.

THE THREE ENERGETIC CHAMBERS OF THE HEART CHAKRA

As we grow spiritually and shift consciousness on a cellular level the etheric geometric codes, sustaining *the template* through which the *heart chakra* functions also shift. These codes determine which dimensions of the gridding the heart and all chakras can access and obtain. As we emotionally and intellectually reach higher levels of consciousness via the chakra system, a deeper chamber of the heart can open. It is only through the *heart chakra* that we can absorb universal energies and knowledge.

> *The heart therefore protects Nature's sacred energies, knowledge and powers.*

THE FIRST CHAMBER OF THE HEART CHAKRA

The first chamber of the heart chakra resonates through the **Green Ray** and stimulates the emotion of *love*. It creates a general healing process in the physical body and a subtle refinement process in the etheric and emotional body. At this time most of us are working through and towards mastering the first chamber. The patterning and energies of the lower and higher chakra system that weave through the first chamber of the heart are what characterise our humanity.

Attributes

Ninety-nine percent of the population is working towards mastering the first chamber of the heart. To continue healing and spiritually evolving on Earth and through Nature we need to begin to master our Lower Self by fully engaging in physical, mental, emotional and spiritual life experiences on Earth, such as eating, loving, sharing, exercising, working, procreating, raising children, learning and connecting with Nature. Before we can move into the second chamber of the heart we also need to master the ability to 'heal thyself.'

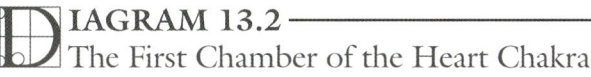

DIAGRAM 13.2
The First Chamber of the Heart Chakra

Copyright 2005 Alexis Cartwright, Keeper of the Crystals Pty Ltd.

THE SECOND CHAMBER OF THE HEART CHAKRA

The second chamber of the heart resonates through the Pink Ray and stimulates the emotion of unconditional love. Those who are now working towards becoming masters (about one percent of humanity), during this time of transition, are working towards opening, functioning from and mastering the second chamber of the heart chakra.

DIAGRAM 13.3
The Second Chamber of the Heart Chakra

Copyright 2005 Alexis Cartwright, Keeper of the Crystals Pty Ltd.

As the patterning and electromagnetic energies of the higher chakra system weaves through the second chamber of the *heart chakra,* our consciousness evolves and we begin to create the 'cosmic lightbody' and Merkabah system, which establishes us as being 'Christened'. We are then able to access, through higher consciousness, what is needed to understand the purpose, meaning and direction of our life. We are also able to evolve and ascend into higher levels of consciousness by anchoring through artistic, psychic and spiritual gifts and talents and create a more profound healing response and process for ourselves and others by channelling universal insight and energies.

Attributes

At the beginning of the transition from 1999-2012, only one percent of the population was working towards mastering the second chamber of the *heart chakra.* They are supporting the rest of humanity to do so over the upcoming years. They are not only channellers of the light, 'Lightworkers', but are generally mastering in their day to day lives and are, in some way, of service to humanity.

As we master the attributes of our inner Nature, while living within the third dimension or physical body, the second chamber of the *heart chakra* begins to weave and anchor through more of the higher chakra system. The seven chakras are then working on a higher frequency and enabling us to reach beyond space and time to co-exist within higher levels of consciousness. We are therefore able to communicate and co-exist with the higher dimensions and realities sustained within the seven parallel universes, which are part of our evolutionary process, and assisting us at this time.

THE THIRD CHAMBER OF THE HEART CHAKRA

The third chamber of the heart chakra resonates through the radiant **Blue Ray** and stimulates the emotion of *compassion*. Very few on the planet are working from, or running their consciousness through, this third chamber of the *heart chakra,* as we must first embody the dimensions of the first and second chambers.

To integrate and live by the consciousness of the third chamber we must:

* Be *living in* higher consciousness.

* Be practicing and living in spiritual service to humanity in some way.

* Embody and master the new dimensions of the new anatomy or Adam Kadmon - the template of the fifth dimensional physical human body.

* Have anchored certain degrees of the lightbody and Merkabah and therefore be living in a higher and more multidimensional level of consciousness as an ascending master. (*Ascending masters* are a step beyond those who are mastering on this plane.)

DIAGRAM 13.4
The Third Chamber of the Heart Chakra

Copyright 2005 Alexis Cartwright, Keeper of the Crystals Pty Ltd.

The third chamber of the heart chakra only opens with assistance from the four upper chakras - **stellar gateway, soul star, causal and earth star chakras** - which exist beyond the seven main chakras. They anchor through higher artistic, psychic and spiritual gifts and talents which create *'genius'* levels and qualities of the mind and spirit, as well as creating the dimensions of the Christbody and Consciousness.

DIAGRAM 13.5
The Eleven Chakras

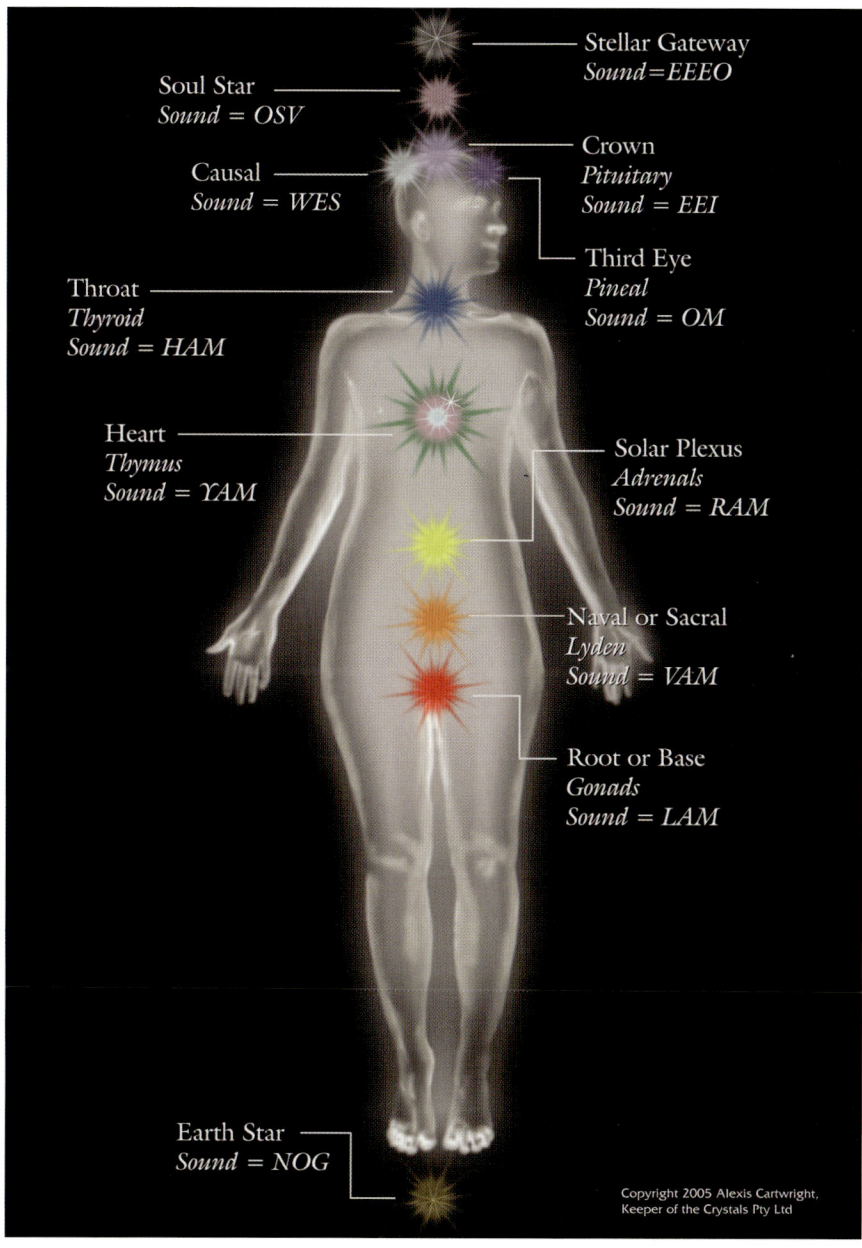

Stellar Gateway
Sound=EEEO

Soul Star
Sound = OSV

Causal
Sound = WES

Crown
Pituitary
Sound = EEI

Third Eye
Pineal
Sound = OM

Throat
Thyroid
Sound = HAM

Heart
Thymus
Sound = YAM

Solar Plexus
Adrenals
Sound = RAM

Naval or Sacral
Lyden
Sound = VAM

Root or Base
Gonads
Sound = LAM

Earth Star
Sound = NOG

Opening the third chamber of the *heart chakra* indicates that we are being 'Christened' *to not only embody the finer frequencies and cosmic consciousness of the lightbody* but also the *Christbody* and *Consciousness*.

Attributes

Since the beginning of the transition of 1999-2012, only one percent of the small proportion of Humanity who are mastering the second chamber of the *heart chakra*, are working towards opening the third chamber of the *heart chakra* and running consciousness from that level. Only a few will do so during this lifetime on Earth. However, they will be the *principle* people helping the Earth and humanity create the necessary energetic resources to survive and achieve the universal death and rebirth, to enter into the next dimension. They have come to Earth specifically to ascend into a state of Mastership and embody the necessary energies to become an *ascending master* at this time - and while doing so become a vital support system for the Celestial Christ on Earth.

If we tap into this higher aspect of the Self we become master healers, teachers and channellers on the planet. We are also able to grid-through, anchor-in and access the higher energies to be of service to others and support the planet itself. As grid channellers we are of service on a universal level. We become master initiates and create massive changes in the Earth and humanity's evolutionary process.

THE SEVEN CHAKRAS AND SECOND CHAMBER OF THE HEART CHAKRA

SUMMARY

We are spiritual beings living within seven parallel dimensions while in a physical body on Earth. Through the seven main chakras we co-exist within the physical and spiritual planes to master the inner and outer dimensions of our nature through integrating our lower and higher chakra systems.

Through integrating the energies of the chakra system and evolving in consciousness by mastering the attributes of the **second chamber of the *heart chakra,*** we can personally grow into a more unconditional level of consciousness and a more perfected physical and spiritual state of being. We can more effectively create and maintain health, longevity and freedom of spirit. We can also become more refined in nature and like a master, live without personal and financial struggle and without painful lightbody symptoms.

> **The old concept 'to be spiritual is to suffer' is no longer a reality within our New World.**

When we begin to master the *heart chakra* and open the second chamber, we bring through a more evolved emotional state of being which enables unconditional love to flow through. The **Pink Ray** begins to resonate through and we begin to master our gifts and talents to become not simply a *'master'* but begin an *'ascending Mastership on Earth'*.

To utilise and benefit from these deeper chambers of the *heart chakra,* we need to live in a multidimensional reality by participating in our spiritual growth process. We can do this by working through karmic relationships; working in a humanitarian or spiritual way; travelling and participating in global change; communicating through higher levels of consciousness with like minded people and also perfecting our channelling ability, and intuitive and telepathic gifts and talents.

RE-ESTABLISHING A LOST LEVEL OF CONSCIOUSNESS

To evolve into higher levels of consciousness, we need to be living all the multidimensional levels of ourselves in mind, body and spirit - from a heart-based perspective. The etheric body, 12-strand DNA and corresponding seven chakras regulate and reconnect all multidimensional (Earth, elemental and galactic) aspects within us. As we master and integrate more of the dimensions of the seven main chakras through the *inner chambers of the heart chakra,* we will become more quasi-dimensional like in Lemuria and Atlantis. We will no longer be restricted by third dimensional gravity, space and time as we have since the fall of Atlantis.

A REVELATION

In the same way as the ancient word and sound, **'OM'**, is a vibrational tool which creates the correct dimensions of the electromagnetic field of the *heart chakra,* **YHWH,** the Hebrew word for God, meaning **'I AM THAT I AM',** is a vibrational tool which can help us take the next vital steps in evolution - at this time of 'universal death, rebirth, and ascension into the next dimension.'

> **I have channelled that geometric frequency of the word YHWH creates the perfection process of the three chambers of the *heart chakra* so that all dimensions of the *heart chakra* can integrate and work in *harmony* with the other six chakras.**

'YHWH,' is therefore the key sound or word to unlock and perfect all three chambers of the *heart chakra* so the main chakra system can work more effectively.

The higher chakra system integrates with the lower chakra system through the *trinity* of the three templates, levels and chambers of the *heart chakra*. When functioning together and in harmony with the main chakra system, these three chambers of the *heart chakra*, create a state of consciousness that reflects absolute *'Truth'* and *'Compassion'* so therefore a *'Revelation'* can be obtained.

> **'I AM** - lower chakra system (Truth)
>
> **THAT** - heart chakra (Compassion)
>
> **I AM'** - higher chakra system (Revelation)

A 'Revelation' is a divinely orchestrated realisation, obtained from a *heart-based perspective,* through which a core knowing of absolute truth comes into consciousness.

By saying this Hebrew word while in a state of meditation an optimal level of perfection can be obtained within the geometric formations of all the chakras simultaneously. This enables the etheric/physical body to access the necessary energies and coding system to receive a 'Revelation'.

(I also channelled that YHWH is the word which initiates the healing and ascension powers symbolised and encoded within the 'Book of Revelations'. When I looked up the 'Book of Revelations' I found that the 'chakras' are frequently mentioned or symbolically referred to in many of its verses.)

MEDITATION

A powerful meditation is to say the sacred word YHWH in Hebrew (pronounced yod-he-vav-he) and each time it is repeated, visualise the colours corresponding with each chakra - as described below.

Close your eyes:

1. Say the Hebrew name 'YHWH'.

VISUALISE GREEN going through the lower chakras (base, naval and solar plexus). Say the key 'I AM **Truth**'

2. Say the Hebrew name 'YHWH'.

VISUALISE PINK going through the higher chakras (throat, third eye and crown).

Say the key 'I AM **Unconditional**'.

3. Say the Hebrew name 'YHWH'.

VISUALISE GREEN, PINK AND THE RADIANT BLUE LIGHT going through the heart chakra.

Say the key 'I AM **Compassion**'.

4. Say, the Hebrew name 'YHWH'.

Draw the symbol of each of the four letters of the Hebrew word YHWH (appearing below) directly into the HEART CHAKRA to complete the integration of the seven chakras through and into the three chambers of the heart.

יהוה

5. Sit and let the energy integrate for a couple of minutes.

- PART 3 -
REVIEW

This section does not simply review chapter 13, but also gives more information on the creative source, principle and properties of creation itself.

Some of these key points explain the spiritual science involved in the creative process.

I advise that you read each key point as a separate reading and you review these points at different times to better understand the essence and power behind the creative principle.

1.1   **Genesis: The origins of life created by sound from geometric disc-like templates**

1.2   **The Transference 'Master Christ Template Set'**

1.3   **The Laws of Genetic Engineering**

1.4   **The 'Crystal Prism' of Lyra**

1.5   **Crystal Alchemy**

1.6   **Grid Points into Inter-dimensional Kingdoms**

1.7   **The Seven Levels of the Chakra System**

1.8   **Universal Healing through the 'Heart' of Earth and Nature**

1.9   **Expanding into Christ Consciousness**

1.10 **Heart Mastery**

1.1 GENESIS

ORIGINS OF LIFE CREATED BY SOUND FROM ETHERIC DISC-LIKE GEOMETRIC TEMPLATES

In the beginning, before the Earth began its formation process, a genetic coding system from *etheric* **disc-shaped geometric templates** began to resonate into space from Lyra. (See chapter 14 for more details). Each separate disc had a unique geometric technology inside.

So, even before the 'Big Bang' there was a form of high frequency etheric crystal technology which co-coordinated the whole creation process. The initial discs or templates co-existed within our level and area of space but within a higher frequency. Therefore, the frequencies of 'sound' which initially transmitted from these cosmic discs or templates resonated within the ethers of space, before time and matter existed within our space-time or dimension.

THE BIG BANG

However, through the compression of energy released by the Big Bang, these templates were able to filter through into our dimension of space, the *internal technology* to co-ordinate the creation of the first particles - electrons, protons, neutrons - and their antiparticles.

Optional Reading: **How Physical Matter was Created**

> **A personal and original concept of the Big Bang and the creation process of the first forms of matter within our Universe -** *Alexis*

It is important to note that all of the key creative steps mentioned below, occurred simultaneously and almost immediately at the time of the Big Bang - and still exist or occur today, as a vital part of our co-creative and evolutionary process.

THE INNER CORE POINT AND CIRCUMFERENCE OF SPACE

The inner core/centre point/Void is the area in space where the Big Bang exploded. Imagine that the point in the centre of a circle sustains the dimension or area where the Big Bang occurred and the circumference is the outer proximity of where the 'sound particles' were dispersed.

THE ALCHEMICAL PROCESS

Within a very short time *after* the Big Bang, certain areas of space further away from the *centre* of the explosion cooled down more rapidly than those closer to it. **The difference in temperatures** caused certain vibrational frequencies I call 'sound waves or *particles*', to begin to vary the intensity at which they were resonating and this variance created *electrical charge which in turn further stimulated the temperature changes.*

While the centre point is a much smaller, compressed area than the circumference, it holds the same proportion and **volume** of *energy* of *resonating 'sound particles'* as the *outer circumference* which sustains more space. (Although, at that time, nothing as yet physically existed within space, in a *physical* third dimensional sense – this can be compared to the physical structure of planet Earth whose core sustains more density, matter or gravity than the outer, surface layers of the Earth where the minerals and compounds are lighter and the temperatures cooler).

The centre point is denser, hotter, more *magnetic* and *vibrational* in nature - *vibrations* move *horizontally* eg. when 'sound waves' move through heavier volumes of energy. Its heat and heavier vibrational resonance produced the heavy proton particles.

The circumference is lighter, *cooler* and more *electrical* in nature – its *frequencies* move *vertically* eg. when 'sounds waves' move through lighter or more dispersed volumes of energy. It produced the electrons which carry a negative electric charge, and the neutrons.

Therefore, at the time of the Big Bang, a divinely orchestrated alchemical process occurred. Higher *crystal frequencies* of 'sound' were resonating through and into the Void from another dimension - the crystal **Prism of Lyra** (explained more in chapters 13 & 14) as temperatures were changing and creating electrical charges, and energy levels were building and dispersing as the explosion released the pressure.

Through this process, the first properties and compounds of physical *light* and *matter* slowly began to come into manifestation in our dimension. As the frequencies were changing, the different particles were coming into existence on parallel levels to the elements. Heavier protons corresponded with 'earth and water' while lighter electrons and neutrons corresponded with 'fire and air. The elements were the first third dimensional particles of light and matter to come into manifestation.

CREATION OF THE ATOM

*Heavier positively charged and more **vibrational*** energies were resonating from the Void while *lighter, negatively charged* and more ***electrical*** energies were resonating from the outer dimensions from where the Big Bang occurred.

This polarity or opposition of electrical charges is what influences a proton to pull an electron in towards itself to create 'atoms,' the building blocks of matter. As the levels of frequency and temperature decreased, the weight of the initial electrons *increased* so the protons could capture them to form the 'atoms'.

Meanwhile the higher *crystal frequencies* of 'sound' were still resonating through, from the other dimension - the crystal **Prism of Lyra**. They contained the internal technology and very fine, higher frequencies necessary to create the *crystal and light hologram* of the **Global Grid Matrix.** The matrix continued to relay the internal technology necessary for *each* atom to build and manifest through, within a third to fifth dimensional hologram, the creation process of our whole world and reality. The Global Grid Matrix and our holographic world and reality still continues to evolve today, through and from this point in time and space.

The world was beginning to come into physical manifestation through the crystal technology and ethereal resources filtered through by the Global Grid Matrix. Elements were forming and changing, temperatures cooling and the electrical charges continued to blend, weave and attract different particles together into atoms. This created a divinely orchestrated 'mutation' and transference process necessary to create the combination of elements and properties of which our body, consciousness and world or reality are made of and continue to evolve through and from.

OVERVIEW ON THE CONCEPTS AND PRINCIPLES OF GENESIS

I believe the internal technology of these 'sound waves' and their etheric substances - the negative and positive *electric* and *magnetic* (electromagnetic) properties and forces sustained *within* every atom - sustain a whole untapped dimension of higher frequency particles within each of the millions of tiny atoms from which we are made. This storehouse of very fine etheric matter contains the 'unformed' substance within the Void from which all dimensions of our physical anatomy and body, reality, elements and kingdoms within our expanding solar system and Universe - are co-created from and through.

This unformed storehouse of matter within each atom, also sustains the *resources* necessary for us to evolve and will eventually come into manifestation, as we filter it through and into our body and consciousness. We will then ascend into a more evolved state of being. Our body will become lighter and lighter but as we still sustain the essence and technology of neutrons and protons, we will still maintain gravity and form. The bodies we are evolving into and the worlds we are coming to co-exist within have less restriction and more freedom. We will *crystallise* light and sustain more 'ether' within our body, to maintain less gravity and duality.

THE NINTH TO ELEVENTH DIMENSION

Therefore the necessary internal technology and resources are available from within us to continue our evolutionary process for eons of time, until we enter the ninth dimension. The atomic co-creation process will continue until we have attained this level of existence. (Explained further in 'Revelations').

The Universe is continuing to expand because the compression of energy continues to be slowly released and while doing so filters through higher frequencies of light particles into our body, consciousness, reality, world and Universe so everything can finally evolve into a ninth/eleventh dimensional body and its holographic reality. This level of existence is far beyond the fifth/seventh dimension, lightbody/Christbody and Consciousness and is the Celestial Christbody and Consciousness.

ΠATURAL MUTATIOΠ

Nothing ever dies only transforms or mutates, so we all hold within us the creative energies of the core/centre point or Void through which we continue to co-create ourselves on all levels. The third dimension is a hologram through which we can see and identify the lessons we need to learn to *balance* within, in order to evolve. We can reach into the core of our inner being (which sustains itself within a principle gravity point within the etheric body) to filter through from source the many levels and layers of frequency, energy and substances necessary to continue to sustain our existence and our co-creative and evolutionary process.

To see or touch the Void from where all resources are accessed and information is obtained, we must do more than look outside ourselves using only the external senses and a rational, scientific level of consciousness. Rather than just studying the planets, we must *see* the compounds that are visible in our own anatomy and rather than just talking about the light - as many people within the spiritual industry do – we must look honestly into the depths of our Soul, to see more of who we really are and thereby work to change and perfect ourselves.

We all sustain the technology, resources and inner power source to co-create within but to master this we need to look beyond the rational mind into the unknown. We also need to listen to the Universe and live not only on an intuitive level of consciousness but also by the laws of Nature and the Universe. Through this level of consciousness we can gain knowledge from a 'higher source', manifest a new 'gift or talent', and heal/cure the incurable.

STARS: THE FIRST FORM OF VISIBLE ENERGY OR LIGHT

> In the beginning, when God created the universe, the Earth was formless and desolate. The raging ocean that covered everything was engulfed in total darkness, and the power of God was moving over the water. Then God commanded, 'Let there be light'- and light appeared.
> God was pleased with what he saw.
>
> ### Old Testament: Genesis 1

In the beginning 'stars, light and crystals' slowly came into manifestation. These initial 'star' elements of light were just a physical manifestation or 'lower vibration' of core elements whose 'sound' technology filtered into our level of space before the matter that eventually formed the Earth was even created. These 'sound' frequencies were geometries or 'crystal templates' holographically filtered through from the crystal **'Prism of Lyra'** **and its holographic dimension.**

1.2 THE MASTER CHRIST TEMPLATE SET

Some of these geometric power symbols are etherically encoded into the five master symbols of the Transference Healing **'Master Christ Template'** set.

Refer to page 197 to find out how you can purchase your own Master Christ Template Set and incorporate this tool into your home or work environment.

DIAGRAM 13.6
The Master Christ Template Set

Copyright 2005 Alexis Cartwright, Keeper of the Crystals Pty Ltd.

The templates within this set are **The Master Christ Template** which is assisted by the geometries of the three **Black Ray Templates** and the emerald green **Crystal Cross Christ Template.**

The information I channelled through the Templates, holds a vital key to access and hold the powers of 'alchemy'. Through these templates we can obtain the internal knowing to access:

- The natural resources to co-*create* a healing that transfers the compounds of the elements within matter in the physical plane while filtering, embodying and *crystallising* light that reflects through from the Void and the non-physical plane.

1.3 THE LAWS OF GENETIC ENGINEERING

By working with the technology of the Master Christ Template Set (specifically the 'Three Black Sisters Templates') we are creating a *natural and divinely orchestrated* form of genetic engineering.

The technology of these templates orchestrates the shifting of the elements in the body so the *new* Adam Kadmon body can materialise. On a parallel level they also co-create the lightbody system, so we can take the next vital step in the evolutionary process.

The procedures I have channelled through as part of the Advanced Level teachings of Transference Healing hold a healing technology created and supported by a higher level of consciousness than our own *(refer to page 485 to learn more about Transference Healing Workshops)*. On the other hand, the unnatural, man-made genetic engineering process created and performed on Earth, controls and prevents a divinely orchestrated evolutionary process from developing. It is still trying to manipulate an old genetic template when the human body is now naturally changing on a molecular level into a new genetic template.

This is a similar scenario to what happened and partially created, the fall of Atlantis, when crystal power and technology was used by and for the *will* of *man* instead of being applied according to the *will of Nature and of the God/Goddess.*

1.4 THE CRYSTAL PRISM OF LYRA

We are becoming co-creators as we learn to heal ourselves and ascend through and by the light. Earth crystals are physical tools of light we can work with to help us in this healing and ascension process.

The template set has been channelled through me at this vital time of transition to support humanity in a different way. They hold the geometry of a specific crystal, known as the 'Crystal Prism of Lyra' which has not yet come into *physical* manifestation on Earth. It is 'diamond shaped' and harder and clearer than a diamond, but of a finer frequency. Although this crystal already co-exists with us etherically on a much higher frequency within our universe, it has not yet been able to physically create itself within this dimension because there is not enough hydrogen, oxygen and ether in our atmosphere. This crystal sustains some of the technology that is utilised and used within the dimension of Lyra to support not only the creation process of some of their holographic reality in which they live in, but also certain aspects of their complex lightbody/ Christbody system. *(This dimension is explained in more detail in the next chapter)*.

However, as the Earth ascends into a higher frequency, this crystal will be able to mineralise itself more effectively. It will then be used as an alchemical tool to help with a natural mutation and co-creation process of the 22-strand DNA, the lightbody Christbody system and opening of the fourth eye.

Procedures to work with specific crystals and the Master Christ Template set will be taught at the Transference 'Mystery School' beginning in 2006. These teachings will therefore be available before this crystal is physically born or formed on Earth. This will support the awakening and educational process of those who are to master and help the Earth and humanity at this vital time of transition and co-creation.

1.5 CRYSTAL ALCHEMY

Alchemy is the hidden force and technology that infuses energy, light and elements into a continual transformation and **co-creation** process.

The original etheric 'discs or templates' of codes, geometry, frequencies and 'sound' which existed before the 'Big Bang,' created:

♦ The technology of the Earth and cosmic crystals which embedded the genetic coding system for all life to evolve on Earth.

♦ The *Universal Laws* and principles through which life and consciousness create the ongoing steps in a divinely ordered evolutionary process.

This original and universal coding system from Lyra still exists within the Earth and cosmic crystals that sustain different degrees and levels of technology, of the 'Crystal Prism of Lyra.' They also sustain knowledge of creation and create an energetic connection to the ethereal worlds which still exist within the dimensions of Lyra itself. DNA was created from this very complex coding system. So, crystals therefore sustain within them the genetic imprint of Earth and all its inhabitants. *(This dimension where all life began in our Universe is explained further in chapter 14).*

1.6 GRID POINTS INTO INTER-DIMENSIONAL KINGDOMS

The Earth and cosmic crystals hold the inner technology to create the *Global Grid Matrix* which sustains the *etheric body* and weaves through the correct proportions of elements necessary for the maintenance and creation process of the *physical body* within this dimension. This inner technology also creates the geometry of the *etheric grid points* of this Global Grid Matrix which exists within and around the Earth and Cosmos.

The etheric grid points usually exist where *sacred sites* are established on the Earth and where stellar gateways are located within the Cosmos. They enhance our ascension process by giving us the internal spiritual technology to access not only into higher consciousness but also into higher dimensions. They create access points, etheric *Doorways* and portals into and between parallel dimensions.

These grid points look like 'crystal discs' and reactivate themselves when specific stargate activity occurs. In this way the necessary resources are etherically woven and filtered through to create the new dimensions of the DNA so we can continue our physical and spiritual evolutionary process.

The specific geometric dimensions of these *grid points* actually *reweave* the necessary *codes* into our **DNA** so the Earth and cosmic energies - from the inner and outer dimensions - can co-create the necessary dimensions of the lightbody and Merkabah. (The Merkabah is the etheric vehicle in which the lightbody travels through space and into parallel dimensions and co-existing worlds within the Earth and Cosmos).

The Merkabah body allows us to *connect in consciousness* to other parallel realms - ethereal and galactic civilisations, co-existing with us in this dimension within different frequency levels of the Earth and Cosmos itself. These realities and worlds are a part of the totality of our DNA and our past and future selves. They are known biblically as the 'Kingdoms of Heaven' and are the dimensions of the elemental, galactic and angelic planes.

1.7 THE SEVEN LEVELS OF THE CHAKRA SYSTEM

The seven main chakras were designed to sustain us in a physical body here on Earth and help us maintain wellness. They also enable us to integrate the human and Divine aspects of Nature in order to evolve and ascend. The perfection of the integration of the lower and higher chakras develops and opens deeper energetic chambers of the *heart chakra* so it can heal all dimensions of the body and integrate the electromagnetic frequencies for the etheric body to crystallise into the lightbody.

1.8 UNIVERSAL HEALING THROUGH THE HEART OF EARTH AND NATURE

Earth was created as a universal and multidimensional healing centre where lightbeings could evolve by obtaining and mastering the resources of Nature and a physical heart and *heart chakra*. As they evolve through the *heart chakra* they obtain a deeper spiritual perception as well as the resources from the Earth itself to heal the etheric/physical body and consciousness.

Lightbeings come to Earth because *it is possible* to access and integrate all 'aspects' of their multidimensional selves to emotionally heal, purify and evolve their DNA and eventually perfect their body and consciousness. This state of perfection is the Christbody and Consciousness.

1.9 EXPANDING INTO CHRIST CONSCIOUSNESS

- Matter shifts and integrates into a new sense of wholeness and completeness.

- Mind and body transform into 'ether' and spirit so we can embody the state of perfection - of the God/Goddess.

- Forgotten aspects of our multidimensional existence are revealed and integrated into Oneness.

- Past life memories are encoded into the DNA. As we become more enlightened or conscious of our Higher Self, we manifest internal gifts and talents. This enables us to reconnect and perfect aspects of our 'forgotten and past self' to shift into higher levels of consciousness and embody more of our 'higher and future self' while incarnated. We will ascend by embodying our 'future self' while still in a state of physical manifestation.

• Universal experiences and self-realisations can occur while reuniting with loved ones in other dimensions.

• We can co-exist with and experience other dimensional realities such as the galactic, elemental and angelic realms.

1.10 HEART MASTERY

We have entered through the 'cosmic Doorway of the core of the Earth' to incarnate on and into the Earth in order to:

• Materialise and perfect the etheric/physical body and electromagnetic/lightbody.

• Perfect an emotionally based, spiritual level of consciousness.

The evolution of *the heart chakra* is the key to the healing and evolutionary process of both our emotional and physical bodies. Through the evolution of the *heart chakra* we can heal, evolve, create a spiritual enlightenment process and obtain a more *humane nature* as we shift into higher consciousness.

The human *heart chakra* resonates with the crystal core of the Earth and is the key through which all *vibrational properties* and *natural resources* can be obtained from the Earth and Nature itself. Through receiving both vibrational and therapeutic properties from the Earth and Nature, the body can evolve on an emotional as well as a physical level and this creates a more *heart-based* consciousness rather than one based solely on intellect.

However, the human *heart chakra* is also the *control centre* of the human chakra system. It 'encodes' the whole chakra system and therefore the etheric/physical and evolving lightbody system with this new technology obtained from the Earth's core. The body and consciousness can not only:

* Obtain a gravity point from the heart to sustain its life force within this reality and world.

* Evolve by integrating this new technology from and through the Earth's core and heart into and through the chakras themselves, so the cellular level of the body can sustain more depth and evolve further on an emotional level.

What makes human beings such a unique race is that the evolution of the heart chakra allows us to run our intellect on a more emotional level of consciousness rather than the instinctual and intellectual levels of consciousness of those who exist within other parallel worlds within the third to fifth dimension.

> **On Earth we have the opportunity to live all of our multidimensional aspects from a heart-based perspective, activate Christ Consciousness and ascend through the Divine healing and ascension powers of the Celestial Christ.**

IMPORTANT: Completion Ritual

*Before you stop reading this chapter, run your finger from **right to left** across the sacred language below. This procedure will assist you to finalise the energies from this chapter.*

Your action, intent and the sacred vibration of this powerful language, will greatly assist you to fully integrate the information you have just read.

ᒧ⅄ᑕ∪ᗰ ᛕ⅄ᒣᛋᒣᛕ
ᛕᑕᒣᒣ∪⅄Ⴙᒣ ᛕ⅄⅄ᒣᒣ
∪ᒣᛋ∩Ⴙ⅄∪ᒣᒣ ᛕᗰ⅄ᛕᑕ⅄ᒣ

IMPORTANT: Commencement Ritual

*Before reading chapter 14, run your finger from **left to right** across the sacred language below.*

Your action, intent and the sacred vibration of this powerful language, will ensure that you are fully open to receiving and integrating the information within.

ꙄꙆꙆⲤꙄꙞꙆꙆ

ᏸᏨꙆꙄꙆ∩ᏆꙆƎᏌꙆ

ꙄꙆᏸꙆƎꙆꙆᏆᏸꙆ

Written above are the words "Doorways", "Grid points", and "Dimensions" using letters from the Angelic language called 'The Enochian Alphabet', which is a Language of Light that reflects the wisdom of Enoch.

These symbols will filter or weave through the necessary *Earth* and *cosmic grid points* and *ley lines* of *light* to support your reconnection process to the Divine and co-existing Kingdoms of the Lyran, Arcturian, Pleiadian, Orion and Sirian dimensions. This gridding process will enable you to filter through the necessary *crystal* and *cosmic codes* that will support your *DNA* in its mutating process so that you can physically anchor through more of your **celestial lightbody** system.

THE EARTH'S GRID POINT CONNECTIONS TO THE PARALLEL DIMENSIONS OF THE ANGELIC, ELEMENTAL AND GALACTIC WORLDS

FROM THE AUTHOR

Chapter 14 is very spiritually complex but I have included it for people to understand the source and origin of their own existence - the worlds, levels and realities they have and will come to live within - and through this process eventually understand more about the essence of the Christbody and Consciousness.

The technical nature of this chapter might not appeal to everyone, but will appeal to those interested in 'gridding'. It explains specific grid points or gateways in space, their origin and purpose in our dimension and where they connect through and into. These grid points and parallel dimensions play a vital role in creating and maintaining our divinity.

*It is not important to **consciously** comprehend the details in this chapter as you will receive a coding or 'gridding' process. As the codes filter into your DNA, they create a healing response so you might feel strange sensations through the middle ear, third eye area and the base of the back of the brain. I therefore advise you to 'ground' yourself after reading these chapters, or even parts of them, by going into a short meditation:*

Visualise a small star a few inches beneath each foot; then, from the base of each foot, extend a silver line to join down into the point of a V at the earth star chakra, six inches beneath the feet.

CHAPTER OVERVIEW

In this chapter you will discover:

- What existed in our space zone before planet Earth.

- That extra-terrestrials have etheric/lightbody systems, they are genetically connected to us and are an integral part of our genetic DNA system. They co-exist within the elements of a planetary system, living within the forces of nature that sustain their universe.

- Grid points also known as stellar gateways and how they connect up all co-existing worlds and create an inter-dimensional maze, which partly makes up the Earth and cosmic Global Grid Matrix.

- How universal 'Doorways' opened so entities could enter the Earth to obtain the healing and ascension process to become more 'enlightened', taking the next vital step in their evolution.

- Lyra is the cosmic Doorway through which the most evolved lightbeings known as Archangels entered our universe. Learn how these Cosmic Archangels were connected to Atlantis and how they created the 'elemental and galactic' races and worlds within Arcturus, Pleiades, Orion and Sirius . How they support a more cosmic aspect of the Global Grid Matrix and humanities evolution in consciousness.

- Arcturus is another stellar gateway, connected to Lyra through a grid line. Here tall ethereal Earth Angels & Archangels exist and work closely with the Elemental Kingdoms to heal the crystal grid lines of the Earth itself. They were connected with Lemuria and now support the global changes occurring as we shift into the fifth dimension.

- The Pleiadian stellar gateway connects to Earth through space, by a grid line directly through to Vega in the constellation of Lyra. This gateway allowed entities from outer evolving worlds to enter Earth as it was being created, so that they could weave in the necessary geometric coding system from the Earth Global Grid Matrix to mutate their DNA into the new double helix human DNA. This Doorway still allows terrestrial/galactic lightbeings to enter Earth.

- How we began to genetically evolve from the Pleiadian gene as well as, higher and lower frequency extra-terrestrials, and how we are continuing to evolve to our new 12-strand DNA system, a process due for completion in 2012.

- Earth and humanity have been in a state of descension since the time of Lemuria and Atlantis. However, since 1999 we have begun a rapid ascension shift back into the fifth dimension and beyond.

- The Sirian stellar gateway filters light into Earth for sustaining and evolving the lightbody. While Orion anchors the etheric physical/lightbody into a more crystallised state, so the body can ascend into higher frequencies of matter and therefore sustain itself in a higher dimension.

- At this point in time Sirius supports the more non-physical worlds that are more electromagnetic and angelic. While Orion supports the more physical worlds that are more ethereal and galactic in nature. These worlds co-exist and work very closely together.

- No dimension is more important than another and all co-exist and support the whole evolutionary process of our past and future self.

- Earth Masters and Ascending Masters are in a state of initiation to ascend into the higher dimension of Orion.

- We are all connected and one.

CHAPTER 14 GLOSSARY

I have given a small glossary and brief description on a few words that are used through out this chapter, so that the context to what has been written is not miss-understood because of general interpretation.

Terrestrials: a lightbeing that sustains a complex and unique DNA and etheric system that enables a more mineralised body to be formed that is created from specific compounds and elements from worlds and dimensions that are more embedded in 'matter'. They are therefore more *elemental* in nature than other comic beings.

Lightbody: is a body that also has a complex genetic and etheric system but is made of more *refined elements* and *electromagnetic frequencies* of *light* and is therefore more ethereal in nature and so is not so embedded, anchored or sometimes even so restricted, in matter.

Extra-terrestrial: Because the lightbody sustains the consciousness of the Soul a terrestrial body cannot sustain a life force and body without a lightbody, so therefore extra-terrestrials have a co-existing lightbody just like human beings.

The extra-terrestrials referred to in this chapter are lightbeings sustaining a consciousness that has an organically formed and temporary body that is sustained and created within, and by another parallel world or reality to our own.

Although the extra-terrestrials referred to in this book and specifically this chapter, also sustain a more physical body as we do, their body is built geometrically differently to our own, as well as being built from different compounds. They are also genetically connected to us, so are an integral part of our genetic DNA system or make-up.

They also co-exist within the elements of a planetary system just like human beings, living within and by the forces of nature that sustain their universe. Their bodies are born from the elements provided by their Earth, so that they can obtain a temporary vehicle through which they can live for a period of time on their planet, before evolving through their lightbody system into another world or reality. The internal technology of their evolving etheric/lightbody system then enables them to co-create new physical formations through which they can then live within their Earth and parallel realities or worlds and by doing so, continue to evolve in consciousness.

Galactic: is a being that has a consciousness and complex etheric system like a terrestrial being but their physical body is sustained more within a cosmic body rather than a more Earth or elemental one. It is made up of the energies and matter that are more alchemically refined therefore sustaining more 'ether'. The galactic body is therefore made up of and living within worlds where the substances sustain more electromagnetic and cosmic light frequency so it can live within worlds that are sustained more by light rather than denser levels of matter or even gravity. However like a terrestrial being they also have a co-existing lightbody system that enables them to go through a co-creation process by evolving into and through parallel worlds.

Christbody: is a lightbody system sustaining a Soul and consciousness like the galactic and terrestrial being, but is a more perfected aspect of both.

A 'Christbody' is therefore made of equal proportions of matter and light. The elements and substances sustaining the body have been alchemically refined and perfected through evolution, so therefore their bodies are more *crystallised* while being sustained within a co-existing lightbody system that is also made up of very high and pure cosmic frequencies of light. (Crystallised matter is solidified light). It is a state of being where one has mastered and obtained the necessary elements of nature, to become physically immortal.

DIMENSIONS FROM OUTER SPACE

Before planet Earth existed in our space zone, there was only space. However, there were parallel universes existing at different frequency levels beyond our space zone. Rotating planets existed within parallel universes, before Earth and our dimension were even created. These parallel worlds sustained and supported each other's evolutionary process and connected through and to each other, by **electromagnetic grid lines** connecting up different frequency points throughout all of space.

GRID POINTS IN SPACE

Over time, the *key* frequency 'connection' points became the *grid points* or centre points in space around which the stellar gateways formed. These gateways **create** energy vortices, 'corridors' or wormholes which connect up all the co-existing worlds and create an interdimensional maze of latitude and longitude electromagnetic grid lines which *partly* make up the **Earth** and **Cosmic Global Grid Matrix.**

STELLAR GATEWAYS OR STARGATES

The star constellations (a temporary or permanent alignment of stars) also manifest from and through these gateways. Stellar gateways are star constellations acting as two-way channels, allowing us to both receive energy from the Divine realms - which exist on higher frequency levels within parallel universes - and also channel healing energies through and from Earth and humanity to other 'galactic beings and ethereal realms'. They form an interdependent network of energies, resonating a healing and enlightenment process into all matter, life and consciousness within our dimension.

THE LOWER WORLDS

Before the creation of Earth was completed, the pre-existing worlds were in a chaotic state of evolution. However, their evolutionary process was divinely orchestrated on a subliminal level. (The *Science of Chaos* refers to this as the study of apparent random motion or events which reveal a much deeper level of order below superficial observation.) The entities or beings existing within these different worlds and realities have been identified as 'aliens, extra-terrestrials or grays,' ranging from reptilian ET's through to entities we identify as 'mythical' - half-human/half-animal creatures.

After these existing realities and worlds evolved to a certain level, their global consciousness resonated this level of growth and frequency out into space. These frequency tones then energetically activated certain *grid points* which became *cosmic Doorways,* into a new **evolving** planet called Earth. Universal 'Doorways' were therefore opened so existing worlds could connect and enter into our dimension and Earth/solar system, as it was being divinely created. It became a haven for entities to enter into (through their lightbodies) to obtain the necessary healing and ascension process to become more 'enlightened.' This literally means they could crystallise, perfect and materialise their physical bodies, lightbodies and consciousness, into a higher level of frequency, and therefore continue to evolve.

> **Our planet, dimension and Universe provides the necessary resources for entities/beings to take their next vital step in evolution.**

Some of these interdimensional worlds and entities have evolved and ascended into higher levels of manifestation and consciousness because of the creation process of Earth and her dimensions.

Others still exist within evolving *parallel* worlds, connecting
through *grid points* within and around the Earth itself, but *below
the third dimensional frequency* of Earth and humanity. In the 'Book
of Revelations', these struggling planets and lower worlds are
identified as the Abyss.

THE HIGHEST WORLDS CONNECTED
TO OUR EVOLUTIONAL PROCESS

THE CREATION PROCESS OF THE ANGELIC WORLDS
AND DIMENSIONS

1. THE ANGELIC LYRAN LIGHTBEINGS, GRID POINT
AND DIMENSION

The 'stellar gateway' or 'stargate' system of **Lyra** is the *cosmic
Doorway* through which the most evolved lightbeings known as
Archangels come through and into our universe.

They co-exist within realities and worlds of crystal and light that
are sustained within the dimension of Lyra itself. This is the highest
dimension through which a spirit can live and sustain a *physical*
life force, which is of the Christbody and Consciousness. These
dimensions still exist within our universe, beyond the grid point of
Vega and its stargate system of the constellation of Lyra.

The Archangels lived and still live within this dimension and the
existing ethereal worlds beyond our space-time. Their lightbodies
stand over 16 feet tall and are made of the finest crystallised
properties of light. Metatron comes from and also resonates the
frequency of light that emanates from this dimension.

They were the founders of the many '*elemental* and *galactic*' races and worlds within the dimensions of Arcturus, Pleiades, Orion, and Sirius to whom, the *Earth and humanity* are related.

To be able to begin the physical co-creation process, these Archangelic lightbeings *transferred* themselves ethereally into our evolving Universe, through the *grid point* known as the star/planet **Vega,** which is one of the stars that symbolise 'the seven strings of the Lyre'.

When entering our space zone they began to filter and weave through the energies to co-create the *crystallised gridding system* of the *Global Grid Matrix*. This globe of grid lines of crystal and light sustains the internal technology and resources that are still necessary for the co-creation and healing process of not only the Earth but also humanity. It does this by weaving through the energies to re-create, repair and rejuvenate the complexity of the etheric/physical body and consciousness.

These Archangelic beings also channelled through the sacred knowledge of this *Global Grid Matrix* which contains the technology and knowledge of geometry, sound, crystal and light to Thoth himself - so humanity could evolve in consciousness, on Earth. Thoth like Enoch eventually mastered their physical evolution through the support of these beings and eventually transcended back into this dimension of Lyra. This after living within and on Earth to teach and support Earth and its inhabitants and also its parallel worlds and realities, certain steps of ascension.

DIAGRAM 14.1
The Lyran Grid Point, Gateway and Constellation

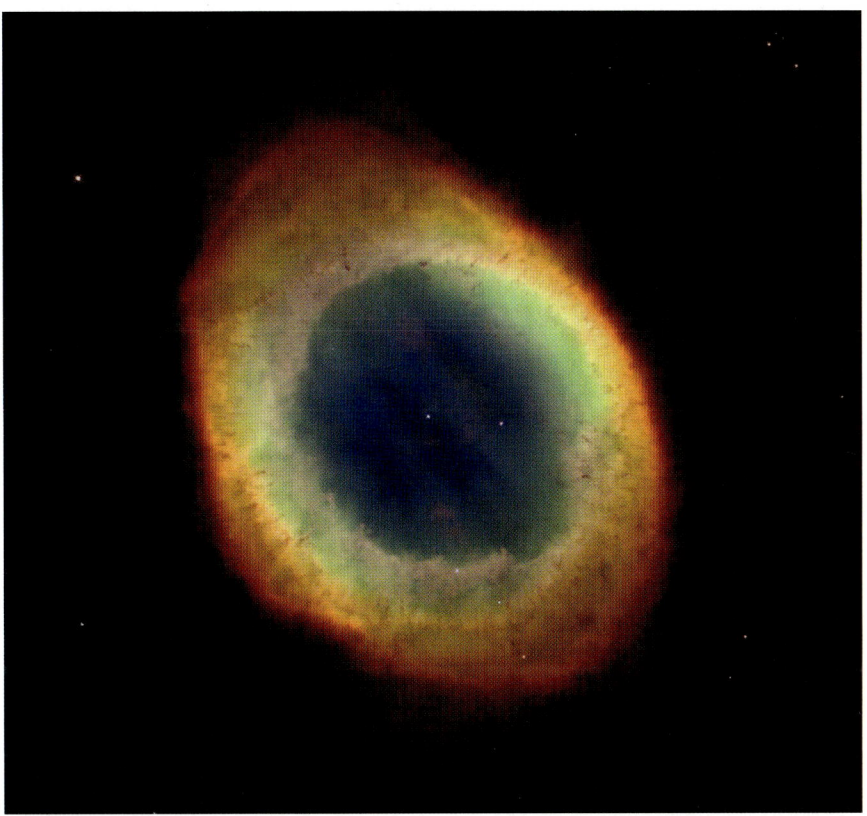

*Vega is the lead star in Lyra and is often called the Harp Star. The other stars are
Deneb in Cygnus and Alter in Aquila. Lyra's other gem, between Beta (B) and
Gamma (Υ), is a patch of gas know as the Ring Nebula (M57). This beautiful
Ring Nebula is called a planetary nebula because when you look at it through a
telescope, it looks like a planetary disc. Courtesy NASA/JPL-Caltech.*

2. THE ARCTURIAN GRID POINT AND DIMENSION

The second grid point that came into existence as a *doorway point* into the angelic realms was Arcturus. It is where the star Arcturus exists today. It is a bright, golden yellow star of 0.3 magnitude.

Both of these stargate systems - the constellation of Lyra and the star Arcturus - are in areas of space creating separate *'Doorways'* into the crystallised realms of Lyra itself, where the highest angelic beings still exist today and come through to support our process of creation, evolution and divinity.

Although these two stargate systems are linked together through a *grid line or corridor,* Arcturus ultimately became a separate dimension to Lyra. *Angelic beings* were then able to maintain a level of crystallised existence (in a Christbody) in Arcturus while choosing to stay connected to and within our space zone and evolving planets and dimensions.

Arcturus therefore became a midway dimension/point or 'cosmic centre'. Those who only stayed for a period of time in Arcturus could enter back into the dimensions of Lyra, beyond our space-time and evolving worlds, *through the grid point of Vega.*

DIAGRAM 14.2
The Arcturian Grid Point, Gateway and Constellation

*Arcturus, or Alpha Boötis, is located about 36.7 light-years from Sol. It is the
brightest star (14:15:39.7 + 19:10:56.7, ICRS 2000.0) of the Constellation
Bootes, the Herdsman or Bear Driver - forming his left foot. Furthermore,
Arcturus the brightest star of the Northern Hemisphere is the fourth brightest
star in the Earth's night sky in Spring. Its name is a variant of the Greek for
"Guardian of the Bear" -- the Great Bear of the Northern Hemisphere known as
Constellation Ursa Major. Courtesy NASA/JPL-Caltech.*

THE ANGELIC LIGHTBEINGS AND DIMENSIONS OF LYRA AND ARCTURUS

Different lightbeings within the Angelic Order sustain different
levels of frequency and consciousness, just like any other race.
Therefore those who are more **'Lyran'** in nature choose to sustain

their reality more within the dimensions of Lyra itself and sustain more of a *crystal-like* consciousness, elemental structure and reality. They are more **cosmic** in nature and support the co-creation of the more cosmic aspect of the Global Grid Matrix. They were also more connected to the civilisation of Atlantis. Some have come to be recognised today as Archangel Metatron, Michael, Raphael, etc.

Those who are more **'Arcturian'** in nature who chose to sustain their reality more within dimensions of Arcturus, are more **Earth** connected in their consciousness, and live within dimensions that are more ethereal and elemental in structure and reality. They support the co-creation of the more *Earth* aspect of the Global Grid Matrix. They were also more connected to the civilisation of Lemuria. They are tall ethereal Earth Angels who are rarely seen, but work closely with the Elemental Kingdoms to heal the crystal grid lines of the Earth itself. They come through and into the Earth to support the global changes that are occurring within the Earth at this time. They are also choosing to come through certain 'Earth channellers' to help not only shift the grid lines of the planet but to also heal and channel through the necessary changes within the etheric/physical body at this vital time of transition. They are now a strong spiritual and energetic support to me when I channel a divinely guided mass healing and gridding process onto the planet, to help support global change.

The 'Earth and Cosmic Archangels' from Lyra and Arcturus are of such a high frequency they are very difficult to hold energetically when you channel them. They are also of such a high frequency and consciousness that they can crystallise or materialise any dimension of their lightbody/Christbody. This enables them to not only connect through to Earth and humanity but also connect, through other grid points within our space zone, to the parallel dimensions and worlds that are evolving and which *will* become part of the totality of our DNA. The 'Earth and Cosmic Archangels' from Lyra and Arcturus are then able weave, filter through and

also crystallise light into the evolving bodies, worlds and realities
of the parallel universes, so these realities can evolve and ascend.

THE HIGHER AND LOWER WORLDS CONNECTED TO OUR EVOLUTIONAL PROCESS

THE CREATION PROCESS OF THE ELEMENTAL, GALACTIC & HUMAN DIMENSIONS

PLEIADIAN ASSISTANCE/INPUT

1. THE PLEIADIAN GRID POINT AND DIMENSION

The stars of the Pleiades were one of the next *stellar gateways*- and
eventually *constellation - to* come into physical manifestation within
our space zone. The other star was Sirius. They began to appear
and evolve as Arcturus was establishing itself more within the
Heavens. The *Pleiades* grid/doorway point is *known* as the '7 Sisters'
star group/system of the constellation of Taurus. This dimension
came into manifestation and connected to Earth through space,
by a grid line or wormhole directly through and to Vega in the
constellation of Lyra.

DIAGRAM 14.3
The Pleiadian Grid Point, Gateway and Constellation

The Pleiadian Star System is the best open cluster of stars in all of the Heavens. This cluster of seven stars, better known as the '7 Sisters', is located in the constellation of Taurus the Bull: 500 light years from planet Earth. The names of the '7 Sisters' of the Pleiadian system are as follows: *Taygeta, Maya, Coela, Atlas, Merope, Electra and Alcoyne. Courtesy NASA/ JPL-Caltech.*

The Pleiadian grid point, gateway, constellation and dimension became the interactive midway point for the lower and higher parallel dimensions or worlds of different frequencies. It was the *'galactic* **midway point',** or *gateway* through which *entities* from the outer evolving worlds could enter into Earth's space zone and the realms of our physical world, as planet 'Earth' was being created with the support of the Lyran and Arcturian lightbeings. These parallel worlds to Earth vary from 2.8D frequency through to 5D frequency.

HUMAN

Many extra-terrestrial races came through and from the cosmic dimensions of the Pleiades (in their lightbodies) to enter the Earth via the *stellar gateway of Taurus,* to receive/weave-in more of the necessary geometric coding system from the Global Grid Matrix of Earth - to mutate their DNA into the new double helix, human DNA.

These extra-terrestrial lightbeings actually came into this dimension to deliberately co-create the new DNA so they could weave through the necessary elements to create *a new, more evolved* **physical body and consciousness.** Through this new DNA, they could receive the necessary etheric crystal and cosmic coding from the Earth and Cosmos to also anchor through new dimensions of the **lightbody and consciousness** - as they went through a healing and ascension process.

This new human DNA underwent a natural genetic mutation on Earth over many millions of years. The woven Celtic rope above is a symbol of the weaving process of the 'cosmic genes,' from co-existing and evolving worlds, into a more 'holistic' strand of 'human DNA'.

Many strands of DNA were integrated from:

* **lower frequency extra-terrestrials** existing within many worlds of 2D-3D frequency which is below the frequency of Earth and human consciousness today, and
* **higher frequency extra-terrestrials** existing within worlds of 3D-5D frequency, which is above the frequency of Earth and human consciousness today.

In this way, the constellation of Taurus and the Pleiadian dimensions became the **mid-way point** through which both the *lower and higher* terrestrials and galactic dimensions could enter into Earth in their lightbodies. The Pleiadian constellation and dimensions became a *Doorway* through which terrestrial/galactic lightbeings could (and still do) enter through and into the existing inner realms of Earth.

It is interesting that Earth is now in the process of leaving the third dimension and entering more into the fifth dimension at this time of transition. This means we are again in the process of *mutating* extra strands or genes from and through the genetic gene pool of the Pleiadian Race and dimension. These extra strands will create our *new* 12-strand DNA system that will enable us to *physically* change the foundation of our appearance and consciousness even more so, as we evolve and ascend with the planet over the next 1,000 years.

HOW WE BEGAN TO GENETICALLY EVOLVE FROM THE PLEIADIAN GENE

Before entering into the inner realms of the Earth, a 'galactic' genetic mutation began in the dimensions of the Pleiades which created a new and evolved etheric/lightbody. After entering Earth this new ether/lightbody continued to genetically evolve through the support of the inner technology and elements of the planet so that a more *humanoid* lightbody could come into manifestation.

Earth enabled the Pleiadians to sustain a more mineralised etheric/physical and lightbody through which they could begin an incarnation process on Earth to become *human beings*. Through overcoming the forces of Nature and 'duality' over many millions of years these Pleiadian and now humans have and still are perfecting themselves in body and consciousness, to ascend into higher 'Christ-like' realms or dimensions – thereby mastering their ascension process.

This Earth/cosmic or human or terrestrial/galactic genetic lineage explains how and why Earth and humanity became a planet of diversity and duality. While living more within the third dimension and sustaining a 2-strand DNA system, we have continued to play out these many aspects from past existences within distant realities and worlds. However, through this same, ongoing, divinely orchestrated mutation process, we are now integrating, purifying and upgrading an extended 10-strand DNA system while sustaining a life-force in body and consciousness within and on the planet Earth.

Through the continuation of this mutation process of the 2-strand DNA, we are now integrating more past aspects that were and still are sustained, not so much within the lower frequency distant worlds and realities of the third dimension, but the more integral aspects sustained within the higher frequency distant worlds and realities of the fifth dimension.

From this natural DNA mutation process on Earth, we obtain more personal, spiritual growth and a physical healing and ascension process via the ever expanding and evolving Pleiadian Race.

DESCENSION AND ASCENSION OF THE EARTH

It is important to recognise that Earth and humanity have been in a state of descension since the time of Lemuria and Atlantis. Since the fall of Atlantis we have hit the lowest level of frequency that matter can be sustained within, while still existing in the 'light'. The planet and humanity on a global level have been living within a 'Dark Age' of duality and going through a deep state of purification, since the final fall of Atlantis about 12,000 years ago. However, since 1999 we have begun a *rapid* ascension shift back into the fifth dimension and beyond. We are *embodying* more light and accessing a higher level of consciousness that is similar to that sustained in the early civilisations of Lemuria and Atlantis.

It is also important to recognise that Old Worlds and realities, like Earth and humanity, are constantly breaking down and co-creating themselves through a divinely orchestrated, evolutionary process.

As the Earth becomes a new planet and world for *healing* and *enlightenment*, outer dimensions and higher levels of worlds and existence are also being created and evolving accordingly.

This is because everything is interconnected by the technology of the interdimensional Global Grid Matrix system (which is like a huge crystal hologram) through which all dimensions: their worlds and realities as well as all aspects of the etheric/lightbody system, is co-created, evolved by and sustained within. Every impact felt or created from a frequency shift within a particle of sand to a whole planetary system, also therefore is felt and affects the whole, we are all one.

THE PLEIADIAN DIMENSION - EARTH AND COSMIC ASPECTS

1. THE EARTH ASPECT: ELEMENTAL KINGDOMS

Some of the Pleiadian dimension eventually extended through and co-existed within many levels and layers of the evolving Earth. As the Pleiadians or 'intergalactic' terrestrials went through a purification and alchemical mutation and creation process, within the different dimensions of Earth, some evolved their etheric body and became more elemental in nature.

An Elemental is a 'fairy-like' creature or being, symbolically representing a *state of consciousness* existing within an evolving lightbody that is still forming its biochemical compounds so that a new physical formation can be created. It is therefore energetically sustained and supported by the elements of planetary system in which it exists within. It is also very connected to the forces and consciousness of nature.

DIAGRAM 14.4
An Elemental Version of a Pleiadian Being

Copyright Alexis Cartwright, Keeper of the Crystals Pty Ltd.

These *Elementals* lived and sustained their life-force and
consciousness while existing within the natural features and
elements within and on the planet Earth herself; in the streams,
trees, mountains etc as well as the Earth crystals. They lived, healed
and grew through the elements of Nature and Earth within this

dimension, and began their first step in an evolutionary process of becoming human beings.

The Elementals took a more ethereal, humanoid form when they had evolved their energy system enough to support the creation process of a more physical body. This happened on Earth at the time of the end of Lemuria.

2. THE COSMIC ASPECT - GALACTIC KINGDOMS

Some of the elemental lightbodies existing within the inner dimensions or realms of the Earth chose not to evolve onto Earth and to become a part of humanity. They experienced their ascension process through another avenue or reality to Earth, without going through the mutation process of becoming a *physical* human being.

After anchoring enough of the genetic coding system of the Global Grid Matrix into their DNA these elementals evolved directly from the Pleiadian dimensions of *Inner Earth* where they *'mineralised'* their lightbodies to go directly into higher worlds and realities within Orion are made up of a more ethereal or refined 'Christ-like' frequency than where they came from, before entering the many evolving worlds within the Pleiadian dimensions, including Inner Earth.

DIAGRAM 14.5
A Galactic Version of a Pleiadian Being

Copyright Alexis Cartwright, Keeper of the Crystals Pty Ltd.

SUMMARY OF THE DIFFERENT DIMENSIONS OF THE PLEIADES

THE HISTORY OF HUMAN GENETICS

1. PLEIADIAN ORIGINS

As the Pleiadian genetics were the source of humanity's *gene pool,* our initial genes were *extra-terrestrial.* The Pleiadians entered the third dimension of Earth through manifesting and sustaining their life force through and within the crystals. They lived within the Elemental Kingdoms within the Earth. While existing within these dimensions and realities they began to crystallise their lightbodies and mutated a more interdimensional and perfected DNA strand, so the humanoid dimensions of the body and consciousness could evolve.

Pleiadian 'stellar gateway' codes wove through the necessary internal technology (geometry) for the etheric/physical body to materialise and for the physical DNA to create itself into a more perfected strand, so the *human* anatomy and consciousness could be created and materialised even more so. During this process they moved from the inner and more ethereal dimensions of the Earth *onto* the Earth itself, so they could continue their physical evolution.

In this way, co-existing entities (*extra*-terrestrials) living within **lower frequency planets** and worlds can ultimately enter into and through the humanoid template of this new planet 'Earth' and its elements (earth, air, fire and water), to eventually ascend into higher levels of consciousness, light and existence.

Entities (*extra*-terrestrials) co-existing within **higher frequency planets** and worlds to what the 3D Earth is today, also entered into and through the template of this new planet Earth. They came

to complete a natural genetic mutation process - to eventually create
and ascend through an evolving crystallised lightbody, ultimately
create the Christbody and Consciousness and ascend into parallel
dimensions to Earth - higher than where they had come from.

'AS ABOVE SO BELOW'

♦ These *resources (energies* to provide the necessary elements *to
co-create* the new DNA and etheric/physical body) can and will
eventually filter through to all beings, while incarnated on Earth
through the coding system of the grid points of Pleiades, Lyra
and Arcturus.

♦ Through the process of evolution acquired from the Earth and
cosmic energies, beings can also *perfect* their DNA system by
mutating and purifying all strands of the (human/galactic)
DNA, to perfect a physical body in which to live. Jesus Christ
referred to this body as the 'Temple'.

♦ Finally, when the physical/lightbody is able to sustain more
'ether' and higher consciousness they will then begin their
journey into the creation process of the lightbody/Christbody
and Consciousness. This process is supported through evolving
with the planet while also existing within the parallel worlds
that co-exist with Earth but within the higher frequencies of the
Pleiadian, Orion and Sirian dimensions.

THE HIGHER FREQUENCY WORLDS

1. SIRIUS AND ORION

Lyra also created the grid points and stellar gateway codes of Sirius
at the same time as those of the Pleiades were being created. The

Star Sirius is a member of a group of stars made up of the trinity of Sirius, Rigel and Betelgeuse within the constellation of Canis Major. By extending an imaginary grid line eastward through Orion's belt, you come to Sirius, the brightest star in the sky. The dimensions/location of Sirius and Orion are therefore very closely linked.

DIAGRAM 14.6
The Sirian Grid Point, Gateway and Constellation

Sirius is the largest and most brilliant star in the Heavens, 8.6 light years from Earth. It is located in the eye of the constellation of the greater dog Canis Major, and is therefore known in mythology as the 'Dog Star'. Sirius is visible in the evening sky of the Northern Hemisphere from November through April. Courtesy NASA/JPL-Caltech.

LIGHTBODY AND CONSCIOUSNESS

The coding system of the **Sirian stargate or** *stellar gateway* was created from a *grid point* that now filters through the higher frequencies of light into Earth, for sustaining and evolving the **lightbody, whereas** the Pleiades sustain and evolve the physical body. Sirius sustains the eternal life-force and consciousness of the Soul as it goes through a cycle of life, death, rebirth, and the intermittent lives between incarnations on Earth. *Sirius also awakens the powers and consciousness of the Christ within.*

Orion on the other hand anchors **the etheric physical/lightbody** into a more crystallised state – so the lightbody it not just so electromagnetic in nature but has solidified and formed more into a *crystallised* formation of light -so the body can ascend into higher frequencies of matter, and therefore sustain itself more within a higher dimension or more ethereal world.

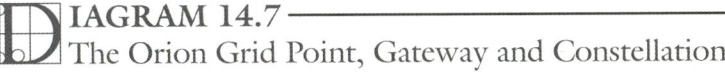

DIAGRAM 14.7
The Orion Grid Point, Gateway and Constellation

The constellation of Orion is one of the most impressive sights in the night sky. It is rich in colour. Its two first magnitude stars, Betelgeuse and Rigel, are both super giants providing a striking colour contrast - Rigel is brilliant white while Betelgeuse is noticeably red. The Star Betelgeuse is one of the biggest stars known, with a diameter of some 400 million km – over 250 times bigger than our Sun. In ancient Greek mythology, Orion was a legendary hunter. Credit & Copyright: Stefan Sip

SUMMARY: PLEIADES, ORION & SIRIUS

> No dimension is more important than another, in the same way that no singular chakra is more important or can exist without another. All dimensions that are referred to in this chapter, co-exist and support the whole evolutionary process, of our past and future self.

1. The Pleiadian dimension will always sustain the **foundations** of our origins, and will continue to be the genetic essence of who we are and how we evolve. The Pleiades gene sustains more of the etheric/**elemental** and physical formation of our *terrestrial* existence.

2. The Orion and Pleiadian dimensions enable us to continue to co-create the process of 'perfecting' our **physical form** as we ascend into higher levels of consciousness and existence within *the elemental, physical and galactic worlds* of the Christ Realm. The

Orion gene sustains more of the lightbody/**cosmic** or *galactic* formation of our existence.

3. The Orion and Sirian dimension enable us to purify, perfect, sustain and crystallise *more* of our **lightbody** and also build the foundations of the Christbody. The lightbody enables galactic and elemental beings including those that exist and have evolved through Earth and also other ethereal worlds and realities of Orion and Pleiades, to enter into a more *non-physical* existence within Sirius to sustain themselves within different degrees of light and consciousness - to enhance their spiritual growth process. The Sirian gene therefore sustains more of the refined dimensions of the lightbody/angelic and crystal or *Christbody* formation of our existence.

SUMMARY OF THE HUMAN DNA AND ITS TRANSITION PROCESS INTO THE DIMENSIONS OF PLEIADES, ORION AND SIRIUS.

1. The Pleiadian dimensions are the *genetic* foundations from which we were, and still are, created. In 1999 the Pleiadians began to reweave another ten strands of DNA for us to take the next vital step in our evolution. From 1999-2012 all of humanity will be energetically forced to reweave the complete 12-strand DNA system through which the new anatomy and lightbody can anchor into our **physical** body and consciousness. We will complete a whole cycle of evolution and begin a whole *new* cycle of evolution as we 'officially' enter into the fifth dimension by the year 2013.

2. The Orion and Sirian dimensions contain the essence of who we will become.

They are the foundation from which we can complete our future ascension process into the seventh dimension. They complete the mutation process of the human DNA into an extended and holistic 22-strand DNA system.

By utilising our lightbody and Merkabah we can then shift in consciousness and travel through all of these gateway-coding systems which not only support our ascension process but are the worlds we will increasingly co-exist within, as we ascend.

MIDWAY POINTS

1. The Pleiadian dimensions are a mid-way point between the lower and higher *extra-terrestrial* dimensions that are *already* part of our genetic makeup. They are also the planets we can evolve into to receive a natural genetic mutation process to access more of the *Elemental Kingdoms* which exist on higher frequency levels to Earth and which are also connected to the many worlds and realities within Orion.

2. The Orion dimensions are the gateway into the higher dimensions of light. This gateway is the midway point between Earth and the higher *ethereal* galactic planes that we are to evolve through and into, *in the future.*

The **Orion star dimension** is the key *grid point* or gateway within our own dimension, through which *lightbodies* on Earth receive the geometric codes necessary for the *new DNA* and *lightbody* to ascend into the co-existing higher galactic and spiritual worlds to Earth.

Orion's galactic beings *do not* have to go through a physical death process between incarnations to access this interdimensional level of consciousness - unlike most of humanity. They learn to master sustaining their life force, existence and consciousness more effectively by simply shifting their vibration when moving into the interdimensional realities from and through Orion & Sirius.

3. The Sirian dimensions are the midway point or plane from which one can experience a lightbody infusion to evolve into the *angelic* planes. Sirian dimensions are a more temporary level of existence or what I would call an intermediate stage of existence

biblically known as 'Heaven,' where we go to learn and develop
our spiritual gifts and talents and co-exist within a state of ecstasy
and light. There is very little duality within this level of existence.

> **When we can access and also *embody* an
> existence within the higher dimensions of
> Pleiades and Orion we can *consciously* co-
> exist more with Sirius.**
>
> **These dimensions also sustain aspects
> of not only our past and future self but
> also parallel levels within us as we evolve
> our etheric, physical, light and ultimately
> Christbody, so we can exist more within
> these dimensions and worlds.**
>
> **This is all part of our ascension process.**

ORION AND SIRIUS

FREQUENCY AND INTERDIMENSIONAL SHIFT

The more light we hold within our body and consciousness and
the more internal resources and codes we sustain within, the more
we are able to channel and access interdimensional lightbeings,
energies, realities and worlds of the higher planes.

At this point in time, Orion **sustains the more** *physical* **worlds whereas** Sirius **sustains the more** *non-physical* **worlds**.

Orion dimensions, realms and worlds are more *ethereal* in nature and of higher levels of consciousness than Earth. They are worlds that are more *galactic* in nature.

Sirian dimensions, realms and worlds are more *electromagnetic* in nature and of higher levels of consciousness than Earth. They are worlds that are more *angelic* in nature.

However, the angelic worlds within the Sirian dimension co-exist very closely with the galactic worlds within the Orion dimension.

WORLDS WITHIN WORLDS

Sirius filters through the necessary ascension codes into all evolving worlds within the inner and outer dimensions of Orion. This includes Earth and its co-existing Pleiadian Kingdoms, as they exist in the very outer dimensions of Orion. However, during the time of the global transference shift from 1999 - 2012, the Earth will become a more evolved planet and will exist within a new frequency level *within* the realms of Orion.

On a global level, we are in the process of physically ascending into a higher dimension of Orion than where we have been before. As we now go through this global and inter-dimensional frequency shift 'Earth' will come to exist as one of the *outer* planets within the dimensions of Orion. Humanity and Earth's Elemental Kingdoms will then be able to comprehend and co-exist more with other galactic beings and planets within Orion.

The parallel worlds and realities of **Orion and Sirius** exist more within 5D-7D frequency levels. We can obtain this interdimensional level of existence by understanding and mastering the elements of Nature and light.

When we evolve to the point of living more within Orion and Sirius:

- There are less and less feelings of separation, fear and grief.

- We don't feel the painful emotions of loss and grief the way most people do on Earth, as we are consciously aware that we are able to re-link-up to anyone in spirit and through consciousness, at any time.

- Those we love who are still on Earth after we have ascended will also be able to be more receptive to us through their own spiritual growth and ascension process.

- We also become *guardian angels* or *guides* to support those we love and are personally connected to on Earth, to also evolve.

EVOLUTION

As we awaken or become more *enlightened*, by anchoring and ascending more into the lightbody and higher consciousness, we become masters on Earth and are therefore becoming an *ascending master*.

At a certain point in evolution the humanoid lightbody and consciousness leaves Earth and transcends through the Pleiadian realms to enter into the higher dimensions of Orion and Sirius, as part of its next step in evolution. There are many worlds within different frequency levels and dimensions of space that exist within Pleiades, Orion and Sirius and it would take aeons of time to experience and learn all that is necessary from these dimensions. Actually, time as we know it on Earth does not exist within these realms.

> **It is important to acknowledge that Earth is also evolving just like the human body and spirit, so at some point we will re-enter Earth when it has evolved into a higher frequency and consciousness. There is a continual global recycling process - so nothing really ever dies.**

EARTH MASTERS

Currently, very few on Earth (only the masters) consciously experience living an interdimensional reality while incarnated on Earth. However, more have and will now begin to because of the lightbody activations occurring on a global level during the transition time of 1999-2012. Masters are those who have *awakened* to such a point they can *channel* through the consciousness of the angelic and galactic lightbeings and experience interdimensional reality shifts while in an altered state of consciousness on Earth. Their lightbodies are therefore being activated and are manifesting through more rapidly than the rest of humanity.

MASTERY

Those who are mastering on Earth are in a state of initiation and preparation to become an *ascending* master. They are in a state of preparation to ascend into higher dimensions. They are already living within parallel realities within the Earth and Cosmos, and will continue to live on Earth for as long as they want, before consciously choosing to leave the planet altogether.

The ascending masters who are mastering the Earth changes at this time have taken many incarnations to get to this point of their ascension process and are here to support the Earth and humanity through the changes. They are usually in a state of service to the planet and humanity, as part of their initiation to eventually enter

into higher dimensions of Orion. They also have to master the ego
and power centre before entering and existing more within the
realities of Orion and Sirius - while still on Earth and co-existing
within the Pleiadian realms.

Orion subjects masters to a maze of initiations to determine the state
of their ego, intent and consciousness, which in turn determines
their level of Mastership on Earth. Orion creates the initiations
of 'empowerment' by creating the universal consequences in their
day to day lives through which they learn to master **duality** in
order to ascend into higher Kingdoms. This process is comparable
to the mythology of King Arthur who mastered the elements of
Nature by being able to remove the sword from the stone.

When we experience altered states of reality by co-existing within
the realms of Orion while in a state of Mastership on Earth, we
become so empowered by the knowledge we gain, that we begin
to live in a state of Kingship/Queenship on Earth. We begin to
live in a state of leadership, service and manifestation, as positive
changes begin to happen more rapidly in our day to day lives. We
live as a spiritual master on Earth and are recognised as such.

However, the Earth is also rapidly shifting its frequency on all
levels to ascend and become a new dimension at this point in time.
Because it is shifting into a higher frequency level or dimension
within Orion, it is now possible for all of humanity, on a global
level, to take a vital step in the path of ascension with the Earth.
In this way, all of humanity and its parallel Pleiadian Galactic
and Elemental Kingdoms will eventually come to live within the
parallel realities and worlds of Orion and Sirius.

**As the Earth and humanity ascends everyone
will come to live as masters within this new
Seventh Golden Age, which will completely
manifest over the next 1,000 years.**

THE DIMENSIONS OF TIME

The lower worlds which exist within *lower* frequency points to Earth and *beyond* the grid point of the Pleiades star system and dimensions are *below* the third dimensional frequency point of Earth. Even though this means their existence in space is beyond and *before* the existence of *time,* they hold aspects of our *past-selves*.

The more present worlds which exist within *higher* frequency points closer to Earth and *within* the grid point of the Pleiades, are the Pleiadian dimensions that exist within and on the Earth as well as on other Earth and cosmic dimensions parallel to Earth existing *within* the third to fifth dimension. They hold aspects of our *present selves* that have or will come into manifestation within our space/time reality on Earth.

The higher worlds which exist within *higher* frequency points beyond Earth and the grid point of Pleiades, are also more evolved beings that have extended/continued their genetic mutation process and now live more within the Orion/Sirian dimension. They are *above* the fifth dimensional frequency point of Earth that exists within the fifth to seventh dimensions. These points in space are *beyond* our space/ time zone and these worlds that now exist hold aspects of our *future-selves*.

> **We are breaking down and through all boundaries of time and space. When we experience different levels of consciousness, we co-exist within parallel levels and worlds through grid points within the Global Grid Matrix which sustains all life.**

> **All dimensions are and will become part of
> our evolutionary experience and existence as
> we evolve through parallel levels, worlds
> and realities.**

THE GRID POINTS OF THE APOCALYPSE

This chapter reveals the hidden 'cosmic or galactic' message encoded within the symbols of the apocalypse. The grid points or stargates mentioned in this chapter, with the corresponding star constellations and dimensions of Arcturus, Pleiades, Sirius and Orion are the key hidden symbols of the apocalypse - the Angel - *Arcturus*, Bull - *Pleiades*, Lion - *Sirius*, and Eagle - *Orion*.

These stargates and grid points and corresponding dimensions are principal power points connecting to co-existing worlds and spiritual beings that are not only part of the totality of our DNA but are supporting our ascension process at this critical time of transition.

They are also identified as the planetary symbols associated with the planets forming/creating the Grand Cross Activation of 1999. Through the information given in this chapter you can therefore understand how the apocalyptic astrological alignment of 1999 energetically activated and re-opened the stargates within these corresponding constellations. These grid points that have now opened are filtering the energies through to assist humanity and the planet to ascend through the templating process of the Christ Light, into the higher dimensions of the Christ Realm.

A MESSAGE FROM LYRA

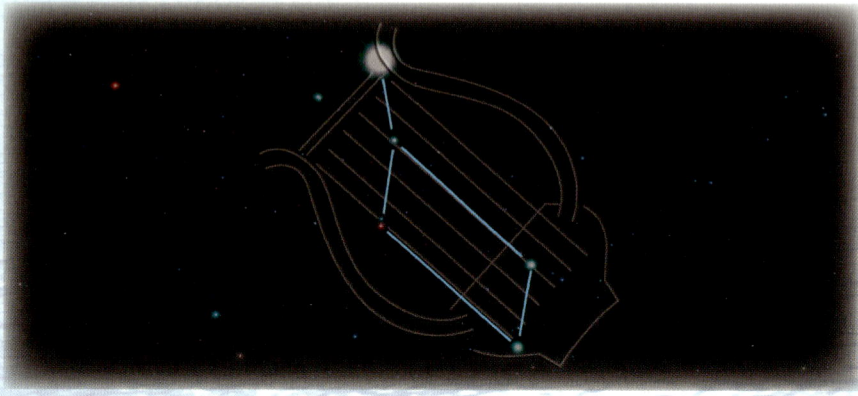

The Archangels or crystal lightbeings from Lyra and their first genetic offspring from Arcturus are our spiritual ancestors

They sustain their life force and consciousness on a much higher frequency level to all existing parallel worlds and realities

From this level, they filter through the codes and purest frequencies, so we can co-create a pure ascension process through both a terrestrial or physical and parallel lightbody/Christbody and Consciousness.

They were the key creators of the coding system or template through which the new DNA and the humanoid physical/light body system came to exist.

Therefore they sustain and filter through, all technology and energetic resources that exist within the parallel dimensions of 'Pleiades, Orion and Sirius,' so that all levels of consciousness, realities and worlds can come into manifestation.

They created the 'crystal, geometry and light technology' for life to exist and the levels of existence that life creates for all beings to evolve through and into a higher state of being.

They are the master co-creators and assist in a divinely orchestrated co-creation and re-creation process.

They initiated the original birth of our immortal inner essence and life force and participate as 'Guardians' as we evolve through many realities and worlds, including Earth, until we eventually return to the dimensions of Lyra herself, from where we have all come - having perfected our life force and consciousness by co-creating and perfecting a crystallised body.

Life is a journey in a physical body and consciousness through which we can experience the true nature of all that exists in creation.

When we master this we will have evolved to such a point that we can participate with our ancestors as Co-creators within the universes.

We can evolve to such a point that we can ascend and enter back through the gateways of Lyra. We will have returned home in a more evolved and perfected state of being.

IMPORTANT: *Completion Ritual*

*Before you stop reading this chapter, run your finger from **right to left** across the sacred language below. This procedure will assist you to finalise the energies from this chapter.*

Your action, intent and the sacred vibration of this powerful language, will greatly assist you to fully integrate the information you have just read.

LEARN TO BE A
TRANSFERENCE HEALER

- Heal and empower your life
- Actively work with your personal growth and ascension
- Heal and empower the lives of friends, family and clients
- Start a new and exciting career or upgrade your skills

There are different workshop levels available to those wishing to really master the Transference Healing® modality.

Fundamental Workshop (Self-Healer)

This four-day workshop will teach you the procedures that will allow you to run the Transference Healing® energy and Christ light. This level of training allows you to heal yourself, friends and family, but does not allow you to become a certified practitioner.

Participants in this workshop will receive a comprehensive practitioners manual and the complete Lightbody Kit of 77 vibrational essences and its associated divination book.

Advanced Level Workshop (Practitioner)

To be a certified practitioner you must complete this three day workshop. This level of Transference® creates a process of initiation to anchor sacred teachings from the Mystery Schools, awaken past life gifts, enhance your ability to channel guides and anchor templates to begin radiating the Christ light.

Participants in this workshop will receive an Advanced Level Workshop Manual, the complete Master Christ Template® Set and five Platonic Solid Essences (that support the Lightbody Kit).

Teacher Level Workshop - for those who would like to be certified to facilitate and teach Transference Workshops.

For more information visit www.TRANSFERENCEHEALING.com

IMPORTANT: *Commencement Ritual*

*Before reading chapter 15, run your finger from **left to right** across the sacred language below.*

Your action, intent and the sacred vibration of this powerful language, will ensure that you are fully open to receiving and integrating the information within.

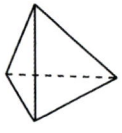 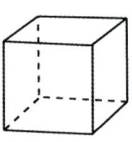 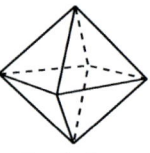 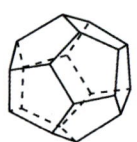 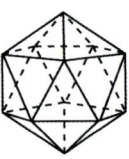

| **Tetrahedron** | **Cube** | **Octahedron** | **Dodecahedron** | **Icosahedron** |
| *Fire / Heat* | *Earth / Solid* | *Air / Gas* | *Universe / Ether* | *Water / Liquid* |

The five geometric formations seen above are known as the five Platonic Solids. They include the hexahedron, tetrahedron, octahedron, dodecahedron and the icosahedron. Platonic solids meet the following criteria; all their edges are equal in length, each of their surfaces have the one consistent angle, while the points of intersection between each surface would fit into the surface of a sphere. They are known to be the building blocks of our body and Universe.

In ancient Mystery Schools, crystals where formed into the dimensions of the 'five platonic crystal solids' like we have today. These platonic crystal solids were laid onto the body in such a way that the more refined elements within earth, air, fire, water and ether could filter through into the body via the crystal and corresponding chakra, so that the body could begin a Divine self-healing and ascension process.

By energetically integrating these symbols you not only begin clearing etheric weaknesses from the body but also activate a deep purification, by clearing low vibrational emotional patterning. You're bodies etheric and electrometric field will resource and can begin to activate the Merkabah or lightbody system and vehicle. Your consciousness can then begin to exist more within the higher realms, realities and worlds parallel to Earth and by doing so, perfect and crystallise the etheric/physical body into a more perfected state of being. These are the steps of consciousness that are necessary to enable you to evolve and slowly anchor through the different dimensions of the lightbody/ Christbody system.

LIGHTBODY
ESSENCES

CHAPTER OVERVIEW

In this chapter you will learn:

- That the Transference Healing Lightbody Kit essences have been channelled and programmed to allow people to begin to work independently on themselves, on a multidimensional level.

- The *complete* Lightbody Kit contains 77 'mother tincture' essences. Essences include single crystal essences, combination crystal essences, alchemy symbol essences, planetary symbol essences, ray essences and elements essences. Crystals are used to program all the essences.

- Using the divination charts and channelled information relating to each essence you can intuitively select a combination of these essences to obtain both an etheric Transference Healing, as well as, corresponding medical-intuitive and spiritual reading.

- Essences are taken internally as drops and filter higher frequency levels of light into the physical body to alleviate internal pressure and create a self-healing and enlightenment process. They also heal specific dimensions of the etheric/physical body, shifting consciousness by clearing corresponding emotional weaknesses embedded at the cellular level.

- Those struggling with the biochemical and DNA changes now occurring in the body are manifesting and mutating viruses and general lightbody symptoms, which are generally not responding to traditional chemical based medicines. The lightbody essences are getting in touch with the source of the disease, both emotionally and energetically, this is why they are profoundly effective. They are *the vibrational medicine of the New Millennium*.

- • You will also be given a detailed overview of common lightbody symptoms now manifesting on the planet.

- • Finally you will learn about the healing and ascension properties of each of the 15 Beyond Doorways Lightbody Kit self-help healing essences.

◆

have channelled and programmed the lightbody essences for people to begin to work independently, on themselves, on a multidimensional level.

The Lightbody Kit itself contains 77 'mother tincture' essences which sustain and create certain aspects of the healing power and properties within *Transference Healing*. The essences include single crystal essences; combination crystal essences; alchemy symbols; planetary symbols; rays and the four elements. Corresponding divination charts enable you to intuitively select a combination essence to obtain both an etheric *Transference Healing* and corresponding medical-intuitive and spiritual reading. After finishing the bottle of combination essence (which takes about three weeks) you have literally fine-tuned, cleared, integrated or embodied the magical healing qualities identified in the corresponding divination reading.

The essences are taken internally as drops. They filter higher frequency levels of light into the physical body to alleviate internal pressure and create a 'self-healing' and 'enlightenment' process. They begin to heal specific dimensions of the etheric/physical body as well as shift consciousness by clearing the corresponding emotional weaknesses embedded at the cellular level.

THE EARTH'S CHANGES

As explained in great detail in this book, the Earth is in a process of great change. It is literally co-creating itself during this vital time of transition from 1999-2012. This global transition is enabling the planet, human body and consciousness to leave a third dimensional reality it has existed in since the fall of Atlantis, to enter into a new holographic realm. This new realm or world which the Earth is *transcending* into has a fifth dimensional template. The Ancients'

referred to this current time of transition from the end of the old world into the new world, as the 'Shift of the Ages'.

THE DNA AND ALCHEMICAL CHANGES

As 'matter' changes, the human body is going through a rapid biochemical, DNA and cellular shift. Abnormally high levels of hormonal and chemical secretions are creating the necessary changes in the etheric/physical body and consciousness for humanity to ascend with the Earth. Blood tests are showing that people are now developing new strands of DNA. Science believes our species is mutating into something 'not yet known', however, this *DNA mutation* process is the beginning of the physical changes necessary for the creation and integration of the new anatomy or lightbody system. This new anatomy is enabling humanity to ascend from the third dimension through and into the fifth dimension - during this vital time of transition.

Those struggling with the biochemical and DNA changes now occurring in the body are manifesting mutating viruses and general lightbody symptoms which are generally not responding as effectively to chemically based medications. The key is to get in touch with the source of the disease, both emotionally and energetically.

> **If we can heal within, through energy and light, the physical body will respond and automatically heal itself.**

THE LIGHTBODY

The new lightbody system is anchoring through on an individual level within the whole of humanity, during the time of the transition from 1999-2012 to enable all to transcend into the fifth dimension or new reality and world.

The essences within the Lightbody Kit not only alleviate, heal and clear physical symptoms but on a parallel level create the new anatomy or lightbody system and enable an enlightenment process to begin to manifest through and into humanity. They not only enable specific past life 'gifts and talents' to begin to manifest through on an individual level but also shift humanity on a global level into a new and higher level of consciousness - Christ Consciousness. *These unique healing and ascension qualities and properties of the essences in the Lightbody Kit make them a vital part of the vibrational medicine of the New Millennium.*

LIGHTBODY ESSENCES

Lightbody essences work on the *biochemical, etheric and vibrational levels* of the body to:

1. Clear underlying etheric blocks to enable the physical anatomy to begin to heal itself.

2. Support the anchoring and creation process of the lightbody.

3. Preventively care against all *new* viruses and *lightbody* symptoms which are just side effects created by the Earth changes and the anchoring process of the lightbody system.

LIGHTBODY SYMPTOMS

Most of humanity is now experiencing some of the following symptoms:

1. Flu like symptoms, high temperature.

2. Unusual respiratory and lung symptoms, sometimes diagnosed as asthma.

3. Colds, hay fevers, runny noses and sneezing for up to 24 hours.

4. Occasional breathing difficulties.

5. Occasional diarrhoea.

6. Immune system changes.

7. Lymphatic system changes.

8. Short periods of intense tiredness.

9. Headaches or even migraines not alleviated by pain killers.

10. Vagueness in the head and an empty feeling in the stomach.

11. Dizziness.

12. Ringing in the ears (Tinnitus).

13. Heart palpitations.

14. Circulation problems.

15. A loss of muscular power and brief periods of weakness.

16. Tingling in arms, hands, legs and feet.

17. Aching bones and joints not responding to antibiotics.

18. Strange symptomatic pain, especially through the back and vertebrae area.

19. Strange skin irritations.

20. Hypersensitivity.

21. Mood swings and bouts of short term depression.

22. Intense fear of separation and loss.

23. Delving into the past and looking at relationships and unresolved personal issues.

24. Intense and symbolic dreams and strange sleeping patterns.

25. Losing sense of time.

26. Feelings of dé jà vu.

The essences from the Lightbody Kit are programmed to clear and *preventively care* against all new viruses and lightbody symptoms now manifesting on the planet.

They clear underlying etheric blocks to allow lightbody integration and manifestation.

CRYSTALS

Specific crystals have been intuitively chosen as the basis of the Lightbody Kit. They tap into the etheric or energetic foundation of the physical body to create a *universal* vibrational healing impact throughout all dimensions of the physical body and consciousness. They effectively alleviate symptomatic pain and naturally create a cellular rejuvenation process within the relevant dimensions of the body. This process naturally begins to rejuvenate, revitalise and repair specifically weak and diseased areas of the body.

Crystals create an *etheric healing* process within the physical body and consciousness. Although Earth crystals are birthed within the planet they are energetically and geometrically formed by the energies of the Earth and Cosmos. The rotations of the planets within our solar system resonate and filter through the *rays* which transmit cosmic colours and universal healing energies from the Cosmos into the forming crystals within the Earth. The crystals therefore embody certain aspects and qualities of the rays. They are *physical tools* birthed by the Earth which then filter specific planetary vibrations, alchemical Earth elements as well as universal colour and sound and cosmic frequencies into each corresponding dimension of the body and consciousness, through the chakra system.

Crystals are therefore very powerful tools for self-healing the etheric/physical body and also for clearing and evolving the emotional body. They are physically formed by the Universe to transmit energy and to not only alchemically shift matter but to also co-create matter and consciousness.

CRYSTAL ESSENCES

Crystals are used in the programming of the Lightbody Kit. They create the fundamental makeup of each essence so that sound/colour, rays and symbols can also be integrated to enhance and create a powerful and divinely orchestrated alchemical healing and ascension process for all who take them.

1. Universal energy and colour can be integrated directly into our body via the crystals.

2. Their etheric patterns, templates and inner technology hold the innate resources and knowledge to heal the body and consciousness on all levels.

3. They also create the alchemical compounds as well as energetic resources to enable the body and consciousness to ascend into the next dimension.

HEALING THE PHYSICAL BODY

Each crystal has a geometric template which energetically corresponds to the internal technology (geometry) of certain organs within the physical anatomy. Crystals create a healing process within corresponding organs by resonating the necessary healing properties from the Earth and Cosmos directly into the energetic or etheric levels of the anatomy. When an etheric healing takes place it then ripples a healing impact into the biochemical and more physical dimensions of the anatomy and body.

HEALING THE EMOTIONAL BODY

The energetic levels of the body resonate different degrees and variations which emanate sound and colour from the body. This tone and colour spectrum of light then resonates out from the body as what we identify as the aura. The different variations of sound and colour within the auric field and dimension of the body therefore create the different combinations and variations of emotions. This in itself creates a 'doctrine or signature' of the uniqueness of our personality, state of emotional wellness and level of consciousness and spiritual development.

Energetically working with the body through crystals not only supports a healing process within the body but also creates a more emotional state of wellness and enables us to shift into higher levels of consciousness. The healing power of crystals creates a sense of balance and inner harmony within our body, mind and spirit through which we can continually co-create our own inner health and purify and develop our emotional and spiritual state of being, on a day to day level.

HEALING THE SPIRITUAL BODY

For those wishing to develop their spiritual powers, the crystal essences heighten awareness. They open and develop the psychic senses to enable you to shift into higher levels of consciousness. They enhance **clairvoyance** - *clear seeing*, **clairaudience**- *clear hearing* and **clairsentience**- *clear feeling* and enable these psychic sensory levels of perception to come more into consciousness.

THE LIGHTBODY KIT

The *complete* Lightbody Kit (as seen below) is only available to those participating in the four-day *Transference Healing Fundamental Workshop*.

However, a smaller *Beyond Doorways Lightbody Kit* has been channelled to support the self-help procedures in this book.

DIAGRAM 15.1
The Complete Transference Healing Lightbody Kit

15 SELF-HELP TRANSFERENCE HEALING ESSENCES

These combination essences support the procedures in chapters 6, 9, 10, 11 & 12 at this time of transition.

1. STRUCTURAL ALIGNMENT ESSENCE

i.   Alleviates back, hip, cranial, limb and joint pain.

ii.   Helps create a structural realignment process to sustain strong physical foundations necessary to maintain *strength, balance and wellness* within the *skeletal* system of the body.

2. COSMIC EYE ESSENCE

i.   Specifically clears any 'webbing' distortion in the third eye chakra.

ii.   Activates a healing process within the 'pineal and pituitary' glands to enable the brain to clear etheric and energetic weaknesses and begin to detoxify so more dimensions of the brain can open.

iii.   Balances the left and right hemispheres of the brain to support a higher level of consciousness to begin to manifest.

iv.   Supports the anchoring and manifestation of the 'lightbody'.

v.   Preventively cares against psychological depletion and weaknesses from manifesting through as lightbody symptoms.

3. AMBER ESSENCE (INDIVIDUAL ESSENCE)

i.   Revitalises the seven master glands so the correct *hormonal* and *chemical* secretion can be created to support an alchemical healing process within the anatomy.

ii.   Begins to clear glandular distortions and viruses ranging from chronic fatigue syndrome through to emotional and psychological weaknesses.

4. RADIANT WHITE LIGHT ESSENCE

i.   Specifically balances the chakra system to enable us to begin to master holding the 'radiant white light'.

ii.   Initiates and activates more of a state of 'enlightenment' so we can stay clear and hold our faith at all times.

5. RAINBOW ESSENCE

i.   Filters the appropriate colours from each chakra into the adjoining organs or areas of the anatomy to enable a *metaphysical* (emotional/physical) healing to occur within the body and consciousness.

6. KARMIC PAIN RELEASE ESSENCE

i.   Specifically *clears energy plays* and *karmic circumstances in* our life.

ii.   Clears the glandular system, creating a purification and self-rejuvenation process so new energies and emotions can be stimulated and created within. (Works with the Transference Healing Harmony Alignment Point 11).

7. COSMIC SHIELD OF CONNECTION AND PROTECTION ESSENCE

i.   Balances and closes *Triangular Star Diamond Doorway Point*, so 'past life,' genetic wounding can be cleared from the DNA and etheric body.

ii.   Clears the fear of *alien abduction*.

iii.   Balances and revitalises the electromagnetic field of the body.

iv.   Clears unusual and bizarre lightbody symptoms when nothing else seems to help.

8. EMPOWERING WISDOM ESSENCE

i.   Clears energy fibres from the *feeling vortex*

ii.   Helps revitalise the etheric/physical body.

iii.   Clears the mental plane so we can sustain a higher level of consciousness.

iv.   Supports us to access/anchor through, Christ Consciousness when taken with the **Crystal Cross Essence**.

9. STAR OF DAVID ESSENCE

i.   Supports us to *embody* the **lightbody** and connect to the Higher Self.

10. CRYSTAL CROSS ESSENCE

i.   Anchors and templates into the body and consciousness the healing elements of the Earth and Cosmos which sustain the 'Christ Light' within our dimension.

ii.   Helps to clear all lightbody symptoms while co-creating the New Anatomy or fifth dimensional Adam Kadmon body.

iii.   Connects us to the Celestial Christ on a *heart* level.

iv.   Supports the awakening of Christ Consciousness within.

11. CHIRON ESSENCE

i.   Supports us when going through a Chiron transit *(see chapter 9)*.

ii.   Supports us to clear the psychological and karmic weaknesses we have embedded into our patterning at the time of birth.

iii.   Supports us when we are being energetically impacted to create a clearing process through our Chiron point.

iv.   Preventively cares against lightbody symptoms manifesting through as we clear genetic or 'past life' weaknesses.

(See chapter 8, written by Lucy Lyne, to understand the nature of your Chiron wounding and how this essence will work for you).

12. RAVEN POWER ESSENCE

Enhances our ability to:

i.   See into the unknown.

ii.   Overcome fear of the unknown.

iii.   Empower the self.

iv.   Purify the intent.

v.   Open and develop the psyche.

vi.   Hold and sustain our light at difficult times of initiation.

vii.   Works with Transference Healing, Harmony Alignment Point 16.

13. DRAGON POWER ESSENCE

i.   Protects.

ii.   Helps build up our *power centre*:

     a. To counteract *direct* psychic attack.

     b. To counteract negative feelings or thought projection against us.

     c. To enable us to start to anchor through unique and Divine 'gifts and talents'.

iii.   Supports purification of the ego.

iv.   Supports us to perfect the nature of our ego, enabling us to embody more Divine Will.

v.   Clears deep feelings of depletion.

vi. Works with the Transference 'Dragon Power' healing procedure.

14. INNER CHILD AND
15. CHILD OF LIGHT ESSENCES

There are two essences that are optional, they include the **Inner Child** and the **Child of Light Essences**. Therefore you need to determine which one of these essences is relative to you or the person who will be taking the essence.

A. Inner Child Combination Essence *for fifteen year olds and over:*

i.   To let go of, and also begin to heal, painful *childhood* memories and wounding from the past.

ii. Supports pure child like-feelings such as joy, love and faith to come back into manifestation and consciousness.

B. Child of Light Combination Essence *for fourteen year olds and under:*

i.   Enables 'transitional children' - those born during this *time of transition* – to obtain a templating and vibrational healing response which helps counteract viruses and lightbody symptoms they could already be feeling physically or becoming more susceptible to.

DOSAGE

Either take seven drops of one of the essences from a dosage bottle before running the energy or doing the meditation of a specific and corresponding procedure from 'Beyond Doorways'.

Or take seven drops of a combination of all of these essences at once.

Do this by putting seven drops of each essence into a 15ml bottle of distilled water (with a small drop of vodka to prevent contamination). Then take seven drops in the morning and seven drops at night until the bottle is finished, which usually takes from 2-3 weeks.

STORAGE & TRAVELLING

1. Store at room temperature in a cool place out of direct contact with sunlight or radiation, such as fluorescent light bulbs, microwave ovens or computers.

2. Travelling on aircraft is safe but after going through a 'property scanner' at airports visualise 'radiant blue light' filtering through the essences and any electromagnetic distortion will be released.

3. Place a pyrite crystal and/ or the Crystal Cross Christ Template on the wall or near the essences, when you reach your destination, to energetically protect them.

IMPORTANT: *Completion Ritual*

*Before you stop reading this chapter, run your finger from **right to left** across the sacred language below. This procedure will assist you to finalise the energies from this chapter.*

Your action, intent and the sacred vibration of this powerful language, will greatly assist you to fully integrate the information you have just read.

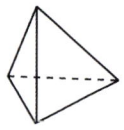 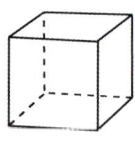 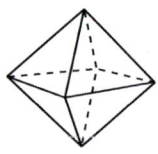 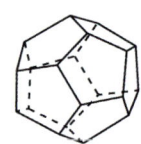 

Tetrahedron	**Cube**	**Octahedron**	**Dodecahedron**	**Icosahedron**
Fire / Heat	*Earth / Solid*	*Air / Gas*	*Universe / Ether*	*Water / Liquid*

THE TRANSFERENCE HEALING® LIGHTBODY KIT

"Vital vibrational essences of the new millennium!"

These essences are programmed to clear and *preventively care* against all the new viruses and lightbody symptoms now manifesting on the planet. They clear underlying etheric blocks to allow lightbody integration and manifestation.

The complete **Lightbody Kit**® contains 77 'mother tincture' essences, which sustain and create aspects of the healing power and properties within *Transference Healing*®. The essences include:

- 28 single crystal essences
- 18 combination crystal essences
- 13 alchemy symbol essences
- Seven planetary, cosmic forces & metals essences
- Seven rays and corresponding masters essences
- Four elements of nature essences

Because these essences are so powerful, the *complete* Lightbody Kit® is only available to graduates of Transference Healing® Fundamental Workshops, however, a smaller **"Beyond Doorways Lightbody Kit"** has been channelled to support the self-help procedures in this book.

If we can heal within, through energy and light, the physical body will respond and automatically heal itself.

Place your order at www.TRANSFERENCEHEALING.com

ABOUT THE AUTHOR
ALEXIS CARTWRIGHT

'BEYOND DOORWAYS' 1ˢᵀ EDITION, 2005.

Alexis was born in 1963 in Mt. Isa, Australia and lived most of her life in Queensland. She is the mother of two children.

PSYCHIC READINGS

She began *intuitive* reading at the age of 19 but as the readings gave her many insights into the energetic and psychological makeup of the human body and consciousness, she slowly shifted her interest to healing.

The 'psychic' or intuitive readings were a counselling tool which gave her clients insight into situations and circumstances in their lives while also providing possible outcomes for them. Information included why they felt a certain way, why certain symptoms were occurring in their bodies and how relationships and finances would work out over the next few years. Universal questions were also answered concerning the direction of their lives and their purpose and destiny, in this incarnation.

Initially, during the readings and healings, Alexis clairvoyantly saw energetic blocks in the body and how and why they manifested into disease. At the age of 23 through a *specific* past life regression channelled through from the planetary influence of 'Chiron,' she was given a deeper and more comprehensive understanding of the *energetic makeup or patterning* of the physical body. In addition, the Spiritual Hierarchy encouraged her to introduce *crystals* as a healing tool for the body and consciousness.

CRYSTAL ESSENCES

Alexis began to combine *crystal essences* with the intuitive readings to clear the energetic blocks and weaknesses she saw in her clients' bodies. This enabled them to not only clear unresolved issues but also to make positive changes to prevent ongoing symptoms and further struggle in their day to day lives.

To help them become more self-sufficient in their healing process, she developed a kit of vibrational healing essences called the 'Lightbody Kit', which could be taken at home. Each essence consisted of crystals, rays, geometry and sound. The healing powers and properties of the crystals within the various essences of the Lightbody Kit helped clear genetic and underlying conditions within the body and consciousness. The essences were chosen from channelled divination charts which gave a therapeutic description and outline of the magical, alchemical and transformational healing properties and powers created by each combination essence.

The Elemental Kingdom assisted Alexis to develop and channel the divination charts which provided the necessary insight and vibration which could solve particular issues and restrictions for her clients. The essences helped to clear the physical symptoms which kept re-occurring throughout their daily lives. The divination charts paved the way for clients to purchase their own essence kit and independently divine and receive a *personal reading and healing* while in their own space and at their own pace. This was a very self-empowering process.

NEW HEALING MODALITY

When Alexis was 29, spiritual guides began to channel *new healing* procedures to her. These procedures *helped* her heal deeper and weaker levels of her clients' *etheric body*, which were creating more severe and long term illness within their body and consciousness. They enabled clients to shift the energetic patterning and master unusual 'transitional' pain and circumstances which she could foresee manifesting more on a personal and global level because of the Earth changes - during the time of the transition, from 1999 -2012. (The "transition" is explained extensively throughout this book).

She came to understand this "transition" as a doorway of opportunity to create radical changes within our body, reality, planet and Universe and that these new energetic healing procedures would also preventively care against "lightbody symptoms" as the new human anatomy evolved.

This new healing modality was anchored onto the planet over a seven year period. During this time new crystals and geometric symbols were also added to perfect and complete the 77 essences of the Lightbody Kit. Together the procedures and essences began to work on *deeper and sometimes more complex energetic levels* of the body and consciousness as they not only worked with the physical body and anatomy, but also the etheric and electromagnetic body.

By the time Alexis was 32 years old, she was no longer just providing readings and crystal essences for therapeutic purposes. She had created a whole new healing modality and established a healings clinic where her clients now came for 'healings' rather than readings. Their needs kept her searching deeper and deeper within herself for answers to help resolve and heal the patterning of their physical, emotional and spiritual bodies.

HEALING SESSIONS

Many doctors, alternative therapists and psychics have referred chronically ill patients to Alexis. She is known to have remarkable results after all orthodox or alternative medicines have failed. Whilst not guaranteeing a cure, her faith in the Universe is unshakable and her clients acknowledge the positive outcomes from her 'clearings'. During the course of a healing session, she disregards any previous diagnosis. She *gives a personal, intuitive reading* to establish the source of pain while co-creating a holistic healing process for 'the individual'. She does not believe in disease, but rather the body being in a state of dis-ease.

DNA

Whilst working with thousands of clients, Alexis could see the new energetic procedures not only healing the clients' bodies and consciousness but also shifting and healing their DNA patterning. This enabled them to achieve more positive healing changes within their own physical body and also their reality, thereby enabling their 'destiny and purpose' reading to come into manifestation at a more rapid rate than what was previously possible. Clients could not only begin to *master* their own health on a daily basis but also transform and master their reality. They could begin to master the ability to **transfer** from one state of being into another and therefore change painful and difficult symptoms and circumstances within their body, reality and life. Consequently this new, channelled technique was named 'Transference Healing' – transformational healing.

This new technique created profound opportunity and potential in Alexis' eyes. She saw positive changes and long term preventative care measures coming through for her clients in the future, at a time when she foresaw on a parallel level, more global chaos and unpredictability because of the Earth changes. She could see Transference Healing was the means of mastering the transformational changes occurring during a vital time of global transition.

Around 1999, when she was 36 years old, she was guided by the Spiritual Hierarchy to write down all the procedures she had channelled and developed over many years so that 'Transference Healing' could be taught to others to make Transference Energy more available on the planet.

'BEYOND DOORWAYS' 1ST EDITION 2005

Alexis now travels extensively within Australia and internationally to practice and teach Transference Healing. The healing format changes in response to her spiritual guidance and the demands and needs of her clients at the time. She has provided individual healings, one-on-one medical intuitive readings, trance channelling 'destiny and purpose readings' and mass healing where she channels a universal healing for audiences numbering 20 to 150 people at a time. She also does presentations, Transference Healing workshops and conferences at difference locations around the world, so that more people can learn to heal themselves and others. Participants at a conference can also receive a unique healing and channelled reading relating to the specific 'gateway' energies of the location, while on location at certain powerful grid points around the planet.

TRANSFERENCE HEALING ENERGY

Transference Healing has taken Chironic (Chiron) Healing onto the next level. It now incorporates and unites all healing energies into one modality by filtering through all natural energies from the Earth, Cosmos and other dimensions into the relevant levels of the etheric/physical body. Running (channelling) Transference Energy via a sequence of set procedures allows clients to master a Divine connection to the Christ and begin to learn how to channel '*Christ*

Healing, Energy, and Consciousness' into the human body and consciousness and onto the planet.

"Transference Healing begins to create the Divine template of the Christ within an individual, allowing them to begin to ascend into a state of inner perfection and higher consciousness. Each time an individual receives a Transference Healing it allows a complete healing and ascension process."

In view of the predicted changes within the Universe at this particular time of transition, Alexis offers her revised book as a practical guide to the transition and ascension, via Transference Healing.

She wishes to be of service to everyone on their journey of self-discovery and self-mastery.